"'Don't trust your heart; tru   in
Street capably demonstrates t   of
the Maker of our hearts for de   *of*
the Heart, we can have confidence that ....   ng
hope and joy. John speaks with great wisdom and unpacks Scripture in a
beautifully relevant way. I commend this excellent book to all those who
struggle with stubborn sexual sins."

> —**Amy Baker**, Author; ACBC certified counselor; instructor and
> counselor, Faith Biblical Counseling Ministry; council member,
> Biblical Counseling Coalition

"It is always a pleasure to read the work of a soul doctor who knows the ailment
he is treating. As a precise surgeon of both Scripture and the soul, John uses
biblical truth to cut deep, revealing the true nature of sexual sin. I finished the
book praising God that a powerful Savior can liberate his people from sexual
enslavement. May the Lord use this volume widely to help those in bondage
by the power of the truths of Scripture."

> —**Ernie Baker**, Pastor of Counseling, First Baptist Church,
> Jacksonville, Florida; ACBC Fellow; Professor of Biblical
> Counseling, The Master's University

"*Passions of the Heart* is the result of extensive and careful research done by
Dr. John Street in the pages of the Holy Scriptures concerning the nature,
expressions, reach, and consequences of sexual sin and all its enslaving desires.
In its faithful approach, the work not only exposes the problem, but also
offers hope and a way to restoration for all who struggle in this area. In days
of such moral permissiveness, this book is a well-timed relief for all who long
to live according to the sufficient provision of God through his Word. It is
a must for those involved in biblical counseling."

> —**Jayro M. Cáceres**, Senior Pastor, Igreja Batista Pedras Vivas, São
> Paulo, Brazil; Director, NUTRA Biblical Counseling and Training
> Center; Director, NUTRA Publishing, a ministry outreach of Igreja
> Batista Pedras Vivas, São Paulo, Brazil

"Dr. John Street is a masterly exegete of both Scripture and the human heart.
In *Passions of the Heart*, he skillfully and succinctly shows how the Word of

God is sufficiently helpful to those enslaved to sexual sin. While it speaks directly to the enslaved, it is also an encompassing guide for the counselor walking beside them. I will definitely be using this invaluable and practical resource in biblical counseling."

—**Jenn Chen**, Adjunct Professor for Master of Arts in Biblical Counseling, The Master's University; former Clinical Instructor, David Geffen School of Medicine, UCLA; ACBC certified biblical counselor

"In a society that is practically enslaved to sexual expression, *Passions of the Heart* is vital work for the student, the counselor, or any other reader seeking biblical means to help those trapped in sexual sin. It has theological depth, exegetical insight, practical applications, effective illustrations, and wise counsel that will benefit its readers and those who apply its principles. John Street's extensive counseling and pastoral experience are evident throughout and complemented by a foundational desire to help people change for their own benefit and God's glory."

—**Carl A. Hargrove**, Dean of Students and Associate Professor of Pastoral Ministries, The Master's Seminary; Associate Pastor, Grace Community Church, Sun Valley, California

"In my many years of counseling, I have noted that sexual sins are the most difficult to overcome. I am thankful for this work, *Passions of the Heart*, written by John Street. The book is not necessarily a 'how to,' even though there are many biblical helps, but it is a 'how come?' Dr. Street gets to the real issue of why people are enslaved to sexual sin: the heart. He has given us an outstanding work on the depravity of man's heart, which produces anger, self-pity, discontent, and fear—often leading to sexual (and other) sin. I was moved to think about my own heart and the need to make sure that I have rooted out all idolatry. I pray that this work aids many counselors in helping those enslaved to sexual passions, and I pray that it helps many men and women to overcome sexual sin."

—**Susan Heck**, ACBC certified counselor; author and speaker

"We've come to trust the biblically wise advice from Dr. Street, and in this volume he applies his confidence in the Scriptures from years of experience counseling those entangled in sexual sin. There is hope, and Street makes clear and practical the path to biblical freedom from the haunting and stern grip of sexual sin."

—**Dale Johnson**, Associate Professor of Biblical Counseling, Midwestern Baptist Theological Seminary; Executive Director, ACBC

"Blending together his decades of comprehensive Bible knowledge and seasoned counseling wisdom, John Street lifts the hood of our hearts to show us in thorough ways how our desires—even those that are initially legitimate or nonsexual—can subtly, progressively, and devastatingly lead to innumerable forms of sexual sin."

—**Robert D. Jones**, Biblical Counseling Professor, Southern Baptist Theological Seminary; ACBC Fellow and certified biblical counselor; author, *Pursuing Peace and Uprooting Anger*

"Dr. John Street has done a marvelous job in writing a book that will assist pastors and others who counsel people struggling with various forms of sexual temptation. It will also provide good homework assignments for people who are being overcome by those same forms of sexual temptation and want to find deliverance. In this volume, John walks us through a thoroughly biblical and practical description of the nature and causes of what many in our world call 'sexual addictions.' In addition, he provides an explanation of the way of deliverance from these destructive practices. I thank God for this book and will certainly use it in my counseling practice. And I will heartily recommend it to my students and others who are either counselors or counselees or who just desire a solid biblical understanding of this increasingly common problem."

—**Wayne Mack**, Founder and Professor of Biblical Counseling, SMTI; Director, ACBC Africa; Member, ACBC Academy; author of numerous books on Christian living and biblical counseling; Pastor of Biblical Counseling, Lynnwood Baptist Church, Pretoria, South Africa

"Dealing with desires is a difficult challenge because they seem to come from nowhere and feel stronger than anything else. Sexual desires are no exception. People suffer from disoriented sexual desires and fall into a pattern of sexual sin. Habitual patterns lead to sexual enslavement, bringing devastating consequences. If you are struggling with sexual issues or if you help people who struggle in the sexual arena, *Passions of the Heart* will help you. Dr. Street presents a biblical perspective of desires applied to sexuality. God's Word is light, and *Passions of the Heart* can help you understand how the Scriptures shed light into the darkness of sexual sin. This book will also help you understand what the Scriptures teach about the origin of sexual struggles, what has gone wrong with our sexuality, and the hope that we have in the Redeemer of our desires. There is hope; we can be sexually pure!"

—**Alexandre "Sacha" Mendes**, Pastor, Director for Vision and
Expansion, Brazilian Association of Biblical Counselors (ACBC);
ACBC certified counselor; member, Board of Directors, Biblical
Counseling Coalition

"John Street has written a carefully researched and helpful book for both men and women who struggle with sexual sin. *Passions of the Heart* will be a helpful tool for biblical counselors dedicated to helping counselees recognize their heart motivations. Diagrams drive the truth home."

—**Caroline Newheiser**, Assistant Coordinator of Women's Counseling
at RTS, Charlotte; ACBC certified counselor; conference speaker

"When addressing sexual sin, John Street goes beyond 'stop it' to address the sometimes hidden or surprising inward motivations that lead to unrighteous expressions of passion. He combines extensive and careful use of scriptural teaching and examples with a wide range of specific contemporary cases that reflect the experience of a seasoned counselor. He also offers practical wisdom for counselors who are trying to help counselees stuck in slavery to sexual sin. This will become an important resource that will help many to be set free to honor Christ with their sexuality."

—**Jim Newheiser**, Director of the Christian Counseling Program and
Associate Professor of Practical Theology, Reformed Theological
Seminary, Charlotte; ACBC Board Member and Fellow

"Dr. John Street is an experienced biblical counselor and a leader in the biblical counseling movement. As such, he believes that the Bible is sufficient in addressing every counseling issue and superior to every other system in diagnosing problems, understanding people, and providing clear, life-transforming answers. In this book, Dr. Street takes the Scripture and does that very thing, tackling the nearly impossible problem of bondage to sexual sin. But he rightly understands that the problem is the heart, not merely the Internet and a culture steeped in sensuality. In *Passions of the Heart*, you will find the Bible's superior analysis of how lust works in the inner man to produce sexual bondage and the Savior's liberating answers that must be found there. Read and profit from this book, and learn the workings of your own heart."

> —**Tim Pasma**, ACBC Board Member and Fellow; Pastor, LaRue Baptist Church, LaRue, Ohio

"'Why do I do what I do, and how can I stop it?' is a common question when it comes to sexual sin. The answer eludes us, and as a result we may be angry, confused, or hopeless. With solid exposition and practical applications, John Street provides a clear biblical answer, eliminating the confusion and giving us hope. If you want to conquer sexual sin and help others conquer it, then this book is for you."

> —**Andrew Rogers**, Assistant Professor and Program Coordinator for Biblical Counseling, Boyce College; ACBC Board Member and Fellow

"Dr. Street has written a solid, pastoral, helpful word. He is clear, Christ-centered, and completely biblical. You will be helped by reading and working through this volume. While Street centers on sexual issues, the truths expounded, explained, and applied can help anyone with any enslavement to any sin. Get the book; wrestle through it; give it away! May the King use it to make Jesus Christ the passion of our hearts."

> —**George C. Scipione**, Adjunct Professor, The Biblical Counseling Institute, Reformed Presbyterian Theological Seminary; ACBC Board Member and Fellow

"There is nothing elementary about this book. My colleague and friend has, in heart-surgery fashion, unpacked well the many fleshly lusts and motivations behind sexual sin. The survey of diagnostic questions is itself worth the price of the book. Perhaps most distinguishing about the book are the real-life stories woven among a study that clearly rests on the Word of God as its authority."

—**Stuart Scott**, Author; Professor of Biblical Counseling, The
   Master's University; ACBC Board Member and Fellow

"This is an incredibly important book for biblical counseling. The mantra of biblical counseling is to watch after one's heart, and Dr. John Street has done a wonderful job in exploring the theology of the heart. This book reminded me of David's prayer in Psalm 139:23–24: 'Search me, O God, and know my heart! Try me and know my thoughts! And see if there be any grievous way in me, and lead me in the way everlasting!' David wanted an X-ray done on his heart so that he would be a genuine man of God. This book is a fantastic tool to make that happen.

"As I was reading the book, I had to remind myself that John was speaking to the issue of sexual sin. Yet the unfolding of the truth about the heart is for any malady of the soul. This book can instruct the reader to develop good devotional and Bible-reading habits to overcome the temptations of sin in all areas of life. This book contains so many jewels for understanding the heart that reading it will be like searching for gold. The search will surely render the reader richer. This volume is for singles and married people struggling with lust. It is for parents desiring to communicate biblically about sex to their children. And it is for counselors wishing to be biblical in their approach to sinners' hearts."

—**Bill Shannon**, Pastor of Discipleship Counseling, Grace
   Community Church, Sun Valley, California; ACBC Fellow

"*Passions of the Heart* by Dr. John Street is a masterpiece! I am not aware of a more thorough treatment of the Bible's teaching about the heart, the well-spring of life. This examination of the heart is accompanied by an insightful description of the way that sexual sin and temptation work. Street masterfully draws out the connections between the passions of the heart and all manner of struggles with sexuality. This book is an invaluable resource both for people who are carried away by sexual passions and for the counselors who endeavor to help them."

—**Tedd Tripp**, Author; counselor; conference speaker

"Any experienced biblical counselor knows that the only way to bring about lasting change is to successfully get the counselee to clearly understand and see his own heart motivations, and then in a practical and biblical manner help him use the Scriptures to bring about lasting change. If we cannot connect the counselee with the reality of his own heart and then with God's solutions, there is little hope. In *Passions of the Heart*, Dr. John Street uses his superior Greek and Hebrew ability and his practical understanding of 'the mechanics of the heart' to tackle (in a simple and clear way) one of the most needy areas in biblical counseling today: that of purifying the heart in an immoral world system with the myriad of temptations that are defeating so many. He demonstrates how lust is fed, how heart idolatry is the real problem, and how the purification process happens. This material not only is comprehensive and biblical, but provides useful diagrams to help the reader picture the truth and practical solutions. Highly recommended for anyone desiring to help counselees with this present and weighty challenge."

> —**Allen Yoder**, Head, Master's of Biblical Counseling Department, SIBIMA Seminary, Fortaleza, Brazil

"When does a thought become sinful? Dr. John Street walks the reader through the deceitful steps along the slippery slope of enslaving sexual desires and sexual idolatry of the heart. Born out of years of the author's pastoral counseling experience built on the solid theological footings of Scripture, this work masterfully addresses the issues pertinent to men and women caught up in the sexual revolution and the resulting gender confusion. Dr. Street not only addresses the issues, but also lays out helpful steps for the counselee and the biblical counselor in purifying the heart of sexual idolatry."

> —**David H. Zemmer**, Former missionary to Brazil, 30 years; current pastor, Riley Bible Church, Terre Haute, Indiana

PASSIONS
OF THE
HEART

BIBLICAL COUNSEL FOR
STUBBORN SEXUAL SINS

PASSIONS
OF THE
HEART

JOHN D. STREET

P&R
PUBLISHING
P.O. BOX 817 • PHILLIPSBURG • NEW JERSEY 08865-0817

Did you find this book helpful?
Consider writing a review online. The author appreciates your feedback!
Or write to P&R at editorial@prpbooks.com with your comments.
We'd love to hear from you.

Library of Congress Cataloging-in-Publication Data

Names: Street, John D., 1952- author.
Title: Passions of the heart : biblical counsel for stubborn sexual sins / John D. Street.
Description: Phillipsburg : P&R Publishing, 2019. | Includes bibliographical references and index.
Identifiers: LCCN 2018042727| ISBN 9781629954028 (pbk.) | ISBN 9781629954035 (epub) | ISBN 9781629954042 (mobi)
Subjects: LCSH: Lust--Religious aspects--Christianity. | Sex--Religious aspects--Christianity. | Christians--Sexual behavior.
Classification: LCC BV4627.L8 S77 2019 | DDC 241/.664--dc23
LC record available at https://lccn.loc.gov/2018042727

This book is dedicated to Christians struggling in the battle for purity, in the hope that they will find lasting change toward Christlikeness. It is also dedicated to biblical counselors who desire to use the Scriptures to help those suffering with enslavement to sensual sins.

Solus Christus

CONTENTS

FOREWORD

Several years ago on a trip to Montana, my youngest son and I decided to challenge ourselves by hiking to the top of a ten-thousand-foot mountain. We started with our group at the base of the mountain and noticed the flowing grass, gorgeous flowers, and flourishing trees growing everywhere. The longer we hiked up the mountain the more we noticed that the vegetation was becoming increasingly sparse. After hours of hiking we passed the tree line, where nothing else grew, and all we could see were the brown and gray of the mountain and the blue of the sky.

As we continued our trek to the top, we came around a corner and saw the strangest thing. Amid the gray expanse of rock, a small yellow flower stabbed through a crack in the mountain. Right where it was not supposed to be, a flower was growing. Exactly where you would expect to find nothing, there was life.

I think about that flower when I think of 2 Peter 1. The first chapter of Peter's second book is about being fruitful. The apostle had studied his Old Testament and knew that fruitfulness was the indicator of a man who was walking with God (Ps. 1:3). He was acquainted with the great prophet John the Baptist, who commanded his hearers to bear fruit in keeping with repentance (Luke 3:8). With all his heart, Peter did not want the lives of Christian people to be characterized by the bitter curse of a failure to bear fruit in their lives before God. In 2 Peter 1:8 he talks about being "unfruitful in the knowledge of our Lord Jesus Christ."

As Peter instructs his readers in the grace of fruit-bearing, he raises one of the most significant tensions in all of Scripture. In 2 Peter 1:4 he says of Christians that we have "escaped from the corruption that is in the world because of sinful desire [lust]." Follow along with me as I make three observations about this all-important verse.

First, Peter admits that corruption exists. When he talks about corruption, he is talking about death. Death and corruption came into the world through the sin of Adam (Rom. 5:17). Now, because of that sin, all people are born dead in trespasses and enslaved to sin (Eph. 2:1). This death is cosmic—that is to say, it affects every person (Rom. 3:23) and every thing (Rom. 8:20–21). Every human being, including every Christian, lives in a fallen world that is defined by corruption and death.

A second observation about 2 Peter 1:4 has to do with the origin of this corruption. Peter says that the corruption present in the world is here because of lust. We often think of the word *lust* as having to do exclusively with sexual sin. But in Greek it is a neutral word that refers to any desire a human being could have. When Peter says that the corruption that is in the world is present because of desire, he is talking about a crucial function of the human heart. The heart wants, it longs, it desires, it lusts.

Nothing is wrong with desire itself, but as sinful human beings our desires can be distorted in *direction* (when we want things we should never want) or in *degree* (when we want good things more than we should want them). The point Peter is making is that the sin and death of the world in which we live is present because of distorted desires. We do not want the things God wants, and it kills us.

This reality is as old as sin itself. In Genesis 3, Satan tempted Adam and Eve to sin by using their desires against them. He appealed to a desire for greatness. He encouraged them to long to be like God in knowing what he knows. Of course, this was not God's design. He wanted them to trust him, but in their greedy desire for more they reached for the fruit, ate of it, and began the process of corruption that we all experience and that Peter addresses in his letter.

That brings us to a third observation about 2 Peter 1:4. Peter says that believers have escaped this desire-induced death. Christians are no longer imprisoned by the corruption that characterizes this fallen world. They have received faith to believe in the righteousness of Jesus Christ, the great God and Savior of humanity (2 Peter 1:4). Jesus Christ has been good on behalf of those who failed to be good in themselves. He has obeyed the law for those who were imprisoned by their disobedience to the law.

As Christians believe in the righteousness of Christ, rich blessings are extended to them. They receive grace and peace in the knowledge of God and his Christ (2 Peter 1:2), they are empowered to live lives that are pleasing to God (2 Peter 1:3), and they are granted promises to share God's own holy nature and so escape the consequences of sin and death (2 Peter 1:4). The point is that Jesus Christ changes the hearts of Christians so that, through his work, they escape the corruption caused by their lustful desires.

I said earlier that Peter raises one of the most significant tensions in all of Scripture, and it is at this point that we really begin to feel the friction. Peter makes it clear that, through Christ, Christians have escaped the death of our sinful desires. We are new. We are different. We are saved. Yet in the very next breath he says, "For this very reason, make every effort to supplement your faith with virtue" (2 Peter 1:5). Immediately after declaring that Christians have escaped the corruption in the world by the righteous work of Christ, he tells us to be diligent to work. Specifically, this diligent work requires that we add to our faith in Christ a list of virtues including moral excellence, knowledge, self control, perseverance, godliness, brotherly kindness, and love (2 Peter 1:5–7).

Do you see the tension? Why, if Christ's righteousness has allowed us to escape the corruption of the world induced by lust, do we now need to work to add virtue to our faith? If we have escaped the corruption of the world, why do we now still have work to do? Why can't we just take it easy and enjoy the escape from corruption that Christ has secured? In other words, why is there an ongoing struggle to be diligent?

The answer to those questions is found in the reality that God has chosen to delay the final judgment of all mankind to a future date known to him alone, creating a gap between the inauguration and fulfillment of our salvation (2 Peter 3:3–15). God inaugurates our salvation with a unilateral work of grace in which we are justified—that is, declared to be righteous through the merit of Christ. But after our salvation is inaugurated, God continues our salvation with a bilateral work of grace in which Christians are called to participate with God in sanctification—our growth in holiness—until we are united with Christ.

Understanding the distinction between God's unilateral work of justification and the bilateral work of sanctification eases the tension in Peter's statement. God has, by the work of Christ, made a genuine escape for believers who are consigned to death by the lusts of their hearts. Yet, as we await the return of Jesus Christ and the fulfillment of our salvation, we are aware that the desires of our hearts are not yet what they ought to be. We have received grace to escape our corruption, yet we must confess with the apostles that we need to grow in grace as it is multiplied to us (2 Peter 1:2).

That is the essence of 2 Peter 1 as well as the book you are holding in your hands. *Passions of the Heart* is about taking what Christ has done in his life, death, and resurrection and applying it diligently to our lives and hearts so that we grow in the grace that Jesus has accomplished. I am excited about this book because it is about the struggle of fighting, by faith, to grow increasingly in the grace purchased for us so that we look more and more like the Christ who died for us.

I am excited for you to read this book not only because of what you will learn but because of who you will learn from. John Street is one of the godliest, wisest, and most faithful men I know. He is a man who has exerted great diligence to supply faith with moral excellence. He is a man who has exerted great diligence in helping others to do the same. He is familiar with the battle, and he knows it is one that cannot be won by mere human effort but must be characterized by radical dependence on the Christ who gives energy and success to every effort we undertake.

As this book points you to the Book and helps you grow in the grace purchased for you by Jesus Christ, remember that flower I saw poking through the mountain in Montana. It was not there because of the mountain, but in spite of it. Against all odds, in a place where it should never be, there was life and growth. The same is true of your heart. The stony face of that mountain has nothing on your hard and sinful heart. You should never think that anything good would ever grow out of it. But, against all odds, in a place where it should never be, life and fruit can grow from your heart. By the grace of God this is exactly what will happen as you learn to grow in grace from this book. Have faith and be encouraged that this is precisely what will happen in your life, and never forget that the fruit of your transformed heart comes from the miraculous work of Christ causing fruit to grow.

Heath B. Lambert

Associate Professor, Biblical Counseling, The Southern Baptist Theological Seminary
Former Executive Director, Association of Certified Biblical Counselors (ACBC)
Founding council board member, Biblical Counseling Coalition (BCC)

PREFACE

As I left my office one day, I was surprised to see a young raccoon in a nearby tree facing me at eye level. I had walked out this door a thousand times and had never been confronted with a sight like this before. He was perfectly still, glaring at me, and apparently awaiting my reaction. Somewhat startled, I froze in my tracks, not quite sure what to do. It was an unexpected standoff! Then I noticed his unfortunate predicament: his right hind foot was caught at the ankle at a fork in the tree branches, rendering him unable to escape. My emotions instantly changed from a gripping fear to tender pity. I had heard that some neighborhood raccoons carried rabies, but he looked so helpless. In fact, he looked desperate, afraid, and exhausted. Overwhelmed with sympathetic feelings, I stepped forward to see if I could quickly release his small hind foot from his hopeless situation and help him go about his day. He was *not* fond of my idea! Even in his exhaustion, he reared up with a growling hiss, showing his needle-like white fangs. I jumped back, momentarily thankful that he was incapable of launching an attack on me. At that point I realized this was not a job for me. I needed an expert, an animal control officer, to help my little raccoon friend. Within an hour, Mr. Raccoon was humanely removed from the tree and allowed to safely return to his freedom.

My reckless young raccoon friend reminds me of the many people I have counseled over the years caught in a stubborn sexual sin. They were willing to risk great danger in order to find some sort of sexual satisfaction, only to get caught in an ever-tightening entanglement. You may know someone who is trapped like this animal, or maybe you are the one so ensnared. Perhaps you have tried everything you know to break the defeating grip it has on you, yet your entire struggle has simply served to tighten its crippling hold. As you read these words you relate to the emotional helplessness of being desperate, afraid, and exhausted. You personally understand the words of Solomon when he explains the experience of a person trapped in sexual enslavement: "The iniquities of the wicked ensnare him, and he is held fast in the cords of his sin" (Prov. 5:22). This bondage is real and deadly.

The desperation of my little friend became acute when I appeared suddenly, unexpectedly exposing his problem. He was startled! Raccoons are mostly nocturnal creatures and love the darkness. The fact that they have a dark mask around their eyes only magnifies their notoriety for stealth and nighttime thievery. Nevertheless, now he was caught in broad daylight and could do nothing about it. There was no denying or hiding his difficulty. In a strikingly similar way, you may have been caught in your sexual sin while you were trying to keep it quiet and under the cover of darkness. You may have tried like Adam and Eve to remain camouflaged, covering yourself figuratively with fig leaves and loincloths when confronted with your sin. But your sin is now exposed for what it is. You are forced to deal with it and determine whether you are going to walk in the light (1 John 1:6–7). You have tried to cover it up and deny it, even to yourself, but now you know you have a serious problem. You need real help!

When I attempted to help that little raccoon, he became fierce and angry. He acted as if he wanted to attack me! I was only attempting to free him from his bondage, but he viewed my approach as a threat. Nothing was further from the truth. I was not intending to harm him in any way. Has someone you know placed this book into your hands as an act of kindness, compassion, and help? If so, what has been your response? Have you reacted to this gesture like Mr. Raccoon, taking a defensive posture and treating their kindness as a threat? In response to their attempt to provide you life-giving, timeless truths and much-needed help to release you from slavery to your sin, you may have turned away. When you return evil to a person who is only trying to do you good, God has a warning: "If anyone returns evil for good, evil will not depart from his house" (Prov. 17:13; cf. 2 Sam. 12:10). Being defensive, easily offended, and protective of your precious sin-child will not change your hazardous circumstances. This fearful attitude and hardness of heart will serve only to move you further away from the real help you need to free you from sin's grip. You need to pray that our Lord will grace your life with a teachable spirit that is willing to accept sincere and loving biblical help.

Think carefully about the actions of King David after his ruinous sin of sleeping with and impregnating a woman who was not his wife (2 Sam. 11:1–21). He tried to get her faithful husband to come home from the king's violent war so that Uriah would sleep with his wife and be deceived into believing the child was his. But Uriah, loyal to his king, refused to leave the battle. This was particularly significant because Uriah was a Hittite, not a part of Israel by birth but only a God-fearing Gentile. Yet he dedicated himself to serving the Lord and the king in this way, while David was dedicated to serving himself. What a vivid contrast: a Gentile who served the Lord and a high-ranking Israelite who disobeyed him. After David ordered Uriah killed on the battlefield, he deceitfully took Bathsheba as his wife, clear evidence of his self-love and unfaithfulness to his Lord. David's sin with Bathsheba was detestable by itself, but his murder of Uriah magnified the hideousness of his sexual sin. Eventually David genuinely repented after being confronted with his sin by Nathan the prophet. Part of his repentance included this prayer to God for a teachable heart:

> Deliver me from bloodguiltiness, O God, O God of my salvation, and my tongue will sing aloud of your righteousness. O Lord, open my lips, and my mouth will declare your praise. For you will not delight in sacrifice, or I would give it; you will not be pleased with a burnt offering. The sacrifices of God are a broken spirit; a broken and contrite heart, O God, you will not despise. (Ps. 51:14–17)

David realized that God wants "a broken spirit; a broken and contrite heart." Up to this time he was not open to help or advice. He was still trying to cover his sin. You might be like David, still trying to cover your sin, but it is time to repent! In order to do so, you first must have "a broken spirit; a broken and contrite heart." Your heart must be teachable.

When I encountered Mr. Raccoon outside my office door, it did not take me long to discover I did not have the equipment I needed to really help him. Although I had good intentions and charitable desires for him, one of us—possibly both—was going to get hurt. I needed to call in someone trained to help his specific problem: in this case, animal control specialists who had all the right equipment and experience dealing with wild animals to handle his predicament in a humane way. The problem you face with sexual sin is going to require much more than good intentions to free you from its bondage. You need to rely on the expertise of God's infallible and sufficient Word. Its transforming truths will bring you lasting change and restore purity to your life. You must learn to trust it as you have never trusted anything before.

This book is written to be a helpful resource in understanding and applying God's truth to your stubborn bondage—so you can be freed! It is the culmination of over twenty years of personal study and many hours of counseling. I have divided it into three major sections. The first section is written to help you understand the complexities of your own heart from a biblical perspective. It is critical to gain God's view of your heart before you move forward in dealing with its desires and the entrapment of lust. The second section identifies eight critical predispositions of the heart that set the stage for sinful sexual indulgence and bondage. A major failure in dealing with sexual sin is ignorance of how heart motivations tend to dominate thinking and behavior. It is too tempting to view the simple deed of sexual sin as the problem. Scripture tells us that the heart's motivations and weaknesses are much more complex. The third section seeks to show how you can biblically address these motivations that fuel sexual sin. It is about the purity of your heart and shows how the misery of sexual bondage can be replaced with the blessedness of purity. "Blessed are the pure in heart, for they shall see God" (Matt. 5:8).

I must point out that all names used for counselees, both in real cases and in composite case studies, are fictional names. This has been done to protect the privacy of others.

I must also point out that I have chosen to use the male gender when naming counselees. This supplies consistency throughout the book; however, the reader should understand my intent to be inclusive of females as it pertains to sexual problems. Similarly, I use the pronouns *he*, *his*, and so on when writing about counselees, purely for the sake of easier reading. I find it cumbersome to continually read *he/she* or *his/hers*. But this is not to imply that this book is only for males and their difficulties. Again, I expect the reader to apply these truths and principles to males and females since both genders struggle with sexual problems.

Finally, I wish to express my sincere gratitude to several for their help with this book. I am most grateful to my wife, Janie, who has painstakingly pored over the manuscript, making sure that my grammar and word choice are appropriate for such a sensitive subject. In addition, I am grateful to Amanda Martin, Karen Magnuson, and John J. Hughes of P&R Publishing for their recommendations, assistance, and encouragement as I completed the manuscript. It was in the final stages of writing this book that my mother, Joan, was promoted to Glory. The grace given for extending the deadline for the manuscript was especially appreciated. Thank you, John!

I cannot express enough gratefulness to my Savior, the Lord Jesus Christ, for the life-changing grace of the gospel, which is the foundation of every critical transformation toward godliness in this life.

Soli Deo Gloria
John D. Street

PART 1

THE NATURE OF THE HEART
AND ITS PASSIONS

1

PREPARING THE HEART FOR CHANGE

The heart of man—that inner being of the one created in the image of God—is by nature so complex that it has for centuries both amazed and confounded the greatest of philosophers and theologians. Invisible to the physical eye, the heart remains elusive and obscure, requiring much study and contemplation to understand its thoughts and intentions. How can anyone really know his own heart? This enigma becomes apparent when an exasperated Christian exclaims, "I can't believe I would ever think such thoughts!"

The obscure nature of the heart is seen as Solomon asks the rhetorical question, "Who can say, 'I have made my heart pure; I am clean from my sin'?" (Prov. 20:9). Scripture says that the human heart is deep, hidden, and clever: "The purpose in a man's heart is like deep water, but a man of understanding will draw it out" (Prov. 20:5). It is also described as dishonest, calculating, and untrustworthy (Prov. 6:12–14). Here the heart is described as *purposing*. The Hebrew word used for "purpose" can also be translated "to plan." Contrary to the world's view of romance and emotion, the Bible says that the human heart purposes and plans.

Yet the heart's chief unsettling characteristic is its capacity for self-deception. It is commonplace for the heart to assume that it is better than it really is; it is customary for the heart to believe its own innocence and to presume the goodness of its own motivations. A self-imposed form of blindness is endemic to the heart because of

3

the effect of original sin. The heart of man labors to hide its wicked intentions from being acknowledged or exposed. If its purposes were brought to light, then guilt would bring unwanted pressure, forcing a fundamental change of direction. People do not want to change when they are complacent—comfortable with their self-determined ambition in life.

Well-meaning voices can be heard telling you to "trust your heart" or "follow your heart," words you have likely heard or read since you were a child. The latest societal push toward this dangerous advice asserts that you cannot be truly authentic or genuine *until* you trust your own heart. Trusting your feelings and allowing them to dictate your choices is the dogma of the day. Further, this culture says you must self-identify—because surely your own heart would not mislead you! A self-determined reality is the only trustworthy reality, according to the philosophical trendsetters. This social construction of reality theory declares that you cannot rely on anything external to yourself— you can trust only self. It is not difficult to see how the push for the "self-defining self" ideology is fueling a culture of self-indulgence and self-gratification. This is the heart turned in on itself, leaving havoc in its wake.

CAN YOU TRUST YOUR HEART?

To underline the critical importance of this issue to the Christian, let us carefully consider some preliminary questions. How much should you trust your own heart? Should you trust your heart at all? You need to resist the temptation to read past this question without giving it proper consideration. From a biblical perspective, the heart is the core of who you are. It is the control center of your life. We can also ask this question, using the biblical etymology of the word *heart*, in this way: How much *do* you trust your own plans, purposes, intentions, and motivations? This is a very difficult question to answer, especially if you are a sincere Christian who strives to be brutally honest with yourself. Consider the words of Solomon as he reveals the peril of self-knowledge: "All the ways of a man are pure in his own eyes, but the LORD weighs the spirit" (Prov. 16:2). A few chapters later he writes, "Every way of a man is right in his own eyes, but the LORD weighs the heart" (Prov. 21:2).

Clearly, self-assessment tends to be intensely self-favoring, which is a manifestation of pride. The proud heart has no difficulty with portraying itself in favorable ways. In fact, this is part of its self-imposed blindness. Essentially, Scripture teaches that it is possible for the pride of your heart to deceive you (Jer. 17:9; 49:16; Obad. 3). Pride is the mask that the heart puts on. It keeps *true* self-knowledge hidden—the knowledge that it is deceitful, that it is wrong when it wants to appear right. Because it actually believes itself to be truly good, the self-deceived heart tends to be cavalier and crafty about the unsavory aspects of its plans, purposes, intentions, and motivations by highlighting the more respectable and honorable ones. This kind of self-assessment can be seen in the Christian who commits sexual sin occasionally yet pridefully evaluates himself based on the multitude of "good" things he does to serve the Lord.

Since you cannot be trusted to assess your heart accurately, you must seek to understand the truth of which Solomon spoke: "the *Lord* weighs the heart." The penetrating truth of Scripture about the sensual heart can be seen in the words of Jesus Christ when he teaches that the heart of an adulterer and the lustful heart are the same heart (Matt. 5:27–28). The adulterer has acted out his lurid fantasies, and the luster has not—but they are the same in God's eyes; no significant difference exists between them. It is dangerously easy to presume personal self-righteousness—until you, by means of Scripture, honestly look at your own heart. God is the One who genuinely sees your heart and all its intentions (1 Sam. 16:7; Jer. 20:12). What does God see when he looks into your heart? When God through his Word reveals the sinful attitudes and prideful assumptions of your heart, your so-called righteous works no longer have any credibility. These deeds are seen for what they truly are—a desperate attempt to excuse and cover up secret and sensual desires.

The heart's natural inclination to judge itself favorably is a serious problem, not only for the openly self-indulgent sinner but even for the most sincere and dedicated Christian. For example, how do you think about yourself when you read Paul's admonition, "As for the one who is *weak in faith*, welcome him, but not to quarrel over opinions" (Rom. 14:1). In leading numerous Bible studies through the years, I have listened to many discussions on this verse that demonstrate that Christians will inevitably view themselves as the *stronger* Christian. *Everyone* in the Bible study is the stronger Christian! Or so it seems. The prevailing opinion is that someone else is the weaker Christian. This illustration reinforces the truth that the heart tends to be willfully blind to its own weaknesses and sinfulness, casting itself in the most favorable light.

This tendency is epitomized in the person who, when caught in an egregious sin, immediately responds by pointing to someone who has committed an even worse sin. You do not have to look very far to find someone who has done something even more atrocious than yourself. The person who adopts this type of reasoning, and continues in it, lives with an ever-lowering measure for goodness in his mind. His self-made gauge for righteousness will eventually become the worst, most vile person who has ever lived. With this kind of thinking, nearly everyone should be able to feel good about themselves because they are, at least, better than the worst person who has ever lived. But that is not to be the Christian's rule of faith and practice! Instead, the Lord Jesus Christ is the Christian's judge of what is good and right; he is the perfect, sinless, and holy God-man whom we seek to please, emulate, and worship (Phil. 3:12–16). Yet this person's heart has led him to create a lower standard for himself than what Jesus demands. Indeed, your heart cannot be trusted!

KNOWING YOUR HEART

How is it that a Christian comes to blindly trust his unreliable heart—even above the authority and perfection of Christ? The person who trusts his heart assumes that he truly *knows* his heart. That leads us to our next question: How well do you know your own heart? Since the character and desires of your heart lead you in every important endeavor and decision in life, this is a critical question. For example, it would be foolish to entrust someone with the care of young children whom you did not know well; it would not be wise to turn your life savings over to someone you did not know; it's not likely that you would eat, drink, or medicate yourself with substances from an unknown source. So when it comes to issues of the heart, why do you assume you know your heart well enough to entrust it with weighty matters vital to your very life and well-being? This assumption is particularly dangerous, given that Scripture demonstrates that your heart will not provide you with the most reliable information about yourself; it will even lie to you so that you are self-deceived.

IN GOD'S SCHOOL OF HEART-KNOWLEDGE

Since we have already seen from Scripture that the Lord God knows our hearts, we look further into his Word to gain *true* self-knowledge. So far, we have noted that the heart is

- Deep, hidden, and clever. "The purpose in a man's heart is like deep water, but a man of understanding will draw it out" (Prov. 20:5).
- Dishonest, calculating, and untrustworthy. "A worthless person, a wicked man, goes about with crooked speech, winks with his eyes, signals with his feet, points with his finger, with perverted heart devises evil, continually sowing discord" (Prov. 6:12–14); "Who can say, 'I have made my heart pure; I am clean from my sin'?" (Prov. 20:9).
- Self-favoring. "All the ways of a man are pure in his own eyes, but the LORD weighs the spirit" (Prov. 16:2). "Every way of a man is right in his own eyes, but the LORD weighs the heart" (Prov. 21:2).
- Deceitful. "The horror you inspire has deceived you, and the pride of your heart" (Jer. 49:16); "The pride of your heart has deceived you" (Obad. 3).
- Seen by God. "For the LORD sees not as man sees: man looks on the outward appearance, but the LORD looks on the heart"

7

(1 Sam. 16:7); "O LORD of hosts, who tests the righteous, who sees the heart and the mind" (Jer. 20:12).

But God goes even further than merely describing the heart of man. He goes to great lengths to reveal what he sees so that he can show us what we cannot see. He often does this by means of adversity, trials, and suffering. When you begin to see your heart through the light of suffering, it is both revealing and humbling.

Consider why God took Israel through forty years of wilderness sufferings. He explains his reason to them: "And you shall remember the whole way that the LORD your God has led you these forty years in the wilderness, that he might humble you, *testing you to know what was in your heart,* whether you would keep his commandments or not" (Deut. 8:2). God did not take them through such difficulties so that *he* could understand what was in their heart. He is omniscient—he already knew what was in their hearts (Pss. 94:11; 139:4). Clearly, he took them through such a troublesome time so that *they* would know what was in their hearts.

The Israelites, like us, believed they already knew their own hearts. This prideful assumption was deceptive; understanding the deep motivations of the heart begins with a settled and convinced attitude of humility. Israel needed their prideful blindfold removed, and it took forty years of hardship to remove it. This suggests that humility is often less a *destination* than it is a progressive learning *process.* Difficult trials, hardships, and afflictions test your spiritual vitality and reveal long-hidden imperfections of your heart. Our God is a God who tests hearts in this way (Prov. 17:3). Why must God test the human heart? Because hardship forces you to look at your own heart honestly, more realistically.

HEART LESSONS FROM THE LIFE OF KING DAVID

After King David's secret disgrace with Bathsheba was revealed by Nathan the prophet, David later explains why this uncovering of sin needed to happen: "Behold, you delight in truth in the inward being, and you teach me wisdom in the secret heart" (Ps. 51:6). God desires truth in your innermost being. But your secret heart is naturally foolish, and wisdom is foreign to it. A few verses later, David explains why it is important for God to take you through the difficulty of these trials: "The sacrifices of God are a broken spirit; a broken and contrite heart, O God, you will not despise" (Ps. 51:17). Your heart needs to break for it to no longer be fake. When you are finally humbled by adversity, you are willing to take a more honest look at yourself, regardless of the consequences. This kind of distress reveals a clearer view of your heart's true intentions and motivations.

The remainder of this book will not have the necessary impact until your heart has been broken by your secret sins. The heart crushed by grief and sorrowing over sin is the prerequisite for real and substantive change. If you are more concerned about the consequences of acknowledging your sin than of the purity of your own heart, then your heart is not ready for change. David was so broken by the awfulness of his secret sin that he cried out, "Create in me a clean heart, O God, and renew a right spirit within me" (Ps. 51:10). He knew what you need to know: that mere external or behavioral change is not enough. It is the heart that needs to change.

On another occasion David, recognizing the craftiness of his heart and its secret intentions, asks and answers this critical question: "Who can discern his errors? Declare me innocent from hidden faults" (Ps. 19:12). David agonizes because he knows that there are hidden faults within himself that he will not see. Within the context of Psalm 19, the answer is clear: it is only God who can truly discern—that is, reveal man's errors and hidden faults. Mankind can do this only through careful attention to God's Word (Ps. 19:7–11). These "hidden faults" are the critical missing aspects of self-knowledge that are deeply hidden within the heart. David eventually learned that he could not trust the promptings of his own heart. Why? Because they are hidden behind layers of self-righteous rationalizations.

Consider the overall story of David's life in the book of 2 Samuel. As you read the first ten chapters, it seems that everything David does is a resounding success. You could liken him to the character King

Midas in Greek mythology; everything he touched turned to gold. In 2 Samuel, chapters 1 through 5, David wins the civil war going on in Israel and successfully succeeds Saul as king. This helps to establish his enormous popularity as the king of Israel who fights and wins impossible battles. Yet, somewhat parenthetically, the text adds, "And David knew that the LORD had established him king over Israel, and that he had exalted his kingdom for the sake of his people Israel" (2 Sam. 5:12). Some translators, in order to heighten the sense of the Hebrew text, write, "David realized that the LORD had established him as king over Israel" (NASB). Could there be a ring of self-righteous pride growing in David's heart over what he had accomplished? Did David falsely assume that he was extra special in God's eyes because he had been chosen as Israel's king? It is difficult to say at this point in the narrative, but the story continues. In chapters 5 through 7, he defeats the occupational forces of Jerusalem and brings the ark of the covenant to his new capital. At that time he receives the covenant from God (2 Sam. 7:8–17). Israel is finally united and now has the leadership of a king who is a skilled military commander. David appears to have the unique blessing of God over all his reign. Following this, he marches out to meet the remaining enemies of Israel (chapters 8–10). He defeats the Philistines, the Moabites, the Arameans, the Edomites, and the Ammonites. There is no battle that David loses; every battle he engages, he wins soundly. Finally, David takes a vacation from his battles (2 Sam. 11:1). He sends out his army to fight his battles under the capable military commander Joab, and David stays in Jerusalem to relax. After winning so many hard-fought battles, David surely believed he had earned his holiday.

The latter half of 2 Samuel is radically different, changing from victorious celebration to devastating heartbreak and discouragement. This begins in the middle of chapter 12 when one of David's young sons dies not long after birth. In chapter 13, David's son Absalom kills his brother Amnon for raping his half-sister Tamar. Then Absalom turns on his father and incites a bloody civil war to rob him of his kingdom. This causes David to flee for his life from Jerusalem, being pursued by the son he dearly loved. In chapters 14–19 Absalom is eventually caught and killed by men loyal to David, who is deeply grieved over losing his beloved son. In chapter 20 another bloody rebellion arises worse than Absalom's, known as Sheba's revolt, which had to be put down by Joab. Then David finally comes to the end of his reign, fighting the Philistines again. But instead of a great victory, like his defeat of Goliath, David becomes exhausted and must be rescued. Other people have to win the battle that day (2 Sam. 21:15–22). Finally, in chapter 22, David writes a psalm of the Lord's deliverance instead of a psalm regaling his great victory. He had become a humble and broken man.

What was the critical turning point of David's life? This occurs in chapters 11 and 12. It is David's sin with Bathsheba! Not only does he sleep with a woman who is not his wife, but upon finding out that she has become pregnant with his child while her husband has been off fighting his battles, he plots to cover it up. If Bathsheba's pregnancy were known, she would be disgraced for cheating on her husband. So David devises a plan for Uriah to return home from the front lines to sleep with his wife, intending to misrepresent the baby as being Uriah's. But when Uriah refuses to leave his responsibilities as a good soldier, David's plan was frustrated. Uriah could not go to enjoy his comfortable home and beautiful wife while the ark of the covenant, Israel, and Judah were still living in temporary shelters. This is even more remarkable since Uriah was a Hittite, meaning he was a Gentile convert to Judaism. This foreigner was more concerned about the honor of the Lord in Israel than was his Jewish king. With David's first plan destroyed, he proceeds to place Uriah on the front lines so that he will most assuredly be killed. Murder—yes murder!—is conceived in David's heart to cover up his sexual sin. This plan succeeded (2 Sam. 11:17), and David thought the cover-up was a complete success.

A secret sexual desire in the heart of David, now acted out, became the turning point of his life. Prior to his sin with Bathsheba he had made numerous compromises in his life (e.g., 2 Sam. 3:1–4; 5:13). Earlier he had fathered six sons by six different wives. He had already collected in his harem many concubines even though God had warned the future kings of Israel not multiply many wives to themselves: "And he shall not acquire many wives for himself, lest his heart turn away"

(Deut. 17:17). But it was David's pride that prompted him to ignore God's commands. He believed in his own righteousness, which motivated his sinful compromises, adultery, and eventually murder. Before David's sin with Bathsheba he was the hero of Israel, but afterward he became a weak and pitiful king. What was the core of his problem? He trusted his own heart, though its sinful cravings were well hidden under several layers of pride, manipulation, and self-righteous rationalizations.

Sensual desires are deceptively hidden within the heart. They are often excused or explained away by a person who has power, prestige, or wealth, any one of which enables him to indulge his provocative fantasies. Many others who do not have great influence or wealth also have the same sensual desires but lack the means to fulfill them. They may delude themselves with self-righteous thoughts, believing they are better than those who have had the opportunity to indulge their secret passions, when the truth is, were they given the same opportunity, they would indulge their lust just as quickly. Indeed, they are no better off. Remember, Jesus said that the heart of a luster is the same as the heart of an adulterer. The major recurring failure here is not taking seriously the sinful condition of the self-favoring heart, whether the lust is acted on or not.

THE CATASTROPHE OF TRUSTING YOUR OWN HEART

The tragic events of King David's life have been replayed countlessly in the lives of many men and women throughout the centuries. Much like David's is the story of a Christian man who ran a massive and profitable business. In the world's estimation he was a huge success in everything he did. Together with his beautiful Christian wife and five wonderful children, they all weekly attended a great church. What more could a man desire? But his whole life changed on the day he was arrested in a police sting for hiring a prostitute, who was an undercover police officer. The following day this devastating revelation was the lead story on all the local television news programs. These broadcasts dragged his name, his family, his business, and his church through the mud. His embarrassed children refused to go to school. His business sales dropped 85 percent in a week, resulting in the layoff of several of his employees. After several months, the banks foreclosed on his business and his home.

All of this occurred even though he fully repented to the Lord, his wife, and his children. Repentance does not always exempt you from the consequences of your sin. While in biblical counseling in his church, he confessed to having years of secret sexual fantasies that he never acted on. These hidden passions had been buried deeply in his heart, artfully disguised as innocent, stress-relieving times of escape. It was not until he had the means and opportunity, afforded to him through his profitable business, that he could indulge his secret pleasures. His years of secret, sensual sins eventually cost him dearly. He was, like David, a seriously broken man!

Of course, these devastating sins of the heart are not limited to men. A Christian woman in her twenties became engaged to be married to a delightful Christian man. The oldest of four children, she came from a solid Christian family; her three younger siblings all looked up to their older sister. She excelled in both athletics and academics at her university. Her fiancé was studying to be an attorney in a prestigious graduate program. Two months before graduation, and three months before her wedding, a young woman living in the same dorm openly confessed to having a lesbian relationship with her. When confronted by her Christian friends, this engaged woman tearfully confessed to her sin. Her parents and siblings were in shock when they heard the news. She lost her athletic scholarship and her grade point average took a severe hit in her last semester. In disgrace, she dropped out of college, her testimony for Christ in ruins. Her fiancé was devastated and quickly ended their relationship when he heard the news. The wedding was canceled. Later in counseling she revealed that this was something she had kept secret for several years and passed it off in her own mind as innocent curiosity. But she had allowed the influence of worldly culture to feed and nurture her sexual curiosity until she had the opportunity to personally explore this in her dormitory. How could she give up so much as a Christian? The answer to this question rests in the fact that she had permitted and even cultivated these sexual fantasies in her heart for a long time. The mind is like a garden; whatever you permit to grow and cultivate will eventually produce behavioral fruit (Gal. 6:7).

In these examples, dangerous assumptions of self-trust led to major moral failures. Neither of these two individuals, at the very beginning of entertaining sexual thoughts, planned to fall into the outward sins of adultery and lesbianism. Both were convinced that they were strong Christians—strong enough to resist giving in to this kind of temptation. This is a fatal error in a Christian's thinking, a grave miscalculation when it comes to the purity of the heart. The apostle Paul understood that such assumptions could be misleading and potentially destructive. He did not trust his own conscience (i.e., heart). He confessed to the Corinthians believers, "For I am not aware of anything against myself, but I am not thereby acquitted. It is the Lord who judges me" (1 Cor. 4:4). In other words, he was not aware of any wrongdoing or unconfessed sin in his life at that time, but that did not make him innocent. His natural, self-approving outlook and insight into himself could have easily blinded him to his own faults. Only the Lord is qualified to be the final judge. Unlike most people in our culture today, Paul rightfully *distrusted* his own heart. The human heart is full of self-justification and self-righteousness (Gen. 8:21; Prov. 16:5). You cannot trust your heart! Its self-diagnostic capability is hopelessly corrupted by the deceitfulness of sin (Prov. 20:9). The righteousness of Christ is the sole standard of what is pure. Like the humbled desire of King David after his failure, there must be a deep longing for a proven purity of heart (Ps. 26:2).

The insidious self-righteousness of the heart and its false presumption of its own goodness is often revealed when unexpected events arise, resulting in reactions that occur automatically and without forethought. These are the unintended words and actions that reveal the false assumption of the heart's innocence. After David was anointed king of Israel, consolidating Israel into one nation and effectively ending a bitter civil war, the Philistines decided to attack. With the Lord's help, David achieved a glorious victory over them (2 Sam. 5:17–25).

With great celebration and rejoicing David ordered the ark of God to be transported to Jerusalem. The ark was placed on a newly built cart pulled by oxen, although the Old Testament law had required the sacred ark to be carried by the sons of Kohath (Num. 3:30–31; 4:15; 7:9). During transport they encountered rough ground near the threshing floor of Nachon, causing the oxen to stumble and the cart to careen sideways. As the ark began to fall to the ground, a man by the name of Uzzah (possibly the grandson of Abinadab, keeper of the ark; cf. 1 Sam. 7:1) reached out his hand and took hold of it to steady it and keep it from falling (2 Sam. 6:6). In that instance Uzzah believed he was doing a good thing. He believed his action would keep the ark from being broken or soiled by the unclean ground. But surprisingly, Scripture says in 2 Samuel 6:7, "And the anger of the LORD was kindled against Uzzah, and God struck him down there because of his error, and he died there beside the ark of God." This was alarming considering the righteous intentions of Uzzah.

Why was the Lord so angered with Uzzah? What does the Lord's response reveal about the heart of Uzzah? Our Lord's quick action treated his deed as a capital offense, even though Uzzah was fully convinced he was doing a good thing. David himself became angry at what had happened, so much so that he named the place Perez-uzzah (2 Sam. 6:8). The Hebrew literally means "outburst against Uzzah!" It is possible that David was angered at himself for allowing such carelessness in transporting the ark by a clumsy oxen cart. But that does not settle the issue of the Lord's anger at Uzzah. To the contemporary mind the Lord's action seems to be entirely unjust, yet this is not the case at all. The Lord brought a death sentence on Uzzah because of his false belief about his own goodness. Uzzah had the audacity to believe that his hand was more holy than the dirt of the ground. He presumed himself to be better, holier than he really was. The Israelites were to treat the ark as perfectly holy; no one was supposed to touch it, under penalty of death (Num. 4:15, 19–20). Uzzah's false belief in his own righteousness, confirmed by his good intentions, betrayed him. If in his heart he believed that no man was worthy to assist the Lord, and that his violation of God's command would defile the ark, he would not have dared to touch it. His attitude toward the goodness of his own heart's intentions became deadly. His heart had deceived him.

He is a fool who believes in the goodness of his own heart. He is a fool who believes that the heart is a reliable guide for life. The biblical doctrine of total depravity means that every intention, plan, and purpose of the heart, no matter how good it may seem, is tainted by sin. This does not mean that the heart is as bad as it could be. Every heart has the capacity to become even worse. But it does mean that the heart is known as being unreliable and untrustworthy because of its sinful mind-set against God in every aspect of its desires. Even the heart of the Christian cannot be fully trusted. The apostle Paul did not trust his heart (1 Cor. 4:4), and the biblical author of Hebrews writes, "Take care, brothers, lest there be in any of you an evil, unbelieving heart, leading you to fall away from the living God" (Heb. 3:12).

Paul writes to the young pastor Timothy about his zealous care over the flock at Ephesus so that he might avoid endless disputes and arguments with doctrinally unsound teachers: "So flee youthful passions [contextually: compulsion to argue] and pursue righteousness, faith, love, and peace, along with those who call on the Lord from a pure heart" (2 Tim. 2:22). If Timothy's heart were reliable, then Paul's warning is unnecessary. But the apostle understood the sinful propensities of his heart and Timothy's chief inclinations. As a young and passionate pastor-theologian, Timothy was inclined to engage these false teachers in debate. He could easily rationalize his purpose as being good. After all, he wants to set these men straight from the standpoint of their bad doctrine and free the church from their influence. Like Uzzah, Timothy's intentions were good on the surface. But you do not win over people to God's purposes by dispute or debate (2 Tim. 2:23–26). That is not the way of the Lord, even though it may seem reasonable to human thought.

THE HEART NEEDS FORGIVENESS AND CHANGE

The Christian will battle evil desires within the heart. This is a truth theologians have understood for a long time. Before a person believes in Christ, his heart is wholly dedicated to sin, fully depraved, and in need of redemptive forgiveness (Rom. 4:3–8; Col. 2:13–14). Such a person is unable to please God from the heart. When God redemptively forgives the unbeliever, theologians call this *judicial forgiveness* because the unbeliever's primary relationship to God is that of Judge. However, after a person becomes a believer he still needs forgiveness from specific sins. Theologians call this *parental forgiveness* because the believer is a member of God's family; God is the believer's loving Father.

When Christians sin, they are not removed from the family, but they will suffer temporal discipline because of God's chastening (Prov. 13:15b, 21; Matt. 6:12; Heb. 12:5–11). These are sins that come from a sinful heart that has been redeemed but still possesses evil lusts and desires. This is a heart that has been judicially justified and placed in union with Christ, so from God's perspective it is perfectly holy— viewed in the perfect righteousness of Christ. But from an earthly perspective it is in the process of becoming more like what it has already been declared to be in Christ. The heart is still growing, changing, and becoming more Christlike through progressive sanctification even though it continues to struggle with pervasive evil desires and lusts. The internal battle of sin in the heart is a reality for the believer. For the unbeliever, there is no real battle, for his heart has not yet been redeemed and given over to God. He remains in bondage to his sin and has no life in him for the battle.

The author of Hebrews describes God's work in the believer's life this way: "For by a single offering he has perfected for all time those who are being sanctified" (Heb. 10:14). When he writes that the believer has been "perfected for all time" (perfect, active tense of τελειόω), he is referring to *judicial sanctification* in Christ. This is a believer's salvation. All sin past, present, and future is paid and atoned for by Jesus Christ. When the author refers to believers as "those who are being sanctified," he changes to a present tense (present, passive tense of ἁγιάζω). This is *parental sanctification* in Christ. Once the believer is saved, God is not finished; he continues to sanctify him to make him more like Christ. It is the very nature of God to finish a task

17

(Num. 23:19; Isa. 55:11). He does not abandon the believer or leave the responsibility of sanctification incomplete. God will see it to the end by revealing the evil desires of the heart, bringing about repentance and a clean heart until the believer's desires are God's holy desires.

THE TRUE NATURE OF THE HEART

What is the nature of the person who continues to harbor known evil desires in his heart even though he claims to be a Christian? Given the character of God and his sustained sanctifying work in the believer's life, such a person has good reason to question whether he is a genuine believer (2 Cor. 13:5). A true believer who persists with lustful desires in the heart will be miserable under the chastening hand of God. This discipline is intended to open his eyes to the truth of his hidden heart desires and to lead him to repentance and a purging of those desires—once and for all—from his life.

The experience of the one who only professes to be a Christian will be different. As time goes on, he will grow increasingly comfortable in his sin because of the hardening of his heart and searing of his conscience. Any unhappiness or misery is the result of difficult circumstances that are a natural consequence of living in sin, not because he is displeasing to God. Perhaps his spouse has discovered his secret, sordid fantasy life and the home is now a place of strife and unhappiness. The unregenerate person, regardless of painful external pressures, will continue to follow the lurid imaginings he has come to crave. Through the deceitfulness of his heart, this false believer will withdraw, retreating to the secret world of his lusts as a comfortable place of escape from the critical eye of disapproving family and Christian friends. Real motivation for change is nonexistent because he is not truly living to bring glory to Christ. Having given himself over to his lust, he lives solely and intensely for self-pleasure. Any claim he makes to be a Christian is due to pride, social expediency, or because he fears death and hell. If you are this type of person, the biblical truths of this book will not bring about the change you need until you sincerely repent and place your faith in Christ alone as Savior and Lord. Pick up the Bible and read the Gospels of Mark and John. You need to know Jesus Christ and become a true follower of him!

In marked contrast, the genuine Christian will mourn the impure desires of his heart. Pleasurable sin is short-lived for the one who is truly "in Christ" (2 Cor. 5:17). His misery will come from an internal sense of guilt and from knowing he is living a life that is displeasing to the Lord he claims to love. Although he may become deeply mired in his sin, he fights it at every turn. His greatest discouragement is found in his apparent inability to overcome serious temptation and sin. His weakness grieves him, and he seeks help even while he is seemingly bound by the cords of his iniquity. If you are this miserable Christian, whom even now the Lord is convicting, then this book is written for you—to bring you hope and biblical change. You *desire* a pure heart because of the Spirit of God within you, but you must also *pursue* a pure heart (Matt. 5:8; Heb. 12:14).

God in Christ Jesus will provide you with the grace you will need for the purification of your heart (Prov. 3:34). But, as I suggested earlier, grace will not come without brokenness. "Therefore it says, 'God opposes the proud, but gives grace to the humble'" (James 4:6). Your soul must be overwhelmed with your vileness and impurities before any real change can take place in your heart and its desires. If this brokenness before God (not just before men) is not present, then you need to cry out to God to restore sensitivity to your conscience, which has been seared by repeated, unconfessed sin. This is a vital prerequisite to substantive heart renewal.

> Submit yourselves therefore to God. Resist the devil, and he will flee from you. Draw near to God, and he will draw near to you. Cleanse your hands, you sinners, and purify your hearts, you double-minded. Be wretched and mourn and weep. Let your laughter be turned to mourning and your joy to gloom. Humble yourselves before the Lord, and he will exalt you. (James 4:7–10)

A heart that is broken because of its sinfulness is a humbled heart. It is a heart that cares about how offensive it is to the holiness of the Lord

19

and that is now ready for real and lasting change. Such a heart becomes keenly invested in purging its sinful and dominating desires. This must be true of your heart before you move forward.

THE HEART'S REPENTANCE: GODLY SORROW OR WORLDLY SORROW?

There is an important distinction that should be made between feeling bad about your heart's impurity and being broken over it. A husband may be horrified and ashamed because his wife has discovered his secret indulgence of pornography on his computer and cell phone; does he feel badly for being caught, or is he broken over his sin? A wife might have been caught in an extramarital affair; is she angry that she has been found out, perhaps even agonizingly grieved over how her sin has injured her husband and children, or is she grieved that she has dishonored the Lord Jesus? A sorrowful pastor might confess to having a homosexual relationship once the evidence is uncovered; is this man in serious depression and anguish over the loss of a place of honor, his position in the church, and his family, or is his heart truly broken over his sin? Many more such true stories could be told. Often the guilty party has a certain feeling of sorrow over his sin, but it is not a sorrow that is according to God; he is not broken in his heart. It is critical to understand the necessary spiritual distinction between *worldly sorrow* and *godly sorrow*. "For godly grief produces a repentance that leads to salvation without regret, whereas worldly grief produces death" (2 Cor. 7:10). The original New Testament language of this verse demonstrates that genuine repentance belongs to the realm of true salvation. Worldly grief or sorrow cannot repent, because it lacks regenerative grace that softens and breaks the heart.

Consider the numerous examples in Scripture of worldly sorrow:

- Genesis 4 records the first murder. Cain kills his brother because he is envious of God's approval of Abel's sacrifice. God judges Cain, and this judgment is so severe that Cain is severely distressed. "Cain said to the LORD, 'My punishment

20

is greater than I can bear'" (Gen. 4:13). Yet he does not repent (1 John 3:12).

- Esau, Jacob's older brother, was sorrowful over the careless disregard of his birthright when he sold it for a momentary meal. He shed many tears over his loss, but he was not truly broken and repentant (Gen. 27:34; Heb. 12:16–17).
- When King Ahab's practice of idolatry was revealed by the prophet Elijah, "he tore his clothes and put sackcloth on his flesh and fasted and lay in sackcloth and went about dejectedly" (1 Kings 21:27, a public and ancient sign of remorse and sorrow), but he was not broken and repentant, because he continued to consult false prophets (1 Kings 22:6).
- After betraying the Lord Jesus Christ, Judas was full of remorse and returned the thirty pieces of silver to the chief priests and elders of Judaism. He even confessed to them, "I have sinned" (Matt. 27:4), but he did not repent. Instead, he proceeded to hang himself.

Being distressed, sorrowful, mournful, dejected, and remorseful are not the same thing as godly repentance. Even though these attitudes may *accompany* genuine repentance, they are not to be confused with it. True repentance is what King David expresses after Nathan the prophet revealed his adulterous sin with Bathsheba: "The sacrifices of God are a broken spirit; a broken and contrite heart, O God, you will not despise" (Ps. 51:17). This must be a reality in your heart for genuine cleansing to occur.

EVIDENCES OF TRUE REPENTANCE

THE PURSUIT OF PURITY

What will be the evidence that genuine repentance has taken place in your heart? How will you know the difference between "godly sorrow" and "worldly sorrow"? The answer to these questions is summed up by the apostle Paul after he contrasts these two types of sorrow in 2 Corinthians 7:10. In the following verse Paul continues to describe the person who has godly sorrow and repentance: "For see what earnestness this godly grief has produced in you, but also what eagerness to clear yourselves, what indignation, what fear, what longing, what zeal, what punishment!" (2 Cor. 7:11). There will be an earnestness and eagerness to pursue righteousness in your life. Repentance sows an undeniable desire in the heart to proactively seek righteousness and do what is good. A broken and repentant heart is not in a static state; it is active—boldly and aggressively pursuing purity. This eagerness then turns to the pursuit of clearing yourself from the remaining stigma of your sinfulness. This does not mean you deny sin's stigma but rather that you seek to remove yourself from any association with your previous sins. In doing so you work to restore the trust and confidence of others who have been hurt or betrayed by your sin. Prior to your repentance you were indifferent and complacent concerning the impurities of your heart, but now you are alert and conscientious to any hint or suggestion of their return.

THE PRESENCE OF RIGHTEOUS INDIGNATION

Another characteristic of a repentant heart is anger! This is what the word *indignation* in this verse means. Your heart is angered over the reproach of your previous evil desires. The fuel of your anger comes from the fact that the sinful desires of your heart have brought shame on the Lord and his people. This is often called righteous indignation or holy anger. It is anger motivated by righteousness in a world filled with unrighteousness. Sometimes you may hear a Christian say in anger, "I can't believe I thought that!" Righteous anger does not make such a self-favoring statement; self-righteous anger does. If you really understood the depth of the sinful desires of your heart and frailty, you would say instead, "I can't believe I don't think that more often!" A broken and repentant heart is easily angered at its own inherent propensities toward unholy desires.

THE PURSUANCE OF A HOLY FEAR

Still another unexpected characteristic of a repentant heart, according to 2 Corinthians 7:11, is fear. The object of this fear is not explained in this immediate verse but can be understood by the surrounding context. There are two equally valid understandings of what should strike fear in the heart broken by repentance. The first is built on the second. The first is the fear of repeating a sin because of the weakness of the flesh. A repentant heart does not want to sin again, but it is fearful because it knows its own careless habits. Second, a repentant heart has a deep and abiding reverence for God that comes from a holy fear of him. He will bring a temporal chastening and judgment on his children. He will not remove a child from his heavenly family, but he will bring hardship into that child's life (Heb. 12:7–11). The repentant person knows that God's chastisement comes from his love for his children. In the first verse of this same chapter Paul explains this more fully: "Since we have these promises, beloved, let us cleanse ourselves from every defilement of body and spirit, bringing holiness to completion in the fear of God" (2 Cor. 7:1). When Paul speaks of the "body and spirit," he is referring to the outer man (body) and the inner man (spirit). Your heart is at the very core of your inner man.

Fear and love are two sides of the same coin. What you love the most, you will also fear the most. It is like a young man who is seriously in love with a young woman. Because he loves her, he is fearful of doing anything that would displease her. Godly sorrow always involves full and complete repentance, and this includes a fear of God that grows out of a deep love for him. You cannot say you love God if you are not fearful of displeasing him. Anyone who truly loves God will be fearful of harboring any sensual impurity within the heart. Therefore, Jesus says, "If you love me, you will keep my commandments" (John 14:15). The repentant heart is a biblically fearful heart.

THE PALPABILITY OF A DEEP YEARNING

Yet another characteristic of a repentant heart in 2 Corinthians 7:11 is a deep yearning, which is an intensely passionate desire or longing to restore those relationships that were broken and damaged by your sin. As a Christian, sin harms your relationship with God. It disrupts but does not sever it. You still have a parent-child relationship with him as your heavenly Father, but it suffers greatly from this disruption. The conscience of your heavy heart is plagued with guilt; repentance is the necessary step to restoring it. When you are repentant you will make every effort to ensure your relationship with God is restored to a better and more intimate state than it was prior to your sin. This eagerness will extend to your attempts to restore any relationship with others that has caused great hurt, difficulty, and alienation. Rebuilding trust is like laying siege to a fortified city (Prov. 18:19). Your broken and repentant heart will do whatever is necessary, for as long as it takes, to rebuild the relationship. Restoring damaged relationships becomes the yearning of a repentant heart.

THE PROPENSITY FOR ZEAL

Still another characteristic of a repentant heart is zeal. This characteristic also comes from a sincere love of God and others (Matt. 22:37–40). Your heart is zealous for God, and you will hate anyone or anything that would bring reproach on him (Ps. 139:21–22). A deep passion for righteousness will grow in your heart that was missing when you were still rationalizing and excusing your sinful desires. You will cringe and be repulsed by all injustice. A burning passion in your heart will motivate you to see that righteousness and goodness prevail. This is not a zealous defense of personal rights that is often fueled by selfish desires; rather, it is a passionate defense of good for others and the righteousness of God. A broken and repentant heart is not passive; it is actively zealous.

A PLACE FOR PUNISHMENT

The last characteristic of a repentant heart in this verse is closely associated with zealousness because it passionately desires justice. It is translated as "what punishment" and means a desire to see punishment applied where it is necessary and appropriate. Sometimes it is translated as a desire for "avenging of wrong." This final characteristic is a critical aspect of a heart changed through repentance. The heart that hides all types of sinful and sensual desires is guarded and self-protective. But the repentant heart does not seek to protect itself. It is so willing to see sin punished or avenged that it does not matter what it personally costs. This heart is open to experiencing whatever consequences that may come about as a result of its sin.

An important qualification is necessary concerning a heart that is eager to see personal sin punished: a rightfully repentant heart needs to understand the theological problem of penance. Some Christians will indulge in self-flagellation when they know they have committed a vile sin. They feel they must pay a kind of emotional penance by experiencing some type of self-imposed suffering. Whether it is through self-denial or by imposing on themselves an attitude of perpetual despondency, they believe they have to pay God back for what they have done wrong. This will often cause a person to wallow in self-pity and adopt a "woe is me" attitude toward life. Good theology will not allow a believer to do this. Jesus Christ has already paid for all the sins of the believer (Heb. 10:10–12). To assume that you can add more payment for your sins by your self-imposed suffering makes the all-sufficient sacrifice of Jesus Christ meaningless. It is a gross violation of good theology because it undermines the atoning work of Christ. Furthermore, it will not be helpful in the prevention of future sin. "These have indeed an appearance of wisdom in promoting self-made religion and asceticism and severity to the body, but they are of no value in stopping the indulgence of the flesh" (Col. 2:23). When Christians practice penance for their personal sin, they betray a misplaced trust in the flesh in order to gain favor with God. This fleshly indulgence in self-appointed suffering will not gain God's favor, neither will it be sufficient to restrain future temptation. Real repentance denies that the flesh has the capability to pay for and conquer sin; instead, it is zealous to see God's justice served even if it involves a personal cost.

THE HEART OF THE MATTER

You cannot trust your own heart to know itself. The only reliable guide for self-knowledge is the Word of God. Your sinful heart is not only difficult to understand but also deceptive—it will lie to you (Prov. 28:26). It is as full of rationalizations for sin as it is prone to cast itself and its motives in the most favorable light. Godly men throughout

Scripture have learned to distrust their hearts while relying only on God's revelation to understand the heart's central motivations (Eccl. 7:20). God is the only righteous judge of your heart. Any dominating desire of the heart that replaces the desire to love and serve God foremost is an *idol*. It may not be an idol of wood or stone, but it is just as destructive. A heart idol will demand worship (1 Cor. 10:6–14). Your heart is full of controlling voices that will call for your complete allegiance. Chief among them are the voices that awaken your sensual desires. They will promise you pleasurable fulfillment but will deliver only death (Prov. 16:25). Your soul dies! Your relationships die! Moreover, your body may die from a sexually transmitted disease (STD). It is time to identify your idol and repent. The remainder of this book provides you with the biblical wisdom and insight in deciphering the impure desires that dominate the worship of your heart. The Lord can purify you of sexual idolatry when you permit the Spirit of God to use the truth of his Word to change your heart.

KEY CONCEPTS

heart of man
obscure nature of the heart
"trust your heart"
self-knowledge
self-favoring self-assessment
self-deceived
self-righteousness
blind to weakness
heart crushed by grief
judicial forgiveness
parental forgiveness
presumption of innocence
total depravity
mourning impure desires
pursuing a pure heart
repentance

godly sorrow
worldly sorrow

STUDY QUESTIONS

1. Using a teaching or example from Scripture, discuss why this statement is true: "The heart's natural inclination to judge itself favorably is a serious problem."
2. Using a teaching or example from Scripture, explain why it can be deadly to "assume you know your heart well enough to entrust it with weighty matters vital to your very life and well-being."
3. God makes it clear to the Israelites (Deut. 8:2) that he took them through the wilderness wanderings so that they would know what was in their hearts. Read the following three passages; then describe what was revealed to be in the Israelites' hearts in each case.
   - Exodus 14:10–14
   - Exodus 16:2–29
   - Exodus 32:1–6
4. "Humility is often less a *destination* than it is a progressive learning *process*." Give three examples of people in Scripture whose failures due to pride demonstrate this truth.
5. In your own words, contrast the person's heart and desires who merely makes a claim to be a Christian with the person's heart and desires who truly is a Christian.

FOR FURTHER READING

Disclaimer: The listing of books and articles in the "For Further Reading" sections of this book is not necessarily an endorsement of every position that each author presents.

Ferguson, Sinclair B. *The Christian Life: A Doctrinal Introduction.* Carlisle, PA: Banner of Truth Trust, 2013.

———. *The Grace of Repentance.* Wheaton, IL: Crossway, 2011.

Frame, John M. *The Doctrine of the Word of God.* Phillipsburg, NJ: P&R Publishing, 2018.

MacArthur, John. *The Gospel according to Jesus.* Grand Rapids: Zondervan, 2008.

Sproul, R. C., Jr. *One Holy Passion: The Consuming Thirst to Know God.* Nashville, TN: Thomas Nelson, 1987.

2

HEART IDOLATRY AND SEXUALITY

What is heart idolatry? This is the first critical question of this chapter, and it needs biblical clarification. If indeed the heart is deceptive, full of self-righteous rationalizations, then we need to go deep in our understanding of it to fully expose sin and live holy lives before the Lord. Christ died for us, not only to give us eternal life but so that "those who live might no longer live for themselves but for him who for their sake died and was raised" (2 Cor. 5:15). We have not been granted forgiveness of our sins just to continue in them. Rather, "His divine power has granted to us all things that pertain to life *and godliness*" (2 Peter 1:3).

You may not be accustomed to thinking of your sin in terms of idolatry that begins in the heart. Your external behaviors—the things that you participate in and can be seen by others—are the problems that weigh heavily on your mind. But if you desire to deal with your sin biblically, earnestly seeking holiness and purity and cultivating a heart that is conditioned by a repentant attitude, you will need to know what the Bible teaches about heart idolatry.

An active pursuit of holiness will characterize a pure heart. Although the *absolute perfection* of this purity will ultimately elude you in this accursed world, it is still something that you should strive for zealously and relentlessly during your time on earth. "For God has not called us for impurity, but in holiness" (1 Thess. 4:7). If you are committed to purifying yourself of ungodly desires—to ridding yourself of heart

29

idolatry—it is vital you understand what God says about how you were made and how your heart operates.

HOW YOUR HEART OPERATES

First and foremost, you are God's creation; indeed, you were created *in the image of God* (Gen. 1:26–27; 9:6). This means that the human being is not an animal. Unlike created animals, you possess intellect, will, and emotions. You have the ability to reason and plan, to realize that your life has meaning and purpose. As a person created in God's image, you even have the capacity to exercise some of the communicable attributes of God: to love, to be jealous, or to be angry (among others). You are not a mere energy force in a meaningless universe. A force cannot love or hate, neither can it intend or purpose.

In addition, you are much more than the sum total of your biological parts. To regard your humanity exclusively from a physiological standpoint is truncated and simplistic. This view places you solely at the mercy of your genetics, your body structure, and the neurochemical processes of your brain. According to this representation of mankind, there is no Creator, no soul. This materialistic view maintains that when the human body dies and brain activity ceases, the entire person ceases to exist. However, this is not the biblical view of a person. The Bible teaches us that when the body dies, the soul lives on. Though the physical brain is dead, the mind continues in the spirit without the limitations of the body. The apostle Paul alludes to out-of-body human consciousness when he declares, "So whether we are at home or away [from the body], we make it our aim to please him" (2 Cor. 5:9). Even though the physiological brain is dead without the soul, the immaterial, spiritual mind continues to function away from the body. It can still purpose, aim, and intend to please the Lord.

All human beings were designed to have a worshipful relationship with their Creator God (Luke 4:8; cf. Deut. 6:13–14). Mankind was created for the distinct purpose of worshiping and glorifying God from the heart (Ps. 111:1). However, as the apostle Paul explains, the human heart demonstrates willful sinfulness and rebellion toward God—a radical change in allegiance from Creator God to created things.

> For the wrath of God is revealed from heaven against all ungodliness and unrighteousness of men, who by their unrighteousness suppress the truth. For what can be known about God is plain to them, because God has shown it to them. For his invisible attributes, namely, his eternal power and divine nature, have been clearly perceived, ever since the creation of the world, in the things that have been made. So they are without excuse. For although they knew God, they did not honor him as God or give thanks to him, but they became futile in their thinking, and their foolish hearts were darkened. Claiming to be wise, they became fools, and exchanged the glory of the immortal God for images resembling mortal man and birds and animals and creeping things. (Rom. 1:18–23)

Instead of worshiping the Creator, the human heart has turned away to find its satisfaction in the worship of creation. The innermost thoughts and intentions of man now crave *self*-gratification and *self*-satisfaction. In order to experience this self-worship orientation, the sinful heart has turned to worship the functional gods of this world rather than the faithful God of glory. This is vital to understand if you are going to deal with the impurities of your own heart. You must have a biblical understanding of the nature of your heart.

The Bible teaches that the heart is the primary "control center" of life. But popular secular concepts, especially in Western culture, have perpetuated a false view of the heart. For many, it is merely the seat of romance and emotion. Greeting cards and candy boxes in the shape of hearts are common expressions of what is in the heart. However, the biblical idea of the heart has little to do with emotion or romance; instead, it is the dwelling place of your thought life. This can be seen in Moses' words as he describes what God saw when he looked on humanity just prior to the flood. "The LORD saw that the wickedness of man was great in the earth, and that every intention of the thoughts of his heart was only evil continually" (Gen. 6:5). The tense of the

Hebrew verb for *saw* indicates this was not just a one-time observation but that God *continually* "saw that the wickedness of man was great in the earth." What God viewed of mankind was more than just continual bad behavior. He witnessed that *the thoughts of his heart* were continually evil. The text describes the heart as having intentionality and thoughts that were full of evil.

You can see a similar wording when Solomon says, "The purpose in a man's heart is like deep water, but a man of understanding will draw it out" (Prov. 20:5). Here the heart is described as purposing. The Hebrew word used for "purpose" can also be translated "to plan." Contrary to the world's view of romance and emotion, the Bible says that the human heart purposes and plans.

While addressing the error of the Pharisees in elevating and equating mere behavior to holy living, Jesus warns that the *heart* of man is the main problem. "And he said, 'What comes out of a person is what defiles him. For from within, out of the heart of man, come evil thoughts, sexual immorality, theft, murder, adultery'" (Mark 7:20–21). In the Sermon on the Mount Jesus further explains, "But I say to you that everyone who looks at a woman with lustful intent has already committed adultery with her in his heart" (Matt. 5:28). For Jesus, the heart's chief function is to think, intend, and lust. Therefore, it is important to conclude that the biblical view of the heart is different from society's emotional/romantic view. It involves intentions, lusts, cravings, purposes, plans, and thoughts. Out of the outgrowth of these, your heart then determines your behavior (see fig. 2.1).

In truth, your heart directs everything you think and do. Whatever is the worship focus of your heart will ultimately determine your entire life. Moreover, your worship focus will determine what your greatest passion is. It will affect all your plans, all your intentions, all your cravings. This, in turn, will affect the choices you make in life. Solomon warns, "Keep your heart with all vigilance, for from it flow the springs of life" (Prov. 4:23). It is contextually permissible to substitute the idea of thought life for the word *heart* in this verse, rendering this translation: "Keep your *thought life* with all vigilance, for from it flow the springs of life." Your thought life reveals what you worship, what controls your

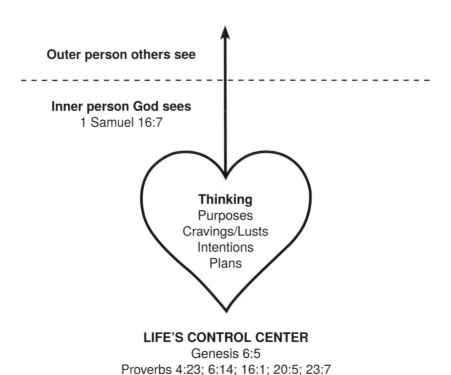

BEHAVIOR
Matthew 7:20–23; 12:34

Outer person others see

- -

Inner person God sees
1 Samuel 16:7

Thinking
Purposes
Cravings/Lusts
Intentions
Plans

LIFE'S CONTROL CENTER
Genesis 6:5
Proverbs 4:23; 6:14; 16:1; 20:5; 23:7
Hebrews 4:12

Fig. 2.1. The Heart: Life's Control Center

passions, thereby revealing what you love the most (Matt. 22:37–40). Your passions will consume your thinking, determine your plans, form your intentions, master your cravings, and focus your purpose.

DISCOVERING YOUR OWN HEART IDOLS

The root of the problem is the sinfulness of your heart, which has twisted your worship away from God. Notice that Scripture reveals that when your heart's chief longings and worship are on anything other than the God of glory, this is idolatry. Many mistakenly think of an idol as only a physical object made of wood, or stone, or some other sort of material. Certainly, tangible objects can become idols, but idols consist of *anything* ruling your heart—whether an object or an idea, whether a statue or an intense longing.

The Bible describes the idolatry of the Israelites after their miraculous deliverance from Egypt. Held in bondage for four hundred years, the Jewish people reveled in their newfound freedom in the wilderness, not by worshiping their Redeemer God but by indulging sinful cravings. "With most of them God was not pleased" (1 Cor. 10:5). Comparing that event to the New Testament believers, the apostle Paul provides a commentary on their idolatry: "Now these things took place as examples for us, that we might not desire evil as they did. Do not be idolaters as some of them were; as it is written, 'The people sat down to eat and drink and rose up to play'" (1 Cor. 10:6–7). These wilderness Jews falsely worshiped "Yahweh" with a golden calf and were condemned by God (Ex. 32:7–8). However, their idolatry went far beyond the worship of a physical idol. Paul says they craved eating, drinking, and playing, which were intangible desires that consumed their hearts. In addition, their idolatry included indulgent sexual immorality: "We must not indulge in sexual immorality as some of them did, and twenty-three thousand fell in a single day" (1 Cor. 10:8).[1] The desire for drink, food, entertainment, and sex can become idolatrous cravings that rule the heart. When self-gratifying pleasure dominates the heart, it has become an idolatrous ruling desire. You do not have to worship a physical idol to be an idolater.

What is so deceptive about these ruling desires is that they seem to be a natural part of one's life. Too many Christians assume they cannot be corrupted by their desires, failing to realize how much these desires have already ensnared their hearts, ruled their thoughts, and now control their ambitions. Evil cravings are often comfortable cravings, easily finding a home in the unsuspecting heart. Nevertheless, a person of integrity is willing to be brutally honest in searching his own heart. "O LORD, who shall sojourn in your tent? Who shall dwell on your holy

---

1. A thousand more died later (Num. 25:9).

hill? He who walks blamelessly and does what is right and speaks truth in his heart" (Ps. 15:1–2).

This search for the truth about your heart can begin by answering the following questions honestly and thoroughly. It will be most helpful for you to write your responses, think about your answers for a while, and then restate them with more clarity and insight. A true portrait of your inner person and its idols will emerge. The idolatrous worship of your heart will become obvious and focused in your understanding.

WHAT WANTS AND DESIRES IN YOUR HEART ARE OPPOSED TO GOD'S WANTS AND DESIRES?

Any want or desire, no matter how innocent it may seem, that is contrary to God's revealed will for your life is a *potential* idol (1 Kings 8:59–61) with the capacity to reign supreme in your heart if you do not turn away from it. While not every sinful desire becomes a *ruling* desire in the heart, the ones that captivate and enslave you are idols, which is one manifestation of heart idolatry. These ruling idols control your thought life and dominate your time and energy in fulfilling their endless demands. If you permit this heart idolatry to remain unabated, unrepented of, you will find yourself in a full-blown rebellion against what God says is best for your life. And when it comes to your defiance against him, God will always prove to be true and you will always be proved a liar (Rom. 3:4).

Many sinful sexual desires easily become idolatrous. For example, a person may for a brief time desire a relationship with another that is ungodly. But when it is acknowledged as being sinful and thereby repented of, it is put to an end. No further thought is given to it. In such a case, the sinful sexual desire was not allowed to rule over that person; it was not permitted to become an idolatrous desire. Conversely, when such a desire has been allowed to become a deep longing of lust in the heart, when significant time has passed without repentance, then it has become a reigning, idolatrous desire—one that shapes and controls every aspect of life. Idols demand worship. What are the sinful desires that tend to dominate your heart?

35

WHAT DOES GOD WANT AND DESIRE THAT AGREES WITH YOUR WANTS AND DESIRES, BUT YOU WANT IT SO MUCH YOU ARE WILLING TO BE UNGODLY IF YOU DO NOT ACQUIRE IT?

Many idols begin as godly and pure desires. For example, the desire for marriage can be a godly desire. However, when this becomes a person's *all-consuming* desire, it can become idolatrous and sinful. Perhaps years have passed and this person is not yet married and has no foreseeable prospects of such. Anger and cynicism is a common temptation. Those who give in to this temptation often become sinfully sarcastic and unduly critical with the opposite sex, by whom they feel rejected. This desire that began innocently has morphed into a sinful craving that demands satisfaction. Some will rationalize their anger by quoting Paul's words out of context: "For it is better to marry than to burn with passion" (1 Cor. 7:9).[2] By quoting this verse they are misusing Scripture to justify their idolatrous desire.

Another example may be applicable. Christian parents love their children and deeply desire to see them repent and follow Christ. This is a desire that conforms to God's moral will as well. However, after years pass and their children walk away from the Lord, many parents' legitimate desire has so dominated their passions that they begin to demand salvation for their children. Often they are angry, sometimes even hateful, becoming manipulative with their children. They are easily offended that other parents have Christian children while they do not. They may blame God for not having "elected" their child. They may be tempted to dilute the gospel in order to ensure their child is covered by their new definition of a believer. This can turn a coerced child's prayer, intended to satisfy the parents, into a false assurance of that child's salvation, often lacking complete surrender to Christ as Lord and Savior. Such desires, which began as godly hopes and dreams, have grown to be controlling idols of the heart. Having a

---

2. Paul is not saying that marriage cures lust. It does not, because a lustful heart can be carried into marriage. The context is a time of great distress for Christians (1 Cor. 7:26) and that it is better not to marry during these distressing times. Yet his statement concedes that for a couple already committed to each other, "it is better to marry than to burn with passion."

Christian child has become more important than being a godly father or mother. What previously good desires in your heart have become sinful and demanding?

WHAT ARE THE CONTROLLING EXPECTATIONS THAT DOMINATE YOUR HEART WITH EVIL THOUGHTS, UNGODLY WORDS, AND SINFUL ACTIONS WHEN THEY ARE UNREALIZED?

Expectations can be the seeds that germinate and grow into mature idols. Of course, not all expectations are evil or sinful. But the ones that overgrow the heart, crowding it and taking over, these are the idolatrous ones. Like the kudzu plant (*Pueraria lobata*) of the southeastern United States, expectations are hardy and robust and can easily grow to cover everything. Some expectations are innately sinful because they are clearly against God's moral law. Any expectation that it is beneficial and even right to steal, lie, cheat, or commit any immoral or ungodly act in certain circumstances is sinful from the start. Malice is a type of expectation that is sinful from the beginning, hoping for the downfall or disgrace of another person. Other expectations may begin righteously but quickly turn ungodly. Perhaps a husband thinks, "I expect my romantic evening spent alone with my wife to be wonderful." This wonderful expectation is in his thoughts all day. But when he arrives home, the house is a wreck, one of the children is sick, his wife called off the babysitter, and they have to cancel their dinner plans at the restaurant. He is upset and angry all evening! It is shown in his sarcastic and angry tone. What started as a good and wholesome expectation turned into a demanding desire. What expectations do you tend to become angry, mean, or hateful over?

WHAT DO YOU CONSIDER YOUR "RIGHTS" TO BE, AND HOW DO YOU REACT IN UNGODLY WAYS WHEN DENIED?

Everyone loves to talk about personal rights these days, and most idols masquerade as rights. Here are a few examples: I have a right to be loved, cared for, heard, respected, considered attractive, honored, promoted, to have a good-looking spouse, to be considered important, to have children, to have well-behaved children, to have children who are successful, to be sexually satisfied—the list could go on. There seems to be no end to what the human heart believes is its right. Yet when you carefully study Scripture, you realize that outside of Christ we have no rights (Gal. 6:3). The rights we have in Christ are only because of his merits, because we are fellow heirs with him (Rom. 8:17), and not based on any merit (rights) of our own. These so-called rights we falsely assume we deserve are idols of the heart. What rights do you believe are being denied you?

WHAT SPECIFIC STANDARDS HAVE YOU SET FOR YOUR LIFE THAT ARE NOT GOD'S STANDARDS BUT HAVE LED YOU TO SINFUL THOUGHTS AND PRACTICES?

Self-determination is a favorite principle promoted by the secular world. Many assume that they are in control of their own future, so they set certain standards for themselves to help them arrive at that desired destination. Many Christians fall into a similar pattern of life. Instead of setting biblical standards and goals for themselves, they adopt self-generated ambitions for life. For example, a person may say that "by the age of forty I will be a millionaire." When age forty arrives and he has not achieved his goal, he is devastated! He is overwhelmed with feelings of inadequacy and failure. Some may even believe that life is not worth living any longer. This artificial, self-contrived standard is an idol they have made for themselves. They may bow down and worship that standard for years. Similarly, a person may set a goal of becoming a star athlete. When years of self-denial and practice end with a debilitating injury, life is viewed as no longer worth living.

Another example can be the person who, during his early teen years, imagines a fictional partner as his future spouse. This imaginary partner has all the perfectly attractive and alluring physical and attitudinal attributes. Such an ideal and unreal person has no imperfections whatsoever. But in reality we are all destined to marry someone with imperfections, falling far short of such an unrealistic standard. Consequently, the person who has set such an impossible standard and refuses to relinquish it to reality finds that the intimacy in his eventual marriage is not as fulfilling as imagined. His unhappiness spills over into the marriage, and his spouse begins to feel inadequate and unloved. Significant conflict arises in the relationship. Where did this come from? It came from a false standard adopted long before marriage that fed his imagination through unrealistic characters in books, magazines, movies, online pictures, and stories. Just to be clear, the sinful mind does not need public and social media to construct the ideal intimate partner; it can accomplish this all by itself. Once the ideal sexual partner is established in the mind, mental and physical desires are mapped onto it. Bodily responses are activated only once this false standard of an ideal sexual partner, programmed into the mind through years of mental rehearsals, is met. It reaps years of disenchantment and unhappiness in marriage. When your heart has set unbiblical standards for personal achievement or desires and those standards rule your life more than God, they are false idols. What kind of ungodly standard have you set for your life that has become your idol?

WHAT MIND-SET HAVE YOU ADOPTED THAT IS OPPOSED TO GOD'S TRUTH AND LEADS YOU TO SINFUL THOUGHTS, PLANS, AND INTENTIONS?

Professing Christians can openly acknowledge their belief in the authority and sufficiency of Scripture but be personally opposed to certain aspects of God's authority in their lives (John 14:23–24). Once you have formed a mind-set that is opposed to God's truth in any matter, it will eventually result in suffering (Prov. 13:15, 21). For example, many Christian men and women enter into marriage with a worldly mind-set regarding their sexual relationship in marriage. It is possible for them to be sexually faithful (having regular relations only with each other) and still be practicing a form of sinful sex with their spouse. The mind-set that sex in marriage is for my personal pleasure and enjoyment alone is one example. Husbands and wives with this type of mind-set seem to be surprised by the blunt way the apostle Paul refers to sexuality in marriage when he says, "The husband must fulfill his duty to his wife, and likewise also the wife to her husband" (1 Cor. 7:3 NASB). Literally, the original language says that the husband has a debt, obligation, or duty (ὀφειλή) to his wife sexually and the wife has an equal debt, obligation, or duty to her husband. How is it possible that Paul refers to this as a duty? This seems strange and foreign to a worldly mind-set that views self-gratification as the goal of sex in marriage. This causes numerous arguments and conflicts in marriage. The goal of intimacy in the Christian marriage is primarily not self-gratification. Instead, it is spousal-gratification. A Christian husband and a Christian wife must have as their primary goal the satisfaction of their mate. It is not wrong to deeply enjoy intimacy in marriage (Prov. 5:19; Eccl. 9:9), but this is secondary to the primary obligation of completely fulfilling the sexual desires of your spouse.

A woman I was counseling, along with her husband, grasped this concept for the first time and sat back in her chair, letting out a deep sigh. "I know where you are going with this," she blurted out. "You want me to make sure my husband is completely fulfilled!" "Well," I said, a little surprised, "it not what I am asking, it is what God is saying!" "I knew it. . . . I knew it!" Then she went on to explain, "It is not my personality to be sexually aggressive!" Immediately I got her implication—"I can't do this because it doesn't fit my personality." In other words, what she was saying was, "God has given me an impossible command to obey!" I responded to her objection by saying, "In Scripture personality is not fixed; it is fluid. We change as we mature in Christ. But this is like anything else in life: Are you going to allow personality or God's Word to reign in your life?" In her mind she understood what God expected of her, but her mind-set led her to believe she could figure a way around it and get out of God's expectation for her as a wife. What mind-set have you adopted in your life that is opposed to God's truth?

HEART IDOLATRY AND SENSUAL PASSIONS

Now we can turn to the important issue of how sexual desires relate to idolatry. Is thinking about sex wrong? Is thinking about *sinful* sex wrong? On the surface, these questions are simple enough, but when counseling a person who is enslaved to sexual fantasies, it becomes a more complicated problem that needs biblical clarification. During one counseling session, a sincere Christian young man questioned, "Is it possible for me to appreciate the beauty of the female form without committing a sin?" Most good counselors are suspicious of such questions. Is this young man trying to justify his sinful behavior and dismiss it with the excuse of artistic appreciation? This sounds like an elaborate ruse to sidestep the sin of sexual lust. Aside from the doubts about how any young man can keep himself detached from such a sensual temptation, his question raises an important issue with which the Christian must grapple. This is especially true when a devoted Christian has a genuine desire to be pure of heart. When does a thought become sinful? Are some thoughts innately sinful? If it is possible to have holy thoughts about sex, when do these thoughts become unholy? In a world convinced of its "rights" to sexual openness and freedom, exploited by advertising executives who know how to appeal to basal desires, how can the true follower of Christ ensure the purity of the inner man as well as the outer man?

The first and great commandment, on which the entire law hangs, should be the desire and goal of every believer: "And he said to him, 'You shall love the Lord your God with all your heart and with all your soul and with all your mind'" (Matt. 22:37). To love the Lord with all your mind implies purity of thought. In the Sermon on the Mount, Jesus said, "Blessed are the pure in heart, for they shall see God" (Matt. 5:8). Paul admonished the Christians at Philippi, "whatever is pure . . . think about these things" (Phil. 4:8). He also instructed the young pastor Timothy to view "younger women as sisters, in all purity" (1 Tim. 5:2). How a counselee thinks about sex issues is critical to his purity.

Sufficient biblical support undergirds the principle that simply thinking about a sin is not sinful. If the mere conceptualization of a sin, even sex or sinful sex, is wrong, then one would have to conclude that both God and Jesus Christ have committed sin since the Bible is full of examples of sexual sin.[3] They are negative examples recorded

---

3. Gen. 19:4–5; 34:2; Lev. 18:1–30; 2 Sam. 11:1–5; 13:11–14; 1 Kings 11:1–8; Prov. 5:1–23; Rom. 1:24–32; 1 Cor. 6:9–11.

41

for our instruction and edification, and we should remember them, be warned, and understand the ugly consequences of sensual ungodliness. Our Lord Jesus Christ spoke on several occasions concerning sex and its associated sins (Matt. 5:27–32; 15:19; 19:9–12; John 4:18). Therefore, to think of sex, or even a sexual sin, is not wrong.

Those who believe any rational thought of sex or intercourse is immoral have made a standard (a rule) for themselves that the Bible has not made. As Christians, they are guilty of sin for imposing a rigid standard of performance that is beyond scriptural admonitions. Such erroneous assumptions concerning sex have led to such things as forbidding Christians to study Proverbs 5–7 and the Song of Solomon. To many of these people, any consideration of sex is wrong because they view sex itself as sinful. But God created binary gender distinctiveness in view of sex and called it "very good" (Gen. 1:27, 31). To label something bad that God has called good is presumptuous and sinful.

The question still remains, "When do thoughts of sex become sinful?" In short, they become sinful when they come from a demanding heart of covetousness. A heart so impassioned that it refuses to accept anything less than the object of its desire is covetous. Sexual pleasure has become the goal of such a heart. All the heart's longings and intense passions are channeled in a sinfully worshipful way; sex has become its functional god. Somatic desires and attraction maintain a perfect cadence with the heart. These enslaving sexual desires of the heart initiate both internal (immoral fantasies) and external (behaviors) activities that become the captivating rhythm of sexual fulfillment.

From the earliest biblical texts, desire (or lust) has carried a dynamic and reflexive sense. The most common Old Testament Hebrew word for desire (חָמַד, *hamad*) is used with both senses.[4] In some cases, this term is used to refer to something attractive or pleasing to the eyes. This is the reflexive use of the word. In English, it would often be translated

---

4. One may distinguish between two functions for חמד: "(a) a usage describing the act. [active], acting subj., and (b) a usage describing the pass. [passive], sought-after obj.; noun meaning fall into the latter category." Ernst Jenni and Claus Westermann, eds., *Theological Lexicon of the Old Testament*, trans. Mark E. Biddle (Peabody, MA: Hendrickson, 1997), 1:434.

"a delight for the eyes" (cf. 1 Kings 20:6; Lam. 2:4; Ezek. 24:16, 21, 25). When the Hebrew term is used in this way, it refers to something precious or pleasurable to view but not necessarily an object of illicit greed or wanton lust. In view of this exegesis, there is an appreciation of beauty or attractiveness that is not sinful, like the appreciation of an exquisite mural or fine painting. In answer to my young counselee's question, it is possible to appreciate beauty and the attractiveness of a woman without entering into sin. But, as we shall see later, it is also a very dangerous line that a person susceptible to sexual sin needs to avoid as much as possible. While he may appreciate beauty in other things, this becomes more difficult when it is the opposite sex because the propensities of the heart and the danger of unholy lust are just too great.

Scripture frequently warns of the dynamic form of desire. Here the same Hebrew term (חמד) is often translated "to covet." This is the more active form that tempts the depraved heart with covetous desire. Unholy lust is sown in the heart when this type of sensual desire becomes vigorous and demanding. This kind of sexual lust is intense, refusing to be denied, and engages the insatiable appetites of the body. Using the same Hebrew word, God warns his people in the Decalogue, "you shall not covet your neighbor's wife" (Ex. 20:17; cf. Deut. 5:21). Solomon advises the fool not to desire or lust after the seductive married woman: "Do not desire her beauty in your heart, and do not let her capture you with her eyelashes" (Prov. 6:25). This reference to "eyelashes" seems to be an unusual statement to our modern thinking, but it was common for women in Solomon's day to cover their entire bodies with a robe and their eyes with a veil. Some flirtatious women would lift their veils or expose their eyes to a man in order to attract his attention. This is active desire that insists on sexual satisfaction, quite different from the detached appreciation of beauty.

The Septuagint translates the Hebrew term *to desire* or *to covet* (חמד) with the Greek, *epithymeo* (ἐπιθυμέω). It, too, is a general term for desire that can express a form of indifferent appreciation (reflexive) or evil covetous desire (dynamic). Occasionally, it is used to speak of intense aspirations that are holy or praiseworthy (Isa. 58:2). However, God prohibits the evil or covetous desires of man in all forms because it amounts to idolatrous worship. "If the tenth commandment (Exod. 20:17) forbids such desire, it is because God desires from men not merely obedience in acts, but also in their words, thoughts, looks, efforts and wishes. He desires love from the whole heart (Deut. 6:5)."[5] Evil desire is dominated by the earthly and the sensual, while holy aspirations seek to love God as the primary, overarching desire. All other desires are defined by and subordinate to the desire to please God.

This idea of the dominating power of evil desire is carried into the New Testament. The apostle Paul uses desire, *epithymeo* (ἐπιθυμέω), as an expression of sinful passion that rules men. In other words, it is a passionate desire that overrules the desire to please God. Paul sees in it the driving power in man's "flesh," *sarx* (σάρξ), his sinful being that has turned from God. *Epithymeo* seeks gratification (Gal. 5:16). It urges man to act on the intense desire. When all is said and done, it expresses the deeply rooted tendency in man to find the focus of life in himself, to trust himself (his feelings, desires, and cravings), and to love himself more than others. Paul equates this tendency with the flesh and the passions (Eph. 4:22), the powers that draw a man away from God.[6]

This "driving power in man's flesh" can be unyielding and relentless in its desire to find sexual self-fulfillment. The man who follows these desires has placed himself under their reign and is described as enslaved.[7] They dominate the individual, ruling and riding roughshod over his life. The flesh now overrules the spirit. Men and women will leave spouses and children, abandon their Christian friends and church, submit themselves to years of debt, and risk deadly disease to find sexual gratification. This is a wicked bondage that exacts a horrific toll.

5. Colin Brown, ed., *The New International Dictionary of New Testament Theology* (Grand Rapids: Zondervan, 1975), 1:456.

6. Ibid., 457.

7. I prefer the biblical terms *enslaved* and *bondage* rather than the more secular *addicted* for at least four reasons: (1) you need to think in biblical terms about sexual desires, (2) the contemporary idea of addiction carries a medical etiology and therefore medical prescription, (3) medical (and demonic) causality to habituated sexual sins assumes a certain unnecessary victimization and irresponsibility, and (4) it is derived from the Latin *addictus*, which means "assigned" or "surrendered," and carries no hope, but there is always an opportunity for liberation from slavery.

SEXUAL IDOLATRY AS SLAVERY

Slavery is a natural and biblical way to think about this problem. A slave must serve or pay tribute to his master. This is his worship. Whatever coerces him to bow to such a master, a slave believes he has no choice. The temptation is too great, too irresistible. He is held captive, under fear of some loss or failure in life, with deeply ingrained sexual habituations that command homage.

Two distinctive types of slavery exist. Similar to the difference between the homeborn slave (Jer. 2:14) and the forced laborer (Gen. 49:15; Isa. 31:8; Lam. 1:1) in ancient Israelite society, there are differences between the two types of sexual slavery. The person who is under complete domination, fully surrendered to these drives, is unregenerate and without the quickening power of the Holy Spirit. No desire within him wants to change his status. He is perfectly content to remain at home as a slave of the household. Roland de Vaux speaks of how ancient slaves were viewed in Israelite homes: "Even slaves do not constitute a class apart: they form part of the family."[8] The unbeliever is perfectly at home with his sexual obsessions unless they get in the way of a greater desire. Normally, he will be happy with his pornography, womanizing, adultery, prostitution, masturbation, pedophilia, homosexuality, fetishism, or bestiality. He is most at home and comfortable here, where he is mollycoddled and soothed. In fact, he wonders why people make such a big deal about his sexual preferences and practices as long as he is not hurting anybody. He views his preferences and practices simply as a matter of personal choice or male nature.

Research statistics provide him with persuasive data to confirm his genetic propensities as a male. The brain circuitry processing rewarding and aversive stimuli is hypothesized to be at the core of motivated behavior. In this study, discrete categories of beautiful faces are shown to have differing reward values and to activate reward circuitry in human subjects differently. In particular, young heterosexual males

8. Roland de Vaux, *Ancient Israel* (New York: McGraw-Hill, 1965), 1:68.

45

rate pictures of beautiful males and females as attractive but exert effort via a keypress procedure to view only pictures of attractive females.[9]

The unregenerate sexual slave argues that certain subcortical and paralimbic regions of the brain instinctually fire because of his inherited evolutionary biochemistry. This instinct is to assure the propagation of the species. He concludes that sexual drives are natural and irresistible; you cannot fight nature. But God says you can!

Biological and genetic models of determinism end in nihilism. Proverbs makes the keen observation, "Whoever pampers his servant from childhood will in the end find him his heir" (Prov. 29:21).[10] Many counselees are kept enslaved to sexual indulgences for a lifetime by catering to their idols with elaborate excuses. What is determinative is not the biology but the spiritual condition of the person. People who are born into the household of wickedness are depraved slaves, and as they give themselves over to their sensuality, they become eager sons of their sensual unrighteousness. They become the true sons of sex.

Those who are concerned about sexual slavery must always be aware of the comfort factor of the person in this sin. Those who persist in sexual sin or repeatedly (or naturally) return to their habits of enslavement may not be regenerate after all. No matter how much they claim to be believers, the dog returns to its vomit and the pig returns to its mud (2 Peter 2:22; cf. Prov. 26:11). Why does the dog return to its vomit and the pig return to the mud? Because their essential natures have not changed. It is the nature of a dog to consume its own vomit and it is the nature of a pig to wallow in the mud. The nature of men and women who keep returning to their sinful sexual activity,

---

9. "Functional magnetic resonance imaging [fMRI] at 3 T shows that passive viewing of beautiful female faces activates reward circuitry, in particular the nucleus accumbens. An extended set of subcortical and paralimbic reward regions also appears to follow aspects of the keypress rather than the rating procedures, suggesting that reward circuitry function does not include aesthetic assessment." Itzhak Aharon, Nancy Etcoff, Dan Ariely, Christopher F. Chabris, Ethan O'Connar, Hans C. Breiter, "Beautiful Faces Have Variable Reward Value: fMRI and Behavioral Evidence," *Neuron* 32 (November 8, 2001): 537.

10. There is no direct reference to sexual sins in this passage, but by way of analogy the broader theological principle is applicable.

after sufficient warning from God's Word, has not changed. Most have never achieved lasting results because they have attempted to liberate themselves from their sexual obsessions through personal efforts of self-denial rooted in self-righteousness, only to experience continual failure. It is easy to dupe yourself into believing you are a Christian; yet, like a boomerang, you find yourself returning to the same sin when the opportunity avails itself. Such men and women cannot help but worship their idol of sensuality because it is a very part of their nature. The homeborn slave has become the rightful heir of his father "gratification" and cannot stray far from his real home.

A second type of slave is the forced laborer, the unwilling slave who has become a casualty of the war between the flesh and the spirit. The opposing side has captured him, but he is not its citizen or son. War is wearisome, and sometimes the person who has been struggling unsuccessfully for a length of time may surrender and attempt to negotiate a truce. With the homeborn slave there is no war, because such sin is natural. But the unwilling slave knows he is in the enemy's camp. Or, having been tricked, he may be seduced into a treaty of peace with the powerful temptation of sensual sin. He finally succumbs to the notion "Resistance is futile!" De Vaux explains what happened with Israel and her enemies during ancient times when they surrendered: "The weaker party, if it accepted the peace-terms, was reduced to slavery. The outcome of a victorious war was always conquest by one side and vassaldom for the other. . . . People, as well as things, fell into the hands of the victor. . . . They would pay tribute, could be used for forced labour, or as public slaves, or as Temple slaves; they could even be sold as slaves to private individuals."[11]

By analogy, this fits the regenerate person who has become weary in his struggle with sexual temptation and in weakness has laid down his weapons in order to bring the conflict to an end. He falsely believes the enemy is too powerful. He will still recognize sexual voyeurism to be the adversary, and he is not at home with the enemy. Nevertheless, he has become its slave. He is a captive in bondage. No hope or answer seems

11. de Vaux, *Ancient Israel*, 1:254, 256.

to bring about permanent change in his condition. He finds himself lapsing into a world of sexual fantasy and surrendering to an aroused body. I am by no means suggesting that everyone who is tempted by sexual desire or sin is a slave. A slave is one who has been captured and is under a tyrannical principle of bondage that threatens loss or harm if the principle is not obeyed. The sexual slave, then, worships the idol of sensual gratification out of weakness and false belief. This is the person who has surrendered to the continual practice of sexual sin.[12]

THE DIFFERENCE BETWEEN SEXUAL TEMPTATION AND SLAVERY

A distinct division lies between the sexually tempted and the sexually enslaved. For the enslaved, sexual desires have become idolatrous—worshiping and paying tribute to their master by indulging every twinge of sensation. By comparison, the sexually tempted may fail, but they do not routinely indulge their desires. Since the sexually enslaved have made a decision to let down their resistance, they find themselves in an ever-tightening downward spiral of degradation and hopelessness.

How can this be true of a believer who, by very definition, is "in Christ" and has been saved to walk in the Spirit? Can a Christian still be seduced by sensually illicit thoughts and acts? What is it in the regenerate man that causes him to turn a listening ear to the familiar call of sexual temptation? In commenting on Romans 8:1, John Calvin explains:

> By walking *after the Spirit*, Paul does not mean those who have completely put off all the feelings of the flesh, so that their whole life exhibits nothing but heavenly perfection, but those who diligently labour to subdue and mortify the flesh, so that the earnest love of true religion may appear to reign in them. Such believers, he declares, do not walk according to the flesh, because wherever the sincere fear of

12. John 8:34 (ποιῶν, present, active participle of ποιέω).

God flourishes, it deprives the flesh of its dominion, though it does not abolish all its corruptions.[13]

This residue of feelings from the believer's previous state as an unbeliever is naturally responsive to the call of illicit gratifications. The new believer is as accustomed to living by these old feelings as a new husband is to being single. He forgets his new station in life and easily returns to those practices that indulged his selfish inclinations. To the degree that he surrenders to these old desires is the degree that he is allowing the flesh to have dominion. Obviously, when he gives in, the fear of God is not flourishing in his life. When a believer has become a slave to his sexual desires, the old feelings of the flesh are having provisional dominion.

My experience in dealing with the sexually enslaved has revealed several factors that can identify and differentiate the sexually enslaved from the sexually tempted. These factors are indicators, not hard-and-fast rules, of sexual enslavement that may grow in frequency as the person becomes more engrossed in his or her sin:

1. A pattern of deceit and elaborate excuses—for time, money, relationships, work patterns.
2. Family and marriage problems—frequent arguments, anger, hate-filled outbursts, discontentment in the relationship and seeking for greater fulfillment in another.
3. Irresponsibility to duties—whether at home or on the job.
4. Attitudinal extremes—from extreme happiness to depression, lethargy, slothfulness (except in appearance), restlessness, anxiety, loquaciousness.
5. Unusual sex expectations of spouse—no interest in sex or a noticeable reduction in sex drive, or a demand for more sex, complaining about frequency or boredom with same techniques.

13. John Calvin, *The Epistles of Paul the Apostle to the Romans and to the Thessalonians*, Calvin's New Testament Commentaries, ed. David W. Torrance and Thomas F. Torrance, trans. Ross Mackenzie (Grand Rapids: Eerdmans, 1973), 156.

6. Suggestive or pornographic entertainment—movies, television, videos, magazines, romance novels, music, internet.

7. On the attack—sexually enslaved men and women will often go on the offensive and become extremely critical of their spouses in order to cover their own sin. After all, "A good offense is better than a good defense." This keeps their spouses off balance and in a state of constant self-suspicion in order to distract them from becoming too suspicious of the accuser.

8. Routine of secretive behavior—always coming home late, getting up in the middle of the night complaining of insomnia, long telephone calls, never allowing anyone else to see phone or credit card bills, on the computer or smart phone all hours of the day and night, establishing a separate bank account, unaccounted mileage on the car.

9. Persistent defensiveness—accuses others of attacking him; takes little or no personal responsibility for feelings, attitudes, and actions; blames others for his own misery.

10. Spends less time at church or around Christian friends—more and more at home, or with nonbelievers, complains about church or the preacher or how uncaring Christians are, personal piety is absent or has decreased considerably.

Yet conceptualization of sexual temptation is not the same thing as yielding the mind and heart to its enticement. Being tempted to sin sexually is not the same thing as being enslaved to sex. Sensual desires become sinful when they overrule the inner man. Sensual desires become functional gods when the believer has given up the fight and the desires assume operative but not absolute rule over his inner man. For the "sexual addict" who is an unbeliever, the rule is absolute. He is a willing subject. In fact, he will offer moderate resistance to his sexual master only to avoid unpleasant consequences or to serve a greater idol. At best, the unbeliever can only trade idols, not abolish them. Only the regenerating power of the Holy Spirit can bring about real freedom and true eradication of idols.

Although cognitively acknowledging sex is not sinful for the Christian, indulging sexual thoughts is. As sin is indulged, it enslaves.

It captures the whole person. The mind, will, and emotions conspiring in concert begin to expect continual indulgence as essential for normal functioning, for the mind cannot conceive of any true satisfaction in life without it. The will becomes increasingly weakened, having begun with the thrill of a simple surrender but now finding sex's appeal demanding and irresistible. An emotional estrangement ensues as the pleasure of its company is denied: the sexual slave feels sick and lethargic, like a lover who has bid final farewell to his love. Lust is a jealous lover. When the whole person is brought under the spell of its pleasurable delights, the body rebels at its forced absence.[14] This betrayal of friendship leaves a residue of regret, anxiousness, and depression (see fig 2.2).

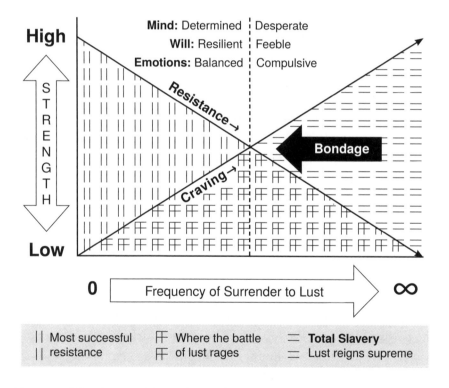

Fig. 2.2. The Point of Sexual Bondage

14. The term *psychosomatic* is an inaccurate description of the effect since it fails to account for the spiritual motivations that govern the entire enslavement condition.

When cravings exceed resistance, a person becomes a prisoner of war to his or her own appetites. Lust takes over its own personal specialization, and the slave yearns for a certain type of sexual fulfillment. Enslavement may begin with simple stimuli, such as catalogs of feminine lingerie for men or romance novels for women, and progress through more intentional hard-core pornographic stimuli to sex shops, strip shows, and even prostitution. Eventually, there develops a deep craving for one particular sexual experience. The brain rewards with pleasurable experiences as it is bathed in endorphins with each indulgence. Its expression can be manifested in masturbation,[15] fornication, adultery, or other sexual perversion, but as the slave surrenders to its delights, he notices its satisfaction has decreasing returns. Therefore, as satisfaction diminishes, frequency is amplified in order to re-experience the same pleasurable reward. It takes an ever-increasing quantity and quality of ecstasy in order to achieve real satisfaction. The deeper the slave wanders into the labyrinth of desire, the greater the lust controls his thinking and the greater is his sense of hopelessness. As the frequency increases, so does the despair. His lowered resistance has been compromised so often that his attempt to find a way out of this habitual activity ends only in frustration.

THE SENSE OF SEXUAL CAPTIVITY

From where does this sense of weakness come? It is the manifestation of God's curse on sin. God intends the errant slave to feel the bondage. The more a person gives himself over to sensuality and lust, the greater the hold these masters possess. As Solomon describes it, "The iniquities of the wicked ensnare him, and he is held fast in the cords of his sin" (Prov. 5:22). These cords include ever-tightening bands of helplessness, weakness, loss of control, agony, insatiable appetites, and undeniable cravings. They are God's index of misery for the

15. Any form of self-gratifying (greed-oriented) sexual activity is sinful for the Christian, including masturbation (1 Cor. 7:3–5; Eph. 5:3–5). It provides immediate bio-feedback for the perfect experience, something a spouse will never have, resulting in dissatisfaction in marriage as well as unrealistic expectations.

sexual sinner. It is part of the human condition and what the apostle Paul calls the "bondage to corruption" (Rom. 8:20–23). The psalmist describes sinful mutineers as "Some sat in darkness and in the shadow of death, prisoners in affliction and in irons, for they had rebelled against the words of God, and spurned the counsel of the Most High" (Ps. 107:10–11). Rebellion always results in God's people experiencing the curse of God through the suffering.

This misery is actually the appetizer in the banquet of death. When the lust-driven sinner's hunger grows to the point that resistance involves great hardship and pain, he is experiencing a foretaste of the grave. Again, Paul explains this as something that should be common knowledge among Christians: "Do you not know that if you present yourselves to anyone as obedient slaves, you are slaves of the one whom you obey, either of sin, which leads to death, or of obedience, which leads to righteousness?" (Rom. 6:16).

The incessant craving for something more vile, dark, and debasing is not uncommon as this person seeks to reclaim the exhilaration that seemed to characterize his initial sin. I have often heard counselees say, "I found myself doing the unimaginable, and when I think about it now, it seems so wicked and degrading." This stricken conscience of guilt is piled on top of a multitude of fruitless attempts to stop. When every avenue of escape is exhausted and a foreboding sense of entrapment sets in, that is when the dark cloud of emptiness and despair begins to hang heavy. One counselee hinted at suicide: "I would rather die than continue living like this." Death is the focus of this curse. Sexual sin has a kind of boomerang effect. The very thing that promised so much excitement in life ends up causing so much death. Physical death may not result, but the fatality of several other important things in life does occur.

HOPE DIES

Despair is common among those in sexual bondage. This is often greater than one might expect since lust is such a private compulsion. Unlike those in bondage to drugs and alcohol, the sex-trapped person is often able to keep his habituation from affecting other areas of his life for many years. There are so few outward observable signs. For years a person in sexual bondage may have made repeated attempts to change, but to no avail. Therefore, it stands to reason that the greater the time of slavery, the greater the sense of hopelessness.

USEFULNESS DIES

Self-gratification renders a person ineffectual. As it consumes more and more of that person's talents and energies, there is precious little left for productivity. This is common for all forms of enslavement. During a counseling session, a young man in his late twenties said he found himself more and more consumed with constructing an elaborate sexual fantasy of all the desirable women at his office into a make-believe plot of greater and greater complexity. Eventually the mental escapes were insufficient, and he found himself making sexually suggestive comments, veiled but purposeful, to these same women, seeking a reciprocal response. He lost his job and came dangerously close to a sexual harassment lawsuit.

CONSCIENCE DIES

Sin defiles the conscience (Titus 1:15). For the conscience to operate properly, it must work from the standpoint of truth. When the sexually tempted surrender to what they believe will give them gratification, they accept a lie that promises life through sexual indulgence but delivers only death. It corrupts the mind and its ability to trigger the conscience. As the mind is defiled, the conscience becomes seared while the sensual desire is indulged. The sexually enslaved persist in practicing lustful ways against the truth. Their consciences become like those of the false teachers at the church at Ephesus who had fallen from the faith "by devoting themselves to deceitful spirits and teachings of demons, through the insincerity of liars whose consciences are seared" (1 Tim. 4:1–2). As mentioned before, some find themselves surrendered to unimaginable sexual filth and defilement.[16] It is doubtful that anyone who habitually practices

16. Sexual desires can be mapped onto almost anything, like those who practice fetishes by being aroused by a handkerchief, lock of hair, or a foot. When there is no sensitivity to the conscience, sexual gratification becomes unimaginably corrupt and seeks satisfaction through a variety of perversions like "telephone scatologia (obscene

such things is a genuine believer, although the apostle Paul admonishes the church at Corinth for its sexual sins: "It is actually reported that there is sexual immorality among you, and of a kind that is not tolerated even among pagans" (1 Cor. 5:1). Depravity debases those who have seared their consciences so much that they may even become proud of their sin. When there is no shame, the conscience is dead.

RELATIONSHIPS DIE

Countless illustrations can be given to demonstrate how sexual perversion has destroyed relationships between people. Selfishness alienates. The most obvious examples are home relationships. Marriage suffers in ways ranging from simple inattention or apathy to severe situations of anger, beatings, and divorce. Newscasts have frequent reports of murders committed by jealous lovers and spouses. Children are often the unspoken victims of the sexual sin of a father or mother. Churches must discipline unrepentant sexual offenders, and Christians are instructed "not to associate with sexually immoral people . . . not even to eat with such a one" (1 Cor. 5:9, 11). Relationships are destroyed because of selfish sexual demands and expectations.

TIME DIES

Lust demands a lot of time. It drains the imaginative energies of the brain, and like the person hooked on drugs, lust expends many waking hours planning and seeking another fix. This loss is irrecoverable. An older man who had worked at a manufacturing plant for several years had a serious struggle with lustful thoughts. His job involved a mindless repetitive activity that took little conscious effort. He calculated the time he spent on an average day living in an imaginary fantasy world of sex to be more than six hours of an eight hour shift. That totaled more than thirty hours per week or 1,560 hours per year (not counting non-working hours) spent on indulging his sexual fantasy.

---

phone calls), necrophilia (corpses), partialism (exclusive focus on part of body), zoophilia (animals), coprohilia (feces), klismaphilia (enemas), and urophilia (urine)." *Diagnostic and Statistical Manual of Mental Disorders*, 4th ed. (Washington, DC: American Psychiatric Association, 1994), 532.

After twenty-five years on the job, this man had racked up around forty thousand hours of ingrained sexual habituation, all of it wasted on a secretive selfish fetish. Several companies have found that their office executives spend a significant number of working hours surfing the web for porn sites. An old expression says, "I am going to kill some time." Well, time is precious, but your life is limited. When sexual cravings consume significant amounts of your time, they kill life.

RESOURCES DIE

Sexual temptation will always seek some type of external expression. Time is not the only resource that is lost. "But a companion of prostitutes squanders his wealth" (Prov. 29:3). Those in sexual bondage can spend hundreds of thousands of dollars gratifying the flesh. From porn material such as magazines, videos, and movies to buying sex at peep shows, strip teases, brothels, and orgies—it all demands cash. The sex industry throughout the world is a billion-dollar enterprise. That is why the credit cards of the sexually obsessed are often at their limit. Their financial credit report is often dismal. The bondage of sexual enslavement is often accompanied by financial bondage.

GODLINESS DIES

Personal piety, if not absent, is often dry and meaningless. Bible study and prayer have long since become formalities. Church attendance is perfunctory at best. Since the sexual sinner has tried to stop his or her obsession with repeated but failed attempts in the past, using the Bible and prayer, they have come to the conclusion that if the Bible does work, it probably does not work for them, and they seriously doubt that the Bible works at all. They may still cry out to God or attempt to bargain with him to break their habituations, but there is no real daily walk with God.

A BODY DIES

Sexually transmitted diseases (STDs) and Acquired Immune Deficiency Syndrome (AIDS) take their death toll on the sexually enslaved every day, yet these are not enough to keep them from

destructive activities. STDs and AIDS are part of the natural consequences of disobeying God's principles of sexuality. Condoms may give
a temporary sense of security, but the sexual obsession of the enslaved
is so great that they will eventually throw caution to the wind. Some
Christian couples have even been known to secretly abort their babies
prior to marriage to avoid the shame of an illegitimate child. This
bondage exacts a death toll. The aim of sin is to take away life, both
spiritual and physical. God's curse on sin was death. This is why the
miserable consequences of sexual sin are a foretaste of the grave.[17] To
yield to its demands is to dig a grave for yourself.

Far too many Christians have easily adopted the thinking that sexual
desire is natural and innocent, no matter what the form or manner of
practice. Yet you have seen how it easily becomes an idolatrous desire
that takes over your heart, demands satisfaction, and controls your life.
As your will is weakened, your resistance diminishes. Your mind and
body become enslaved to its incessant demands. A day without indulging
its desires becomes an abnormal and miserable day. Ultimately, it robs
you of life itself. This is the miserable byproduct of sexual heart idolatry.

KEY CONCEPTS

heart idolatry
self-righteous rationalizations
active pursuit of holiness
image of God
materialistic view of humanity
out-of-body human consciousness
self-gratification
potential idol
idolatrous ruling desires
deep longing of lust
personal rights

---

17. See Ed Welch, *Addictions: A Banquet in the Grave; Finding Hope in the Power of
the Gospel* (Phillipsburg, NJ: P&R Publishing, 2001).

self-determination
covetousness
dynamic and reflexive
homeborn slave
forced laborer
point of sexual bondage
sexual captivity

STUDY QUESTIONS

1. Consider these two statements: "An active pursuit of holiness will characterize a pure heart." "How a counselee thinks about sex issues is critical to his or her purity." Will having a desire for purity be enough for the Christian? Can a Christian truly be pure who primarily focuses on keeping his *actions* free from sexual sin? Explain what process must be active in the pursuit of purity.

2. How does rejecting a materialistic view of human life bring hope to one enslaved to sexual idolatry?

3. The progression of desire of the heart into idolatry looks like this:
   - natural, human desires for drink, food, entertainment, sex
   - become cravings (I *must* have)
   - self-gratifying pleasure begins to dominate thought life
   - resulting in committing acts of sin, whether in the heart or outwardly

   Explain what role *covetousness* plays in this progression from good desire to idolatry.

4. In this chapter, two examples are given of making an idol of something good (marriage / believing children) that God has chosen to withhold (at the present time). Describe and discuss another common good desire that often turns idolatrous.

5. Describe how the influence of the culture's fixation on "personal rights" has exacerbated the dominance of sexual idolatry.

6. Describe the difference between the "homeborn slave" and the

"forced laborer" as it relates to sexual enslavement.

7. The term *sexual captivity* is an accepted idea in society, which leads one to believe that captivity produces heightened sexual excitement. The Bible terms sexual captivity as "bondage to corruption." Explain from Proverbs 5–7 how sexual captivity indeed leads not to more pleasure but to death.

FOR FURTHER READING

DeYoung, Kevin. *The Hole in Our Holiness: Filling the Gap between Gospel Passion and the Pursuit of Godliness*. Wheaton, IL: Crossway, 2014.

Elliot, Elisabeth. *Passion and Purity: Learning to Bring Your Love Life under Christ's Control*. Ada, MI: Revell, 2013.

Lambert, Heath. *Finally Free: Fighting for Purity with the Power of Grace*. Grand Rapids: Zondervan, 2013.

Ryle, J. C. *Holiness: Its Nature, Hindrances, Difficulties, and Roots*, 7th ed. Durham, England: Evangelical Press, 1993.

3

HEART IDOLATRY AND SEXUAL ENSLAVEMENT

The person who seeks to free himself of the bondage of sexual sin must remember that God's Word gives *hope* to those who fear him. This is an important truth because the ungodly world, and even well-meaning Christians, want to convince you that you are a victim—that you cannot help yourself. Contrary to what these people say, your thought life and faith in Christ determine your life—not biology or DNA, even though each of these can have an influence. Biological determinism (the belief that all human behavior finds its source in one's genetic makeup, brain size or function, or other biochemical attributes) produces *despair* and *hopelessness*. Thank God, you are not at the mercy of the chemical processes of your body!

Therefore, the slavery that we speak of in the term *sexual enslavement* is truly one from which a person may be freed. This is the hope that is found in Jesus Christ, whose death and resurrection broke the power that sin held over us. In this chapter we will explore the nature of the enslavement so that we may more clearly see how to apply the truth of Scripture to those in bondage.

THE PARADIGM OF SEXUAL ENSLAVEMENT

Enslavement to sexual desires is an idolatrous relationship with a mood-dominating sexual experience. Some people become entrapped as they use sexual pleasure as an attempt to escape life's burdensome obligations, inevitable troubles, or just suffering in general (Prov. 31:1–7). Others view sexual enjoyment as a means to add exhilaration and excitement to an otherwise tedious and boring life. Certainly there are many who believe that the enjoyment of continual thrilling sensations is a natural right not to be denied, but it is not (Prov. 21:17; Eccl. 2:2, 10; 7:4; 1 Tim. 5:6; Heb. 11:25). In fact, such a philosophy of life culminates in self-destruction.

While it would seem that the enslaved person is addicted to the act of sex, the ultimate source of this bondage is not in the sexual experience itself. Rather, it is within you as a person—it is in your heart. To be precise, it is your heart's worship or love of the experience. Any worship that is not of the true God of heaven is false and idolatrous. And any practice that does not lead us to love the Lord our God with all our heart, soul, mind, and strength is idol worship.

This brings us to another important question. If sin begins in the heart and mind, leading ultimately to death-producing slavery, exactly how does the thought of sex become sinful and enslaving, resulting in death? Is there a recognizable progression? James 1:14–15 gives a four-stage paradigm for all sin, in which sexual bondage may be legitimately included. This paradigm will help you understand how sexual thoughts become sinful, eventually leading to slavery and death.

STAGE ONE: CERTAIN INTERNAL DEPRAVED DESIRES OF THE FLESH ARE STIRRED BY THOUGHT OR EXPERIENCE.

"But each person is tempted when he is lured and enticed by his own desire" (James 1:14). James is clear that the blame does not rest with the world or Satan but with our innate lust. *Man* is fully responsible for his lapse into immoral craving; the cause of blame is deep within. Satan and the world provide the occasion, but the effectiveness of their temptation is totally dependent on the condition and receptivity of your heart. Too many Christian counseling approaches to sexual sin exhaust themselves with the eradication of the external conditions that occasion lust rather than addressing the source. When the etiology is flawed, so is the solution. John Calvin comments, "Since the urge and pressure to do wrong come from within, it is useless for the sinner to seek to hide behind an excuse of outward provocation."[1] Therapy techniques of spiritual exorcism, group accountability used by Sexaholics Anonymous, or the purging of all suggestive media from the environment—these miss the point as well. When these kinds of things are the sole focus of counseling, the real root of lust is never addressed. The twelve-step program's incessant mantra, "Once a sexaholic, always a sexaholic," is well-known in our world. What a hopeless viewpoint! Viewing sexual enslavement this way ignores the real source of sexual captivity, hence the slave is never freed.

Conquering lust is a matter of identifying the right enemy and knowing the battlefield. In the past, the United States of America has gone to war against formidable and threatening enemies. Dates such as December 7, 1941, when Japan attacked Pearl Harbor, and September 11, 2001, when terrorists attacked the mainland, will live in infamy for Americans. Once the enemies were identified and the battlefields pin-pointed, retribution began in earnest. As the battles progressed, media outlets gave reports about the difficulty of finding and attacking elusive Japanese fighter planes over the Pacific and Taliban warriors hiding in caves of the rugged mountains of Afghanistan. Most strategists agreed that the wars would be long and arduous; merely bombing from above would never dislodge the entrenched enemy. As in most wars, it required a perilous and treacherous scheme: dropping foot soldiers into enemy territory, moving cave to cave, rooting out the adversary.

What is the real enemy when counseling the sexually enslaved? It is not Hollywood, *Playboy* magazine, or Satan himself. These only provide the opportunity. The real enemy is your depraved desire—your own lust. Make no mistake, the vehicles of opportunity are indeed enemies of the Christian, but they require an ally within—your heart—in order to be effective.

Counseling approaches that focus solely on the outward adversaries

---

1. John Calvin, *A Harmony of the Gospels Matthew, Mark and Luke and the Epistles of James and Jude*, Calvin's New Testament Commentaries, ed. David W. Torrance and Thomas F. Torrance, trans. A. W. Morrison (Grand Rapids: Eerdmans, 1972), 3:268.

of opportunity are attempting to win the war by the limited effectiveness of high-altitude bombing. This will serve only to drive the enemy further underground instead of rooting him out and killing him. When the superficial bombing stops, he will reappear in another location and continue to wreak havoc in your life. This enemy will appeal and evade; it is elusive and clandestine, hiding in the cracks and crevices of your own heart. Calvin continues, "But we are to note these two effects of lust—it has charms to entice us, and it diverts our attention. And either of these will convict us."[2] Lust makes allies with the world and Satan. The terms of the treaty are catastrophic: total domination of your heart.

What is the terrain of this battlefield? The human heart is rugged, full of stubborn crevices and caves carved out by years of sinful habits and practices. A good counselor is like the special forces soldier who knows how to use his deadliest weapon, God's Word, to make a surgical strike on the heart. He is well-trained in the covert operations of the enemy and understands his elusive techniques.

This is not an easy war, because sexual desires are at home on the heart's battlefield. The heart is familiar territory to sexual desire, and over time it becomes an expert at diversion and camouflage. This is its home turf. As a sincere Christian, however, you should be well aware of your enemy's identity and methods. You must be willing to invade your underground shelters—your hidden areas of the heart—in order to extricate him. Lust embeds itself within your heart behind rationalizations as you yield to its deceitful feelings of satisfaction and gratification. Eventually, lust becomes your closest companion, until you no longer view life as normal without indulging it. However, you have no one to blame but yourself for fraternizing with the enemy.

STAGE TWO: LUST CONCEIVES IN A FERTILE HEART WHEN IT ACQUIRES THE CONSENT OF THE WILL.

"Then desire when it has conceived . . ." (James 1:15a). This is the point in which sin is sown in the heart. The world and Satan

2. Ibid.

may stir the depraved desires, but it is not sin in the heart until the will has granted its permission. A young man may have inadvertently observed an attractive bikini-clad young woman (on a billboard or at the beach), and he knows this sight has the potential to become a sinful gaze because it has stirred something deep within him (awakened depraved desires). But this glimpse is not sinful until he willfully agrees to entertain its enticements. When his mind settles on the idea of her attractiveness and he begins to draw detached sensual pleasure from the vision, sinful lust has been conceived. His eyes respond in obedience to his will's surrender, and he begins to trace her inviting form over and over in his mind. An initial innocent look has aroused his desires. Instead of exercising his prerogative to turn his mind and eyes away, his volition, weakened by the promise of all-consuming pleasure, made a temporary truce with lust. His mind drinks in her image, memorizing its details while his body begins to respond with increasing desire. In fact, desire's growth is so rapid that he is surprised at its sudden power. Lust has commandeered his heart, installing a new potential king who promises pleasure but whose ultimate goal will be enslavement.

Scripture is not silent on the coercive nature of this problem. This is the point at which we find David as he admires the bathing form of Bathsheba from a rooftop vantage point (2 Sam. 11:1–3). In that moment of decision David could have turned away, but he did not. Here is a powerful man who has already satisfied himself with many wives and concubines, yet there is always something more that the depraved desires seek for gratification.[3] Satan has thousands of years of expertise in appealing to these latent desires of the heart. Corrupt desires exist within every heart, like an inactive computer virus, and with the proper trigger they can surface and reprogram

---

3. Kent Hughes captures this instance well when he writes about how this sin was conceived in David's heart: "His *look* became a sinful *stare* and then a burning libidinous sweaty *leer*. In that moment David, who had been a man after God's own heart, became a dirty, leering old man. A lustful fixation came over him that would not be denied." R. Kent Hughes, *Disciplines of a Godly Man* (Wheaton, IL: Crossway, 1991), 26 (emphasis original).

the entire life of the counselee. These desires are so deceptive; they will lie to you.

It has been observed that the Greek terminology used in James 1:13–15 is similar to terms employed to refer to the enticement of a prostitute.[4] For that reason, given the varying degrees of semantic range, sexual lust is a very appropriate application of these verses. Unquestionably, the term for conceive is a specialized word for sexual impregnation (συλλαμβάνω). The assumption made by James is that the heart is a fertile womb for lust's implantation and growth. The womb is perfectly analogous to the sinful heart that becomes the nurturing nest for lust's embryonic seed.

To carry this biblical analogy further, some wombs are fertile, while other wombs are barren and will not permit impregnation. Likewise, a person's heart can possess certain qualities that make it more or less fertile for the impregnation of sexual lust. What characteristics make the heart fertile for sexual sin to be implanted? What makes some hearts more susceptible to the conception of sexual sin? Why is it easier for some to resist sexual temptation than others? How can one person experience the same external sexual temptation as another and successfully miscarry it—putting it to death? These are important questions, and the answers have to do with the fertility differences in the womb of the heart.

Two stages of this paradigm are illustrated in figure 3.1. After the will has surrendered to the initial temptation of sexual sin, idolatrous craving is sown in the heart. Like a pregnancy, it begins to grow if it is not aborted by repentance. As the craving grows, resistance decreases and the struggle becomes less intense. Passion and desire within the heart and body beat hard with increasing intensity. At this stage, there has been no external action taken to satisfy that desire, but as the desire deepens, sinful behavior is not far behind.

---

4. Franz Mussner, *Der Jakobusbrief: Herbers Theologischer Kommentar zum Neuen Testament* (Freiburg: Herber, 1974), in Fritz Rienecker and Cleon L. Rogers Jr., eds., *A Linguistic Key to the Greek New Testament* (Grand Rapids: Zondervan, 1980), 724.

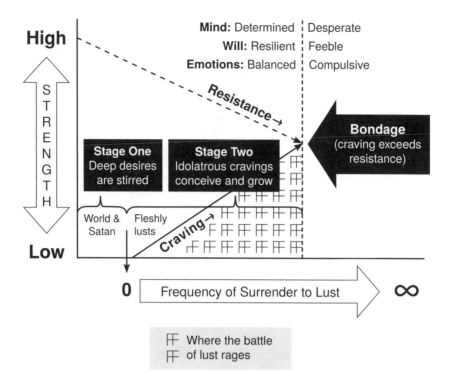

Fig. 3.1. Stages One and Two Leading to Idolatrous Enslavement

STAGE THREE: THE LUSTFULLY IMPREGNATED HEART EVENTUALLY GIVES BIRTH TO VISIBLE DEEDS OF TRANSGRESSION.

"Then desire when it has conceived *gives birth to sin*" (James 1:15). The birth of sexual sin brings about behavioral actions. Your mind gives your body permission to act on its desire. This does not mean that the internal conception of lust in the heart is not a sin; indeed, lust in the heart *is* a sin. Like a full-term pregnancy, however, sexual lust takes on a life of its own and is born as certain perceptible sinful deeds. Just as a baby is not fully seen until birth, sexual sin is not visible until it is born in outward acts of corruption. Calvin clarifies this point:

Perhaps it does not appear quite accurate, indeed rather opposed to scriptural usage, to restrict the word *sin* to outward acts, as if lust were not sin in itself, and every wicked desire that lurks secretly concealed in the heart was not equally "sin." The term, however, has a variety of uses, and there is nothing strange in taking it, in this instance, as in many other passages, for actual sins committed.[5]

It is your mind's choice to allow the members of your body to act in order to satisfy its desire.

James teaches that the natural progression of lust is to seek outward fulfillment through an unrighteous activity. Growing lust will bear sinful behavioral fruit. Sexual lust will be born into the world when it has reached gestational maturity and the womb of imagination can no longer contain it. You may try to suppress its expression because of unpleasant consequences anticipated from the disappointment and disproval of others. Yet it will initially seek a secretive outlet until you no longer care whether others know. It is what your heart wants. Lust cannot remain in the heart forever; it will demand to be brought into the world.

Other forms of lustful enslavement such as alcohol, smoking, and drugs give birth to more ostentatious offspring because they are accompanied by telltale signs and consequences—bloodshot eyes, wounds, lingering odors, bad breath, erratic behavior, fights, quarrels, needle marks on the arm, and so on (Prov. 23:29–35). While these effects are more obvious to others, a serious substance abuser will rarely admit to his enslavement, declaring, "I can stop whenever I want!" But he will be forced to isolate himself from people in order to keep his shameful slavery veiled. Sexual lust also makes you subservient, so that when the impulses of your body begin to demand fulfillment, you cannot resist obeying them, no matter the cost. People in sexual bondage, however, can hide their behaviors and the ensuing consequences for longer periods of time and still appear respectable in more public arenas. In fact, these public settings (involving the world and Satan) are often the sources that fuel their fertile imaginations (see stages 1 and 2). One of the last things a sexually enslaved person wishes to do is cut off

5. Calvin, *A Harmony of the Gospels*, 3:268–69.

the thrill of that public contact. His sexual fantasies demand constant reinforcement and refreshment. Despite this, it is not uncommon for even the closest friends and family members of the sexually enslaved to be totally unaware of the problem for years. I have worked with more than one counselee who has kept his rendezvous with prostitutes a secret from his wife and family for fifteen to twenty years. In some cases, even some pastors have been able to keep their congregations in ignorance concerning their sexual sins for long periods of time.

James's teaching in chapter 1 of his epistle reinforces the reality that the embryo of sin planted in the fertile imagination of the heart will eventually seek to be born through some means of outward expression. Although he does not address through the wording of this verse whether it is immediately visible *to others*, the inevitability of its birth through some external sinful action or behavior is the important point that needs our attention. Your body will act in full cooperation with the dictates of your heart. The applicable Pauline principle is that what you sow, you will reap! "Do not be deceived: God is not mocked, for whatever one sows, that will he also reap. For the one who sows to his own flesh will from the flesh reap corruption, but the one who sows to the Spirit will from the Spirit reap eternal life" (Gal. 6:7–8).[6] Lustful sin in the heart demands to be born.

Christians are rightly ashamed of their ugly sin (child) of sexual obsession. Like the promiscuous single mother who wishes to keep her baby a secret, they will go to unimaginable lengths to keep their habits from public view, especially from the scrutiny of other believers. Sexual sin is a disgrace. Job describes how the adulterer hates the transparency of daylight: "The eye of the adulterer also waits for the twilight, saying, 'No eye will see me'; and he veils his face. In the dark they dig through houses; by day they shut themselves up; they do not know the light. For deep darkness is morning to all of them; for they are friends with the terrors of deep darkness" (Job 24:15–17). Solomon

---

6. The present active participle (σπείρων) specifies the continuous action of sowing and indicates that one who persists in sowing to his own flesh does not possess eternal life. Genuine Christians will battle this sinful habituation and seek to put it to death.

speaks of the naive young man "passing along the street near her [the wayward adulterous woman's] corner, taking the road to her house in the twilight, in the evening, at the time of night and darkness" (Prov. 7:8–9). Why the shadows, secretiveness, and darkness? Because of the guilt and shame of such ungodly behavior. This is especially true if you have a Christian conscience.

Exposure to the light frightens you as much as the terror of thick darkness frightens other people. Your greatest fear is that one of your friends, family members, or fellow believers will find out. A guarded suspiciousness of everyone in your life makes you appear edgy and easily startled (Lev. 26:17; Prov. 28:1). Even so, as the sin is practiced and the conscience is hardened, you will find yourself taking increasingly greater risks of disclosure to satisfy lust's voracious appetite.

Starting small with the baby food of little private deeds of self-stimulation, the child will grow and demand realistic nourishment, seeking additional substantive and solid forms of exhilaration. The sexual slave will progress to specialized types of fulfillment that will require greater public exposure. Whatever you choose to do at this level, the intention is that no one else should know or be involved. There is considerable legal risk at this point as well because stealing, sexual touching, prostitution, and the voyeurism of a "peeping Tom" can result in criminal prosecution. Your mind will leverage the risk and the reward; gradually it will take greater risk because of sin's false promise of a greater reward.

This illegitimate child, born of slavery, is still developing and will eventually gamble greater exposure to achieve a better thrill. The sexual slave will start by seeking a limited number of people who can participate in his erotic escapades. Often this level begins in the bedroom of a married couple. Sometimes a husband or wife will complain of the lack of frequency and variety in their sex, placing the blame on the spouse, while all along they are seeking to appear self-righteous while feeding their own fat baby of desire. In other words, the one so enslaved uses his partner to experiment with new ways to fulfill this overgrown and ever-growing sexual desire. He may become increasingly insistent on sexual techniques of personal bondage, masochism, sadism, or particular types of oral sex that are revolting to his spouse. This is not meant to suggest that experimenting with different sex positions and techniques is forbidden in a godly marriage of mutual love and respect, in which the goal of intimacy is your mate's satisfaction (1 Cor. 7:3–5). However, when a person is in sexual enslavement to his lustful desires, his selfish demands betray an ungodly agenda that is bent on personal satisfaction at all costs, even if it means using his spouse as an object for selfish sexual gratification. You could be intimate with your spouse, which seems biblical compared to adultery, yet still be in sin because your heart motivation is hedonistic greed instead of ministry to your spouse.

Another route that is often chosen at this level of exposure is fornication or adultery with at least one other person. Again, the main operational goal is to keep the circle of knowledge of this obsession as narrow as possible. If this sexually obsessed person is married, the shame of his own perverse thoughts may pressure him to find fulfillment in someone other than his spouse in some type of secret encounter. This encounter is seldom a one-time event but often becomes part of a regular rendezvous with increasing frequency. It may be a heterosexual affair, a homosexual encounter, or the hiring of a prostitute as the companion who will help him achieve satisfaction. At this level, some forms of acquiring sexual gratification, like soliciting a prostitute, are still condemned by some parts of society as illegal and may carry severe consequences of heavy fines and imprisonment.

Nonetheless, this will not stop the driving desires of lust. The demanding child of sexual obsession is still growing and refuses to be satisfied even at this stage. Now more and more people are potentially brought into visible range of his perversity. As he assumes greater risk, the sexual slave desperately attempts to feed this obsessive child who has grown into a self-absorbed adolescent with an incessant appetite. For example, this person might change clothes in front of an open window, hoping to be seen by another person passing by. Or perhaps he may walk around in public places and flash certain (specially chosen) people, deliberately exposing himself. The thought that someone else may be watching brings a temporary rush of erotic pleasure. This level of exposure now involves an unlimited number of potential victims who are included in his illicit résumé of self-gratification, and these victims are most often unwitting and unwilling participants.

Man will attempt to find other ways to hide his sensual activities. A recent manifestation of "respectable" sexual sin has harnessed commerce and technology in producing lifelike automatons (robots), designed for every type of sexual indulgence. These are designed to feel and react just like a live human being, currently being marketed with the pragmatic claims that they will reduce venereal disease, eliminate prostitution, end pedophilia, and so on. However, when you understand that the real problem is rooted in the heart, then this type of perversion will only feed the illegitimate child of desire until it grows into a monster. When sex is viewed simply as a biological activity and not as a form of worship, then the sinful heart's growing demands will socially explode with unrelenting sensual demands that will settle for nothing short of complete selfish satisfaction (Prov. 21:10; Eph. 2:3). Society will become an increasingly hostile place to live because everyone will be seen as an object for self-gratifying purposes.

Regardless of the initial shame that the sexual slave feels as he seeks to satisfy his lust in secret, unrepentant sexual enslavement is always evolving, transforming into increasing levels of insidious behavior, eventually leading to overt actions. Secrecy fades as a priority, and the enslaved person often finds himself committing felony offenses like molestation, incest, rape, sex-murder, and necrophilia—things he never dreamed he would do—until he is no longer fearful of forcing himself on another person in order to achieve self-gratification.

Most psychological models adopted by Christians tend to define these deviancies on the basis of societal norms of acceptance and criminal conduct.[7] We should avoid such an organizing principle because it leads both the counselor and counselee to focus on what the Bible would view as "performance-based standards," emphasizing only the

---

7. P. Roger Hillerstrom, *Intimate Deception: Escaping the Trap of Sexual Impurity* (Portland, OR: Multnomah Press, 1989), 115. See also Frank Minirth, Paul Meier, and Stephen Arterburn, *The Complete Life Encyclopedia* (Nashville, TN: Thomas Nelson, 1995), 507–8.

high risk of adverse consequences. This argument is organized around the motivating principle of *exposure* to highlight both the aspect of personal guilt, evidenced by shame, and the tendency of the human heart to disguise its inward motivations to avoid change. The focus of counseling for Christians in sexual slavery should be purification, not penalties.

Figure 3.2 illustrates the difference between the two approaches and the truth of James 1:15. Lustful sin risks increasing exposure to find fulfillment. It begins with a stirring of desire by the world and Satan and moves to implantation within the heart, where it grows until it is manifested externally in overt behavior. Lust-born behaviors seeking sexual gratification will grow according to the same degree. Sexual lust grows through degrees of exposure, gaining false confidence in its expression and becoming more open while encompassing additional people in its field of influence.

Notice in the diagram below the progression of each level and what determines a move from one level of sexual behavior to another. For the *secular model*, each successive level is determined by a progression of how "serious" society considers the sexual deed to be. In this model, counselees focus on what society thinks about said behavior and bringing that behavior into line with its construct of normative and acceptable behavioral patterns. What is sociologically permissible is deemed to be morally right. In the *biblical model*, each successive level is determined by a progression of how much the counselee is motivated by guilt and shame to keep his conduct hidden. It is correct to observe that both models operate somewhat on what others think (fear of man). But the biblical model of sexual behavior views the downward progression of this behavior to be evidence of greater corruption and captivity instead of moving from acceptable to unacceptable behavior. Like an ever-tightening cord, the sensual impulses gain increasing control until the slave's behavior is beyond the thinkable.

External behavior is always indicative of the heart's condition. In the beginning, human beings were created to be governed by *holy* desires and passions. The ruling principle of the soul should be to delight in God and to make his desires supreme in life. The highest purpose of

	Secular Model Organizational principle: social acceptance & criminal conduct	**Biblical Model** Organizational principle: personal guilt & motivational disclosure
Level One ↓	fantasy, pornography, masturbation, any sexual behavior not classified as a crime, a "victimless crime"	private stimulation, masturbation, collection of erotic clothing, phone sex, voyeurism, sexual behavior that maintains the anonymity of the sexual sinner
Level Two ↓	live pornography, fetishes, and extra-marital affairs, sexual behavior not condoned by society, yet not considered criminal activity	selfish sexual practices in marriage, fornication, adultery, incest, homosexuality, lesbianism, prostitution, sexual behavior that attempts to keep its illicit conduct limited to one other person
Level Three ↓	prostitution, voyeurism, exhibitionism, and other minor sexual offenses, sexual behavior classified as a criminal conduct which involves a victim	multiple victim exhibitionism, molestation, incest, homosexuality, lesbianism, rape, sex-murder, necrophilia, sexual behavior that involves many victims and usually includes the harm of another person's body
Level Four	molestation, incest, rape and other major sex offenses, sexual behavior classified as serious crimes because they cause some type of damage or injury to the victim	mortality, the loss of life, full-grown sexual lust that finds itself caught in a cyclical pattern of meaninglessness and death

Fig. 3.2. Levels of the Progression of Sexual Behavior

man is to yearn for God and the desires that follow from enjoying him. These desires, in turn, are to bear behavioral fruit of righteousness. Our God is a jealous God (Ex. 20:3; 34:14; Ezek. 14:7–8). He will not share his glory or the desires of his people with another "god."

Once an idolatrous craving has been planted in the heart and has begun to rule there, the sense of guilt will lessen proportionately. Next, sexual cravings will behaviorally progress with alarming openness, risk, and vileness. The sexual slave's concern for God, others, and consequences will diminish. Although the sexual slave is unaware of this, bondage to sexual passion leads to self-destruction. It will always cause interpersonal and social causalities. As sexual sin matures, it becomes increasingly characterized by a lack of humility. Sin, by its very definition, is an arrogant affront to the holiness of God. Sexual sinners become increasingly comfortable and confident in their hypocritical lifestyles. They are "Genesis 3" people—constantly running and hiding in the bushes, covering themselves with fig leaves in the hope that God or man will not see. The longer they are able to keep their illicit behavior hidden from the sight of others, the more confident they are in living a double life.

As one married counselee revealed, "At first I was extremely ashamed of my visits to the red-light district of our town, but the more I visited, the easier it became. I grew to believe that my sin was private and hidden, so the consequences of my behavior became insignificant to me. I could go to church with my wife and family on Sunday and sneak away from the office on Monday." During the same time that he was increasing the frequency of his visits to the red-light district, he assumed the teaching of the largest adult Sunday School class in his church. He relished the thought that everyone in his church believed him to be a great Bible teacher. As Andrew Murray said, "The chief mark of counterfeit holiness is its lack of humility."[8] The idolatry of sexual craving numbs the conscience and emboldens the arrogance of the human mind.

8. Andrew Murray, *Humility: The Beauty of Holiness* (Pensacola, FL: Chapel Library, n.d.), 22.

Let us examine the last stage in the progress of lustful enslavement from James 1.

STAGE FOUR: FULLY FORMED SIN ENDS IN DEATH.

"And sin when it is fully grown brings forth death" (James 1:15). Birth usually results in life. But in this case, lust's child grows as though it is alive, but its maturation yields death. Its growth is like that of malignant cancer; ever growing yet leading to death. The effects of death are evident everywhere in the sexual slave's morbid existence—hopelessness, uselessness, dead conscience, broken relationships, wasted time, squandered resources, ungodliness, and diseased and dying bodies.

In King David's case, lust's toll began with the murder of Bathsheba's husband and David's loyal servant, Uriah, and eventually extended to the death of David's infant son (2 Sam. 11:15–17; 12:15–18). Recently I helped a counselor-in-training counsel a man who had hired someone to murder his wife so he could collect the insurance and run off with a woman with whom he had had an adulterous affair. In another case, I performed the funeral of a young homosexual man who had attended a Christian college, was married with children, and had succumbed to AIDS after leaving his home for the gay lifestyle. I also counseled a young woman who tried to commit suicide because her life had cycled from one meaningless relationship with a man to another, with no apparent end in sight. Lust is the worst imaginable thief because it robs you of life. In the state of California, bills have been introduced forbidding the counsel of any person away from a lesbian, gay, bisexual, transgender, queer, intersex, asexual (LGBTQIA) lifestyle; one man wrote that if this bill had been law thirty years ago, "I might have killed myself."[9] Hopelessness, despair, and death litter the pathway of the sexually enslaved.

The analogy of James 1:15 compares the development of lust to a child who grows into adulthood. Much like an adult who matures

---

9. Walt Heyer, "If California's LGBT Therapy Ban Had Been Law 30 Years Ago, I Might Have Killed Myself," *The Federalist*, April 25, 2018.

physically, the child of sensuality has advanced in the ways of this world and, having been well schooled in self-gratification, will finally reach the age of maturity. The English Standard Bible translates this using the English term *fully grown*. Its Greek basis (ἀποτελέω) means "to be complete," emphasizing being "fully accomplished" or "fully formed."[10] This is a powerful analogy. When allowed to live and thrive, lust grows in its skills and abilities as time progresses. It is not dormant, static, or passive; rather, it is constantly learning and adjusting as it seeks satisfaction from its environment. Like a child whose arms and legs are growing and gaining kinesthetic skill, lust develops proficiency in acquiring what it wants. Since its desire is never fully satisfied, it must be driven on to find other sources and avenues for its fulfillment. Sexual lust seeks full formation and is never satisfied with partial or rudimentary pacification. Too many in bondage to sexual desire believe they can appease lust with incomplete substitutes like occasional self-satisfying activities, only to find that while frequency increases, satisfaction decreases.

Death is the result of continually surrendering to lust. While believers will not experience eternal or spiritual death, it is possible that they may experience physical death. Scripture provides evidence of the judgment of God on the lives of sinful believers (1 Cor. 11:30; 1 John 5:16). We have previously demonstrated some of the deathly consequences of being in captivity to sexual lust. Figure 3.3 illustrates all four stages of lust's gradual enslavement.

The overlap of these stages in the diagram is intentional. Multiple cravings operate at different stages in your life. While some stages are fully formed, others are being conceived and just beginning to grow. I have never encountered a counselee who did not have multiple idolatrous desires operating simultaneously in the heart, giving continual birth to various sinful sexual behaviors. For example, it is not uncommon for the behavior of the pedophile to extend beyond the enjoyment

10. James Hope Moulton and George Milligan, *The Vocabulary of the Greek Testament: Illustrated from the Papyri and Other Non-Literary Sources* (Grand Rapids: Eerdmans, 1982), 70–71.

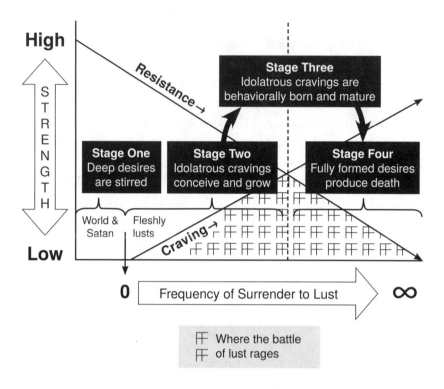

Fig. 3.3. Four Stages of Lustful Enslavement

of interacting sexually with prepubescent children (usually thirteen years of age and younger). While the pedophile's primary thrill and excitement is taking one of the most forbidden things in our society—a young child—this has not been his only compelling, lust-driven sin. The search for illicit thrills may have manifested itself behaviorally when the pedophile was much younger. Unacceptable behavior, such as stealing and skipping school, may have been his thrill-fix at this early age, but now his own sexual drives are mapped on top of this exhilarating motivation and are expressed in the ultimate ecstasy of pedophilia. Added to that is the craving for the thrill of the hunt, the excitement of secrecy, and often kidnapping and/or murder.

The overlap of brackets in figure 3.3 also demonstrates that the experience (sense or feeling) of death occurs at the point that craving surpasses resistance. At that point, a person in bondage has been

mastered by lustful desire. Even though elements of lust are still growing, it is also yielding death-type consequences early in the bondage.
Marriage can experience years of strain, slowly dying, until unrepentant
infidelity results in its death by divorce. I do not believe that James
intended these stages of lust to be strictly consecutive. Because of the
complexity of the human heart, they overlap. But James is expressing a
definite progressive course in lust's development, which elucidates the
point of its inception, growth, and final result.

APPLYING THEOLOGY IN COUNSELING SEXUAL PROBLEMS

Now that Scripture has explained how lust begins and progresses
within our own desires, several misconceptions invariably surface in
overcoming sexual lust. One such problem is the belief that fantasizing
about a potential sex partner is not a sin; it is only the external acting
out of that desire that is sin. This view often comes from a misreading
of James 1:14–15, as if it were saying that the lust is not sin until it
culminates in some physical action, such as physical intercourse. In one
instance, an unmarried college-aged couple who had traveled home
together for holiday break rationalized their sharing the same motel
room with this type of reasoning, along with the claim that they could
not afford two separate rooms. They insisted that since they had not
had sex together, they were innocent of any sin, even though they
admitted to heavy petting and caresses. Many believe that as long as
actual intercourse does not take place, there is no sin. Not only is this
not the case, but we have seen that Scripture actually teaches that the
internal desire feeding the fantasy is the very sinful source and cause
of outward sin.

Another misunderstanding comes when some Christians believe
that fantasizing about other men or women during sex with their spouse
is a legitimate aphrodisiac for the Christian. Again, here we have those
who believe that lust/desire is not a sin, only the behavior produced
by the desire. Often married men believe that as long as their sexual
tensions are relieved with their spouses, then toying with imaginary

women in their mind is only helping improve sex with their wives. As long as they use their own wives as their sexual outlets, they believe they are innocent of any wrongdoing. They retain a conceptual harem to be ready and on-call for occasions in which they may need some mental help in achieving and maintaining the physical process of sex.

Medical science has even entered the bedroom by producing certain hormonal enhancing drugs to artificially arouse men and women for greater frequency and enjoyment on sex. For the men and women who have never biblically dealt with the idolatrous sexual cravings of their hearts, using these drugs is like throwing gasoline on a smoldering fire. Drugs may increase the personal pleasure of sex, but they will also provide additional opportunities to become an even greater slave to sex. Sexual sin is more than just a physical act. It is rooted in the lustful desires of the worshipful heart, not just the body.

Premarital counseling affords couples the occasion to explain their view of sexual involvement without copulation. Often young couples have expressed their view that as long as they practice oral sex, and not intercourse, they are not sinning. Deep sensual passions are aroused and justified as long as they gain control of themselves before "going all the way." "After all," they explain, "it is a monogamous loving relationship, and we intend to get married soon. In God's eyes, we might as well be married, because we love each other. Does a mere piece of paper, called a marriage license, really make any difference in God's eyes?" Their definition of sexual sin is full copulation, and they even potentially excuse it by suggesting that formalized marriage is just a man-made construct, not necessarily a God-recognized covenant. As early as the 1950s, it was beginning to be commonly understood that two consenting adults having sex in a loving relationship constitutes a marriage. These Christian couples who justify their sexual relation have bought into this unbiblical view of marriage. Like the Pharisees of the New Testament, as long as they obeyed the law outwardly—not committing "the physical act" by having intercourse in an uncommitted relationship—they consider themselves guilt-free. Immorality and lust do not seem as shameful when they have "love" as their justification. For many, loving sexual passion divorces the sense of guilt from the fact of guilt.

GETTING TO THE HEART OF LUST

According to Jesus Christ, the lustful person and adulterer share the same sinful heart. The adulterer has acted out his desire (given birth to it, to use our previous analogy), whereas the heart of the luster has kept it within. From God's internal view of man, the two hearts are the same. Nothing differentiates them in terms of craving and desire. The outward expressions of sexual passion are simply the fruits of a preexisting idolatrous heart already surrendered to erotic imaginations. The words of Christ give us insight into the heart of a man who lusts after a woman but has never committed physical adultery with her: "You have heard that it was said, 'You shall not commit adultery.' But I say to you that everyone who looks at a woman with lustful intent has already committed adultery with her in his heart" (Matt. 5:27–28).

The Pharisees of the first century were proud of their external piety since they had not practiced fornication or adultery. They believed themselves to be righteous and acceptable before God because they had not had sex with anyone other than their legal wives. They even taught that this was the essence of the command given by Moses (Ex. 20:14; Deut. 5:18). In these words, Jesus expresses the true intent of the law and exposes their hypocrisy by revealing the real desires of their hearts. While they maintained external sexual control, their hearts were dominated with passionate sexual cravings. Their lust-saturated hearts longed for some external satisfaction, but they did not dare because they would lose their illusion and supposed reputation of sexual purity.

A person who lusts after coitus gratification in the heart is just as evil as the person who commits fornication or adultery. Jesus does not say that a man who merely looks on a woman has committed sin (e.g., the need for the complete covering of Muslim women in the dress code called the burqa), but the man who looks (βλέπω) to "lust . . . in his heart." Christ's words are strong. This man is one who sees an attractive woman and purposes to lust after her in his heart. Instead of using the simple infinitive, Jesus uses the more definite Greek preposition (ἐπιθυμῆσαι) with the infinitive, signifying that this man's ultimate goal goes beyond simple appreciation of beauty. He intends to lust after her. There is purposeful intent in the depraved heart of man that is constantly alert to opportunities that will satisfy a fertile imagination and demanding sexual appetite.

To this, Jesus adds an important adverb that focuses his point on the fact that the real issue with God is the lustful cravings of the heart, not necessarily the external purity of the body. These Jewish leaders were proud of their adultery-free lives, which they believed made them justified before God. Jesus says that if they had lusted after a woman, they had "already" (ἤδη) sinned by way of adultery in the heart. Inordinate cravings of sexual desire in the heart are just as serious a sin as the unfaithfulness of adultery.

Earlier, in the Sermon on the Mount, Jesus had warned those who attempted to make the law achievable by external human behavior. "Unless your righteousness exceeds that of the scribes and Pharisees, you will never enter the kingdom of heaven" (Matt. 5:20). They had tried to "annul" (λύσῃ, to loosen or relax) the law by making it into an externally observable command (Matt. 5:19). They reconfigured the law into a doable standard. In so doing, the effect was to negate the purpose of the law and turn it into a performance-based morality. Jesus condemned their superficiality and highlighted their corrupt practices.

Nowhere are their legalistic practices better exposed than in the divorce proceedings of the day. Since they were not permitted to commit adultery, they had to find a way to deal with the lust that reigned in their hearts for women who were not their wives. So one particular school of rabbinical thought developed a rationale for divorce that made it especially easy to put away a wife and marry another woman. A Jewish husband was at liberty to put away his wife, provided that the proper legal process of granting her a notice of divorce was followed. But the grounds on which a husband might divorce his wife were disputed between the two rabbinic schools of Shammai and Hillel (teachers in first century B.C.) who allowed divorce only for adultery or for marital incompatibility, respectively.[11]

---

11. Colin Brown, ed., *The New International Dictionary of New Testament Theology* (Grand Rapids: Zondervan, 1975), 1:506.

Jesus illustrates how their lust was eventually born through the common practice of granting a certificate of divorce: "But I say to you that everyone who divorces his wife, except on the ground of sexual immorality, makes her commit adultery, and whoever marries a divorced woman commits adultery" (Matt. 5:32). Not only was Jesus clear about lust being a form of adultery, but the fact that they had been "legally" divorced and "legally" remarried did not change the fact that they were practicing the very adultery they were ostensibly seeking to avoid.

It is imperative that lust not have its way in the human heart. The heart is a God-given source of thought and motivation, but because of sin it is both corrupt and impressionable when it comes to raw, selfish craving. Your greatest struggle with sexual desire will be found within yourself, and you must learn to guard the spiritual sensitivities of your heart. Matthew 5:28 is explained well by John Calvin:

> Christ's purpose is in general to condemn the lust of the flesh. So he says that they are adulterers in God's sight who not only have intercourse with others' wives, but who have stained their eyes with unchaste glances. It is an expression by synecdoche, for it is not only the eyes which convict men of adultery, but also the unseeing passions of the heart. . . . Since it is the eyes which most solicit souls by their panderings, and lust reaches through their . . . concupiscence: the word *lust after* shows this clearly. The lesson is, that they are rated adulterers in God's sight who not only by deliberate thought conceive harlotry in their minds, but admit even its slightest inducements.[12]

Certain desires and longings make the heart extremely impressionable to lustful temptation. Calvin says that even the "slightest inducements" are tantamount to adultery. The heart's quiet coup d'état eventually grows into total anarchy. No one knows or sees the lust that fills your heart except God, but it is there, and it is real. This lust soon

---

12. John Calvin, *A Harmony of the Gospels*, 1:188 (emphasis original).

triggers the tiny region of the brain known as the hypothalamus, which in turn ignites sexual arousal in the body. The body and the heart become allies in subjecting a person to sexual slavery. Once this lust is conceived in the heart, it cannot be denied; it can be only temporarily suppressed until an outlet is found for its fulfillment.

These words about lust from the Sermon on the Mount are masterful because they reveal the importance of understanding the role of the heart in sexual desire and demonstrate the danger of preexisting impurities that give rise to inordinate desire. Certain impurities of the heart surrender it to lustful cravings when sexually tempting opportunities arise. After all, a pure heart will have no problem when it sees a beautiful woman or an attractive man, as lust cannot conceive in the womb of the heart that is infertile. A pure heart will abort any notion of enticing the body with provocative mental stimulation. The words of Jesus are indicting because they reveal the preconditioned wicked hearts of the scribes and Pharisees who so easily rationalized lust-driven divorce and remarriage. Self-gratification rules, but it rules for a reason. Behind the motivation for sex is an even more fundamental desire to be self-righteous. Sexual cravings are mapped onto this desire. Self-righteousness encourages, rationalizes, and, yes, even fuels heart-based longings for sexual satisfaction.

Both the self-righteous and self-gratifiers are obsessed with living for self. The driving purpose of personal self-righteousness caused the scribes and Pharisees to arrogantly rewrite the demands of the Mosaic law into a more workable measure of holiness. Jesus elucidates that this fundamental motivation also resulted in supporting, justifying, and nourishing a lifestyle of lustful cravings. Eventually these desires could not be contained in the womb of the heart but were visibly born through the behaviors of divorce and remarriage.

Preexisting impurities of the heart are embedded in covetousness. In fact, covetousness is what makes the heart/womb so fertile for sexual temptation. Impurities of the heart twist God-given sexual drives into covetous, dominating, and demanding desires. Once these desires captivate the mind and enslave the body, the sense of bondage overwhelms the lustful person, and he or she believes there is no hope for lasting change. The next chapter will expand on the most common impurities that set the stage for sexual slavery.

KEY CONCEPTS

biological determinism
hope
victim
sexual enslavement
self-destruction
innate lust
depraved desire
idolatrous craving
coercive nature of desire
hedonistic greed
holy desires and passions
fantasizing
heart of an adulterer

STUDY QUESTIONS

1. Explain why the sole use of techniques of spiritual exorcism, group accountability in twelve-step programs, and the purging of all suggestive media are only marginally effective at best.
2. The predominant view of sexual "addictions"—by both secular therapists and Christians alike—is that man is a victim. He is basically good, but other people and events have led him to do things he would otherwise never have done; therefore, his sexual sin is not his fault. James 1:14 teaches otherwise. Explain—using various Scriptures—the truth of the statement "*Man* is fully responsible for his lapse into immoral craving; the cause of blame is deep within."
3. Consider these two statements: "Your body will act in full cooperation with the dictates of your heart." "Lustful sin in the heart demands to be born." Explain these statements

in light of James 1:13–15; Psalm 7:14; and Proverbs 14:14; 17:20; 21:10.

4. What is hedonistic greed, and how is it often manifested within marriage?
5. Describe the difference between the purely psychological model of help for sexual deviances and the biblical view of such sin.
6. Describe several ways in which sexual sin, which promises a fulfilling and blissful life, actually leads to death.
7. What is unbiblical about the claim that "two consenting adults having sex in a loving relationship constitutes a marriage"?
8. According to Matthew 5:27–28, God takes issue with the heart of an adulterer as much as he does outward sexual sin. Discuss how sinful lust, self-gratification, and self-righteousness hide in the heart of the adulterer, making it an abomination to the Lord.

FOR FURTHER READING

Beale, G. K. *We Become What We Worship: A Biblical Theology of Idolatry*. Downers Grove, IL: InterVarsity Press, 2008.

Burk, Denny. *Transforming Homosexuality: What the Bible Says about Sexual Orientation and Change*. Phillipsburg, NJ: P&R Publishing, 2015.

Lundgaard, Kris. *The Enemy Within: Straight Talk about the Power and Defeat of Sin*. Phillipsburg, NJ: P&R Publishing, 1998.

Welch, Edward T. *Addictions: A Banquet in the Grave; Finding Hope in the Power of the Gospel*. Phillipsburg, NJ: P&R Publishing, 2001.

4

HEART IDOLATRY AND DEEP PASSIONS

As you learned in the previous chapter, the enslaving dynamic of sexual sin is a consequence of the fall of man into sin. When God created man, he gave him many abilities that would prove essential to living a productive life on earth. One of those abilities is the capacity for habituation, which is the ability to complete routine behaviors without focused thought or concentration. The brain, in cooperation with the "muscle memory" of the body, enables you to accomplish mundane, repetitive behaviors, such as tying your shoes or combing your hair. No forethought or conscious focus is required for these types of functions, because they are habits formed through repeated practice. Because of this capability, as you finish your habitual routine of getting ready for your day, you can direct your conscious thought to review important things you need to accomplish that day. These habituations of your usual routine enable you to make wise use of your time, truly a blessing to mankind!

SINFUL HABITUATIONS

But with blessing often comes the curse of living with a heart influenced by sinful desires. The ugly side of this God-given capability of forming habits is that covetousness brings defilement, redirecting what is usually a blessing into a curse. In addition to habits that help and bless, the heart develops enslaving habits of self-gratification. This is illustrated in Scripture when the apostle Peter describes the false teachers of his day, saying, "They have eyes full of adultery, insatiable for sin. . . . They have hearts trained in greed" (2 Peter 2:14). It is clear that these false teachers, who claimed to be Christians, were habituated in sexual sin and leading many astray.

The habituation of sexual sin is rewarded in the brain's neurotransmitters with pleasurable endorphins that benumb receptor neurons with feelings of euphoria. This increases the likelihood of repeating the behavior again in order to receive the same experience of euphoria. Sinful habituations easily become a deeply embedded enslavement to a sinful sexual experience. As you already read in 2 Peter 2:14, this is not primarily a physiological enslavement; it is first and primarily an enslavement of greed. With the proper motivation of the heart, the body will deny itself a pleasurable experience because it will do only what the heart gives it permission to do. Christians should not believe in biological or chemical determinism. While brain chemicals can greatly influence your decisions, they cannot determine them. Rather, it is the greed of the heart that emboldens the body to repeat the pleasurable behavior over and over again, even if the conscience deems it sinful. Far beyond biologically driven hormones, it is the deeper issues of the heart and soul that determine the course of a person's life. However, it is important to understand that these desires and cravings of the heart can be complicated, concealed, and highly developed.

Some time ago I counseled a young husband by the name of Frederick who had been married to his wife, Robin, for three years.[1]

---

1. All names used for counselees, both in real cases and in composite case studies, are fictional names. This has been done to protect the privacy of others. I must also point out that I have chosen to use the male gender when naming counselees. This supplies consistency throughout the book; however, the reader should understand my intent to be inclusive of females as it pertains to sexual problems. Similarly, I use the pronouns *he*, *his*, and so on when writing about counselees, purely for the sake of easier reading. I find it cumbersome to continually read *he/she* or *his/hers*. But this is

Our previous counseling appointment had not gone well, and the present one appeared to be even worse. I had been meeting with this twenty-six-year-old man for almost six months, and his problem with masturbation seemed as bad as ever. He was faithful in completing his homework, studying the Bible, praying fervently, but he reported only a slight decrease in the frequency of this self-gratifying habit. He was at the point of becoming very discouraged. Hopelessness hung in the air of my office like a dark, cold fog. Frankly, as his counselor, I was as discouraged as Frederick.

Several sessions previously, I had concluded that his lack of progress must be due to the fact that he simply was not a Christian. I probed his profession of faith, as I had done successfully with other counselees, expecting to find a crack in his supposed Christian façade. Of course, I know that no human counselor can see the heart the way God can. Almost any counselee can fool the best of Christian counselors concerning the reality of his or her faith. But as I had grown over the years as an experienced pastor, knowing how easily I could be fooled, I had become especially alert to fakers. Kingdom criteria for genuine Christianity raced through my mind as I questioned Frederick and listened to his response to the gospel (Matt. 5:3–12; 7:13–27). I reminded him that genuine believers walk in the light and confess their sins (1 John 1:5–10). He reminded me that he had been completely honest with me, as well as his wife, and he was willing to confess his sin to God and seek his forgiveness every time he succumbed.

Using 1 John, I reasoned with Frederick that a person cannot be a Christian if he continues to practice willful sin. "No one who keeps on sinning has either seen him or known him. . . . Whoever makes a practice of sinning is of the devil. . . . No one born of God makes a practice of sinning, for God's seed abides in him, and he cannot keep on sinning because he has been born of God" (1 John 3:6, 8, 9). I explained that the Greek tense does not mean Christians do not sin

---

not to imply that this book is only for males and their difficulties. Again, I expect the reader to apply these truths and principles to males and females since both genders struggle with sexual problems.

at all. That contradicts what John has already said in 1 John 1:10. It means that a genuine Christian, having the holy seed of righteousness in him, does not *continue* in sin.

"But pastor," Frederick almost came out of his chair, "you make it sound like a true believer can never be enslaved by a sinful habit!" And he was right. I was beginning to give him that impression. The apostle Paul spoke of the struggle he had with conflict between the flesh and the spirit. He would find himself doing things that his spirit did not want to do (Rom. 7:14–25). He also described other believers "caught in any transgression" as needing another helpful Christian to come alongside with "a spirit of gentleness" and help to restore them (Gal. 6:1). I knew that sin could have a temporary controlling power over a believer, but I also knew that sin has absolute dominance over the unbeliever.

After two full sessions of some intense probing concerning his profession of faith, I finally concluded that Frederick was a genuine believer as best as I could determine from a human standpoint. He had a real desire to be pure and to live for Christ, but he had more failure in this one area of sexual enslavement than in any other area of his Christian walk. But why? After so many weeks of biblical help and insight, why did Frederick continue to have more failures than successes? This sticking point continued to mystify me as a counselor.

I proceeded in this counseling session to review the biblical principles of repentance and replacement (putting off and putting on from Eph. 4:20–24), radical amputation (Matt. 5:29–30), total self-denial (Matt. 16:24–28), and repentance and change for sex that had become an idolatrous desire (1 Cor. 10:6–8, 12–14). Frederick was, by now, well acquainted with these verses and had voluntarily committed many of them to memory. That was when he made a very insightful comment. "You know," he said during one of those thoughtful pauses when I was trying to decide where we would go next, "I have discovered that I sin sexually when I get frustrated and angry about something going on in my life." "Would you repeat that?" I asked, leaning forward across the desk. "I sin sexually when I am frustrated, upset, or angry about something in my life."

THE HEART CONTEXT OF HABITUAL SEXUAL SIN

This was my "a-ha" moment as his counselor! Now those things I had learned about Frederick's past were beginning to make sense in relationship to his sexual habits. I had known for some time that he, like many others who seek self-gratifying sexual activity, had a problem with dissatisfaction and discontentment in life, but now this admission of anger began to open up a different perspective. Frederick did not commit sexual sin simply for the sexual thrill itself. Certainly that was part of the hold it had on his life, but there was a deeper, previously hidden motive that drove his sinful activity. It became clear to both of us that masturbation was also an expression of his anger. The source of that anger was rooted in his whole life perspective and the way he had learned to deal with disagreeable people and situations. The sexual expression of his problems was just the veneer. Below the veneer was a more fundamental problem that extended to every area of his life but primarily manifested itself in sexual ways.

Sexual idolatry always has a heart context that can come from a wide range of idols. As a counselor, I had not looked carefully for the heart context of Frederick's problem. In my seminary training, I had learned one of the critical maxims of hermeneutics: "A text without a context is a pretext for a proof text." Proper exegesis of a biblical text includes a careful study of the entire book, its genre, and its immediate textual environment as well as the text itself. In Frederick's case, I should have been paying closer attention to the context—the surrounding environment of my counselee's heart. Instead, I had focused solely on the compulsive tyranny of his masturbation and the idolatry of its pleasurable sensations. A broader heart context included a history of experiences that fed his increasing appetite for self-gratification.[2]

Reworking the hermeneutical maxim, we might say, "A heart problem of idolatry without a context is a formula for continuing idolatry."

---

2. See Prov. 20:5. The purpose or intention (motivation) of the counselee's heart here is defined as being deep, indicating that a counselor of true understanding will go beyond the immediate surface expressions of the problem, using legitimate biblical discernment in discovering and exposing all the motivations that fuel the problem.

Frederick's sexual habituation was idolatrous, but it was idolatrous because it was plotted on a character map of perceived deprivation. He was a man given to angry passions at times. This was not apparent in his demeanor or attitude; externally he seemed kind, even timid. Masturbation, however, had become his chosen means of expressing his displeasure with life.

BIBLICAL INSIGHT INTO IDOLATROUS HEART DESIRES

As I grew in my understanding of Frederick's life, it caused me to ask questions of Scripture I had never asked before. Does the Bible provide insight into the complexity of human motivations that feed sinful habituations? Are there complicated, often hidden layers of idolatrous desires in the human heart that must be addressed for purposes of sanctification? As soon as I asked these questions, a part of me reacted skeptically. Even careful interpreters tend to see things in the biblical text that are not there and can unintentionally depart from the authorial intent and its theological implications, sacrificing divine authority. Was I seeing things in Frederick's heart that were not there? That was a danger I wanted to avoid. When you do that, you begin to give your counselees your opinions rather than God's judgments.

Conversely, asking experience-prompted questions of Scripture can help us see things in the text that *are* there but have been ignored or misread because of a lack of engaging a strategic battle for holiness in the lives of the people we minister to, and even in our own lives. Each person carries a certain knowledge of the text into addressing problems, but as we are faced with the realities and struggles with sin, like Frederick's behavior, our own insight into the Word grows. Wisdom dictates skillful application of that Word in an appropriate manner and time. Richard Pratt believes that good interpretation of the text involves appreciation of the fact that it occurs in a war zone.

> Not only does studying the Bible affect our spiritual condition, but our spiritual condition also helps and hinders our study of the Bible. . . . Each of us reads the Bible in a foxhole surrounded by the fire of

a cosmic war between evil and the Spirit (Ephesians 6:10–18). . . . Beliefs and opinions are often formulated, confirmed, and modified in the context of practice. . . . Similarly, Liberationists point to the influence of praxis, active engagement in the world, on interpretative perspectives. They insist that their interpretations cannot be adequately evaluated in the comfort of an air-conditioned study. They are right; struggling with social oppression leads interpreters to ask questions of the Bible in a way that others may never consider.[3]

The battle against sexual enslavement will have the same effect. An active ministry of the Word will cause you to look at Scripture in new and fresh ways, asking questions of the text you would not normally ask in the ordinary flow of life. The apostle Paul strikes a similar tone when he says, "and I pray that the sharing of your faith may become effective for the full knowledge of every good thing that is in us for the sake of Christ" (Philem. 6). Full understanding and insight into Scripture cannot be achieved through a detached, academic, or non-ministry study. Rather, it comes through an active ministry (κοινωνία, "fellowshipping" or "sharing" of faith) that deals with the practical problems of life. Frederick's persistent problem forced me to return to the Word, asking critical questions regarding motivations that undergird the idolatrous habituations of sexual sin.

Are there motivations and desires of the heart that *predispose* it to unholy sexual lust? If the term *predispose* is too fatalistic, then are there motivations and desires that cause the heart to be *vulnerable* to unholy lust? Is it biblically legitimate to say that otherwise honorable desires for sex can be mapped on top of preexisting idols of the heart? If so, once sexual lust has conceived, does its motivation continue to energize lust's enslavement (see fig. 4.1)?

The book of 1 Corinthians was written to a struggling church, with sexual sin being a prominent feature of its struggle. Immorality plagued its fellowship and was proving to be the ruin of more than

---

3. Richard L. Pratt Jr., *He Gave Us Stories: The Bible Student's Guide to Interpreting Old Testament Narratives* (Phillipsburg, NJ: P&R Publishing, 1993), 45, 49.

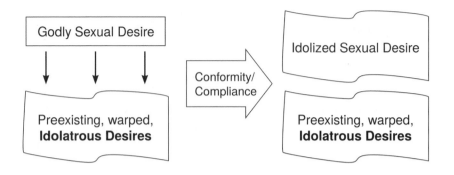

Fig. 4.1. Heart Idols Energize Lust's Enslavement

one Christian (1 Cor. 5:1–6:20). Like ancient Israel, the Corinthian Christians were misusing their freedom and were in danger of becoming overconfident in their walk before God. In the case of ancient Israel's forty-year desert experience, in which there was a forced abstinence from food, their newly discovered freedom to eat lacked self-discipline and soon gave way to craving evil things. Paul warns, "Now these things took place as examples for us, that we might not desire evil as they did" (1 Cor. 10:6). God was not pleased with them because, contenting themselves with freedom from the brutal treatment of their Egyptian masters, they then gave themselves over to rest and relaxation only to indulge their sensual desires.[4]

These Jews, having lived their entire lives under the harsh extremes of bondage and hardship, longed for the indulgent pleasures enjoyed by their taskmasters. The effect of the Jews' punishing labors instilled within them more than a desire to be free to worship the God they served; they wanted to be free to enjoy unrestricted pleasures. But God had delivered them to be his people, not the people of good times. Obviously, their desires became greater than loving and serving God, despite the fact that he had miraculously freed them. Once delivered, the Jews soon gave themselves to serving idolatrous gods: the Egyptians

---

4. 1 Corinthians 10:5, "they laid low" as on death beds (καταστρώννυμι); 10:7, they ate, drank, and played (παίζω, to play, to indulge and amuse one's self, to dance).

had patterned for the Jews an enjoyment of sensual fulfillment through indulgent living (Ex. 32:4, 6). Paul warns the Corinthians, "Do not be idolaters as some of them were; as it is written, 'The people sat down to eat and drink and rose up to play'" (1 Cor. 10:7). Ancient Israel's experience in Egypt had stirred up certain heart expectations and desires that made her vulnerable to sexual idolatry when freedom was acquired. Her disobedience was to be a forewarning to the Corinthians, and all Christians afterward, of the danger of cravings and desires becoming idolatrous.

The Israelites mapped their physical desires onto this layer of comfort idolatry. The fact that they had a desire for food and sex was not wrong, but since this comfort idol was worshiped through their physical appetites, it escalated into inordinate physical cravings. "And the people spoke against God and against Moses, 'Why have you brought us up out of Egypt to die in the wilderness? For there is no food and no water, and we loathe this worthless food'" (Num. 21:5). "While Israel lived in Shittim, the people began to whore with the daughters of Moab" (Num. 25:1). The apostle Paul says they put the Lord to the test, grumbled, and committed immorality (1 Cor. 10:8–10). God hated their idolatrous ways and severely judged them: over twenty-three thousand died on one occasion, several died from snakebites on another, and many were destroyed by a plague (Num. 25:9; 21:6; 16:49). In this case, it is clear that their sexual immorality had a context and was fed by cravings for comfort and easy living, which they believed had been denied them in Egypt. The Jews' unhappiness directly paralleled Frederick's sense of being deprived of the childhood he deserved. Sexual behavior becomes one way in which previous heart idols actualize themselves. Then sexual enslavement becomes its own idol.

Our apostle proceeds to warn the Corinthians in strong terms. "Now these things happened to them as an example, but they were written down for our instruction, on whom the end of the ages has come. . . . Therefore, my beloved, flee from idolatry" (1 Cor. 10:11, 14). Frederick's struggle with his sinful habituation took me back to the text, seeking additional insight into human motivation and behavior.

95

I began to see that the human heart has layers of reasoning, purposes, and motivations that are rooted in a strata of complex cravings. The examples in God's Word of those who preceded us in the faith are recorded to save us, including Frederick, from such slavish idolatry and its temporal judgment.

IDOLATRY IN THE LIFE OF KING DAVID

In a similar fashion, David's infamous sin with Bathsheba illustrates a heart that was already ripe for adultery. David did not go out one evening and innocently and suddenly fall into sexual sin upon seeing her naked form. Other idolatrous desires were already present when the tempestuous opportunity presented itself. To use our previous analogy from James 1:14–15, his heart was already a fertile womb in which the seed of lust could be implanted and grown. A well-established history preceded David's sin. Prior to his adultery with Bathsheba, David had compromised his heart many times, and in various ways, because of his high expectations and longings. All of these were present long before Bathsheba came into view.

David was a sensual and passionate man. He had a great love for his people and the preservation of the nation. Soon after his coronation as king over Israel, he solidified his reign by a systematic process of establishing political treaties with neighboring countries whenever possible (2 Sam. 5). Part of the arrangements he made included taking concubines and wives into his household, a practice in direct disobedience to God's prior commands (Deut. 17:17). These commands were especially given to the future kings of Israel. The main reason God gave for not taking many wives and concubines was "lest his heart turn away [from the Lord his God]." Custom dictated that these international alliances be formalized by intermarrying aristocratic families. A king whose daughters were married to a neighboring king would think twice before waging war on his grandchildren. David purposefully laid aside the Word of God to follow the customary practices of royalty in establishing peace between Israel and her neighbors. David was a man of war, having defeated more of Israel's enemies than his predecessor.

He had seen a considerable amount of bloodshed in his life and longed for the day when Jerusalem would be at peace. However, his desire for peace exceeded his desire to please God.

With the defeat of Ammon and Aram, David's desire for peace was mostly realized. The defeat of these foes was Israel's greatest victory because its greatest threat had been neutralized.

> And the Syrians fled before Israel, and David killed of the Syrians the men of 700 chariots, and 40,000 horsemen, and wounded Shobach the commander of their army, so that he died there. And when all the kings who were servants of Hadadezer saw that they had been defeated by Israel, they made peace with Israel and became subject to them. So the Syrians were afraid to save the Ammonites anymore. (2 Sam. 10:18–19)

After such a resounding victory, in which the dreaded Ammonites and their allies, the Syrians, were so soundly defeated, David was ready for a break. He wanted time to relax and enjoy some peace. Although David was courageous, hardworking, and a skillful tactician, he believed he deserved the fruits of his labor.

After Israel achieved this partial peace with such a great enemy, we read, "In the spring of the year, the time when kings go out to battle, David sent Joab, and his servants with him, and all Israel. And they ravaged the Ammonites and besieged Rabbah. But David remained at Jerusalem" (2 Sam. 11:1). David stayed behind—to relax! The general of the army—the king of the great nation—wanted to personally experience some of the peace he had worked so diligently to achieve. He was convinced he deserved a little diversion and relaxation.

Peace and pleasure are sisters with the same parent: ease. David was a hardworking man who had spent himself fully, putting his own life on the line for the sake of others. He considered an occasional self-indulgence well-deserved. But there was a difference between this sexual union and the previous ones, which were consummated for the safety and peace of his people. He may or may not have wanted to be with these women of political expediency. But Bathsheba was different. He wanted *her*. This union was totally for the purpose of self-gratification. The life of ease, for which he had fought so hard and compromised so much, was the idol that would express itself in sexual greed with Bathsheba (2 Sam. 11:2–5). It would so consume his life that he would arrange to have Uriah, Bathsheba's husband and one of his own devoted soldiers, murdered (2 Sam. 11:6–27). It would be the idol that would bring unending grief to himself and his family for the remainder of his life:

> In the first half of 2 Samuel the story is about David's rise to power. Everything is going great for David. He wins the civil war and succeeds Saul as king (chs. 1–5). He conquers Jerusalem, brings the ark to his new capital, and receives a covenant from God (chs. 5–7). He wins all his battles, defeating the Philistines, Moabites, Arameans, Edomites, and Ammonites (chs. 8–10). Life is good for David and his nation.
>
> The second half of the book however, is incredibly different. Events in that half are almost all negative for the king. David's oldest son Amnon rapes Tamar, Amnon's half-sister, prompting Absalom, Tamar's brother, to kill Amnon (ch. 13). Next, Absalom, a son whom David loves, conspires against him, creating a bloody civil war. David is forced to flee Jerusalem. Eventually Absalom is defeated and killed, but David remains heartbroken (chs. 14–19). Next another rebellion arises (ch. 20). David then ends his career by fighting the Philistines again (ch. 21). In contrast to his earlier defeat of the Philistines (and his single-handed defeat of Goliath), David becomes exhausted and must be rescued by his troops; other heroes kill the giants this time (2 Sam. 21:15–22). . . . The pivot event is in 2 Samuel 11–12. David sins by sleeping with Bathsheba and having her husband Uriah killed. Prior to this episode, David cruises through life as the beloved, respected, national hero; afterwards, David's magnificent reputation begins to unravel.[5]

5. J. Scott Duvall and J. Daniel Hays, *Grasping God's Word* (Grand Rapids: Zondervan, 2012), 98–99.

David's adultery with Bathsheba was the crucial turning point of his life and reign. His life and family were never the same. In fact, the operative god of ease, on which his sexual drives were mapped, exacted a costly toll. He was transformed from a national hero to a Peeping Tom, adulterer, murderer, liar, and eventual failure as a husband and father, all because of the idol of ease sown in his heart from the earliest days of his reign.

IDOLATRY IN THE LIFE OF KING SOLOMON

David's son Solomon followed his father's reign and reproduced his habitual sins. In rebellion against the restrictions of Deuteronomy 17:17, he took to himself many wives and concubines. But in Solomon's case, the text is more explicit—Solomon "*loved* many foreign women" (1 Kings 11:1). This was something that was never said of his father. It seems that Solomon too married for political purposes, but he also did it out of deep, romantic passion for these women, despite the clear prohibition of God: "From the nations concerning which the LORD had said to the people of Israel, 'You shall not enter into marriage with them, neither shall they with you, for surely they will turn away your heart after their gods.' Solomon clung to these in love" (1 Kings 11:2). He exceeded his father in his sexual desire for many women.

Solomon was a womanizer. "He had 700 wives, princesses, and 300 concubines. And his wives turned away his heart" (1 Kings 11:3). Because he was able to enjoy a relative time of peace during his reign, he did not long for the ease for which his father had lusted. Solomon's quest and longing to a much greater degree became personal satisfaction and happiness. "I also gathered for myself . . . many concubines, the delight of the children of man. . . . And whatever my eyes desired I did not keep from them. I kept my heart from no pleasure, for my heart found pleasure in all my toil, and this was my reward for all my toil" (Eccl. 2:8, 10).[6] For a time Solomon was the consummate

---

6. Addressing the argument of whether Solomon was the original author of Ecclesiastes is not my purpose in this book. Even those who deny Solomonic authorship

99

hedonist. He believed that true lasting satisfaction and meaning in life could be acquired "under the sun."[7] He adopted a materialistic cosmology, elevating earthly things to a level of worship.

His god of seeking earthly satisfaction expressed itself in many ways, including his sexual lust for many women. He gave himself to them and "clung to these in love." Eventually he found that intimacy with many women did not bring any lasting satisfaction or meaning to his life. In fact, it brought bondage and captivity. "And I find something more bitter than death: the woman whose heart is snares and nets, and whose hands are fetters. He who pleases God escapes her, but the sinner is taken by her" (Eccl. 7:26). Strangely, he writes in Proverbs 5:15–19 that a married man should seek satisfaction from his wife—not wives! The singular "wife" is significant and telling. The man who embraces an adulteress will find himself trapped like a prisoner: "The iniquities of the wicked ensnare him, and he is held fast in the cords of his sin" (Prov. 5:22). Solomon understood that a beautiful woman could be captivating, but he also put the blame in this verse where it belonged—a man's own "iniquities." The culpability of a man's own heart is the real reason for enslavement to sexuality.

God's blessing on Solomon made him the wealthiest king of Israel. Instead of being eternally thankful, Solomon allowed his heart to be drawn away into a quest for even greater wealth and influence:

> Thus King Solomon excelled all the kings of the earth in riches and in wisdom. And all the kings of the earth sought the presence of

---

advance the argument of an impersonator (Qohelet) who is attempting to assume the persona of Solomon by describing his vain quest for purpose and meaning from "under the sun," like his sexual conquest of women. See Tremper Longman III, *The Book of Ecclesiastes* (Grand Rapids, MI / Cambridge, UK: Eerdmans, 1998), 2–9. "Ecclesiastes may well have been written by Solomon himself; this is the most natural way to read the Biblical text." Philip Graham Ryken, *Ecclesiastes* (Wheaton, IL: Crossway, 2010), 18. Ryken believes that Ecclesiastes is an autobiographical polemic written by Solomon himself. Later ancient Jewish revisions could have added updated Hebrew terminology.

7. Hebraic shorthand for everything temporal or earthly that is part of this fleeting life.

Solomon to hear his wisdom, which God had put into his mind. Every one of them brought his present, articles of silver and of gold, garments, myrrh, spices, horses, and mules, so much year by year. (2 Chron. 9:22–24)

Wealth provided the opportunity for Solomon to acquire anything his pleasure-seeking heart desired. On his profligate idol was mapped his sexual desire, which found its expression in the many women he loved, even though he eventually realized that his own idolized heart had led him into the snare of sexual bondage.

THE SUPREMACY OF THE IDOL OF COVETOUSNESS

Abundant evidence from the Scriptural accounts of David and Solomon supports the assertion that sexual lust is fed by deeper motivations possessing authoritative seniority. These motivations are broader and more generalized heart themes, but they form the perfect staging ground for sexual sin. In the pantheon of heart deities, they have been around the longest. They feed, nurture, and support the constant conception of new sexual gods that want to set up permanent altars in the heart (see fig. 4.2). At the top of this lineup of deities is covetousness. This idol nourishes all other functional gods. Covetousness is at the root of all sexual sin, and it produces in the heart new and refined idols. Serving and gratifying self is its core expectation. Although it manifests itself in a number of different attitudes and expectations, greed is its main appeal.

Thus we see that unholy sexual lust first finds its primary source in a demanding heart of covetous greed. In the book of Galatians, the apostle Paul says this is the desire of the flesh that sets its desire against the Spirit (Gal. 5:16–17). The flesh is myopic, seeing the fulfillment of its desire as the only worthy focus of life. Fleshly desire has been the condition of man since the fall of Adam and Eve and continues to reside in the Christian as he struggles to submit the flesh to the Spirit. The Decalogue (Ten Commandments) anticipates this basic greed of the heart and warns, "you shall not covet your neighbor's

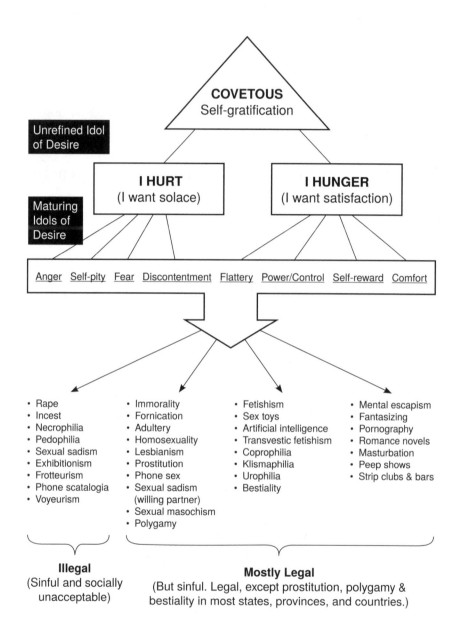

Fig. 4.2. Pantheon of Heart Idols

wife" (Ex. 20:17). Greed expressed as self-gratifying expectations and desires is the raw core of sexual sin. Greed is the supreme idol in the array of functional gods of desire. In the book of Ephesians, the apostle Paul connects forbidden sexual pursuits with greed. Christians should not follow the practices of the Gentiles who "have become callous and have given themselves up to sensuality, greedy to practice every kind of impurity" (Eph. 4:19). A few verses later he states, "But sexual immorality and all impurity or covetousness must not even be named among you, as is proper among saints" (Eph. 5:3). Self-satisfying sex is, by its very definition, sinful. The rationalization that masturbation is permissible, as long as it does not hurt another person, carries no biblical weight. Masturbation is one sexual act that is an expression of pure greed.

Counselors who understand the complex yearning of the human heart will be aware of the two broad categories of desire that greed may assume in sexual lust. The more common is the *craving for pleasurable satisfaction*. A human heart naturally longs for fulfillment, but the selfish sinfulness of the heart idolizes that longing, demanding to be satisfied. Returning to Galatians 5, Paul says literally, "For the desires of the flesh are against the Spirit, and the desires of the Spirit are against the flesh, for these are opposed to each other, to keep you from doing the things you want to do" (Gal. 5:17). Now this is the critical idea: "to keep you from doing the things you want to do." When this lust reaches the point at which personal resistance fails, it becomes an idol. Greed has worked through its incessant craving to secure an altar in the heart that requires allegiance and personal worship. Four specific types of idolized desire seem to orbit around this craving for sexual satisfaction:

- Flattery
- Power/Control
- Self-Reward
- Comfort

They all fuel the desire for sexual sin in whatever evil way the heart chooses to manifest itself.

Another, often overlooked route that greed may take to sexual expression is through the *longing for solace*. Here the person has some perceived hurt demanding to be redressed that is causing his sexual misconduct. Many situational determinative approaches to sex therapy attempt to rectify this injury by making the person face his "hidden past" in order to accept it and express repressed anger for its damage. The biblical model does not deny the pain of the past—if it is a reality, not the result of a therapist's encouragement of a false memory. When there is a genuine painful memory, such as "I was molested by my grandfather," it must be handled with tenderness, mercy, and grace, helping the victim walk biblically through a repentance/forgiveness/reconciliation process.[8] It is imperative that the person who has been violated or molested should be helped to see not only that people do sinful things to us and we suffer because of it, but also that the sinfulness of our own hearts contrives evil ways of dealing with these memories. A covetous, sinful heart insists on being compensated for the loss, which may have been innocence, childhood, happiness, virginity, a sense of safety and security, or a combination of these. Consider the young woman who has been abused or neglected by her father. As she matures she desperately longs for a man to care for her; she is even willing to give herself away sexually to men in order to receive their attention and adoration. A young man who was reared in a home with a father who rarely showed him any affection or approval might eventually and earnestly seek affection from other men in homosexual relationships. In any case, the heart deeply desires solace and will seek it in many ways. The quest to alleviate interpersonal emotional pain can be seen in four idolized desires that may seek sexual expression in your life:

- Anger
- Self-pity

8. Dealing with a history of molestation must include addressing the abiding anger and vivid recollections of this criminal activity. Victimized people can, through the grace and mercy of Jesus Christ, live without being plagued by oppressive memories or sinful anger (Gen. 50:20; Ps. 37:8; Eph. 4:26; Phil. 4:6–8; Col. 3:8; 1 Peter 2:21–25; 4:19).

- Fear
- Discontentment

Continuing in Galatians 5, the apostle moves our thinking from the inward longings of the heart to the more outward expressions, from the *desire* of the flesh to the *works* of the flesh (Gal. 5:19–21). Among the more than fifteen "deeds of the flesh," he specifically inventories ten that are either directly or indirectly associated with sinful sexual practices:

- Immorality (πορνεία)
- Impurity (ἀκαθαρσία)[9]
- Sensuality (ἀσέλγεια)
- Idolatry (εἰδωλολατρία)[10]
- Enmity (ἔχθραι)
- Strife (ἔρις)
- Jealousy (ζῆλος)
- Fits of anger (θυμοί)
- Drunkenness (μέθαι)
- Carousing (κῶμοι)

It is obvious from Paul's list that these are more refined expressions of "the works of the flesh." He also says that this is not an exhaustive list, because he concludes with "such things."[11] So there are many different types of "the deeds of the flesh" that manifest "the desire of the flesh," and several of those are sexual in nature.

9. "[Early] Young Christianity regards the sexual immorality of the Hellenistic world as ungodly ἀκαθαρσία (R. 1:24ff.; with πορνεία, 2 C. 12:21; Gl. 5:19; Eph. 5:3, 5; Col. 3:5; cf. Rev. 17:4). ἀκαθαρσία is ἔργον τῆς σαρκός (Gl. 5:19), i.e., it is an expression of the nature of the unregenerate man whose action is determined by commitment, not to God, but to natural ἐπιθυμίαι." Gerhard Kittel, ed., *Theological Dictionary of the New Testament*, trans. Geoffrey W. Bromiley (Grand Rapids: Eerdmans, 1965), 3:429.

10. Early Christians were well acquainted with the common practice of temple prostitution.

11. Galatians 5:21, ὅμοιος, that which is like another.

People who persevere in practicing these deeds need to be cautioned that they do not have the Spirit. Paul says to the Galatians, "I warn you, as I warned you before, that those who do such things will not inherit the kingdom of God" (Gal. 5:21b). He repeatedly reminds them of this judgment of God that awaits ungodliness. The participle "those who practice" is present active in its Greek declension, meaning that unbelievers are the type who continue in their sexual misconduct unabated. A Christian, like Frederick, may struggle with sexual enslavement for a time, but if he is a genuine Christian, he will not persist without resistance and change. Indeed, as a Christian he is seeking godly counsel to be freed from his enslavement.

Paul has already said to the Galatian Christians experiencing this war between the flesh and the Spirit that, for a time, "the desires of the flesh are against the Spirit, and the desires of the Spirit are against the flesh, for these are opposed to each other, to keep you from doing the things you want to do" (Gal. 5:17). Christians can, for a time, seem to be at the mercy of the flesh, not doing what the Spirit wishes, but they will not remain there. Those who remain at the mercy of the flesh are demonstrating that they were never believers to begin with and will continue to be plagued with increasing sexual debauchery.

A HEART CONTEXT OF ANGER

Even though he had not seen a lot of progress, Frederick was still willing to "fight the good fight" against his self-indulgence. I now understood what fed his sexual bondage. Frederick had been reared in a home of hostility. He could not remember a kind word his mother or father ever said to the other. As a young child, he could remember running to his room and hiding when the fights broke out between his parents. He was never abused, but his parents would get rather physical with each other. This was especially true when they had been drinking. I could not help but reflect on the grace of God in Frederick and Robin's home now that he was a believer. He was a kind and loving husband and father, something I know he did not experience when he was growing up.

106

His parents would fight for hours. Frederick admitted that as a young boy he would stay in his room and sob, never allowing anyone to see him cry. Eventually he learned that he could escape with comic books, reading silently in his bedroom closet and closing off the outside world so that he would not have to think about the pain. This became his regular routine. He took special notice of how these comic books enhanced certain female attributes, and they captured his intrigue. His parents divorced when he was twelve, and even though he welcomed the peace, he was angry about what had happened. Why could he not have a normal childhood like the rest of the kids he saw at school? Deep in his heart, he wanted more than anything else to have parents who could get along. His mother married his stepfather less than a year after the divorce. She had met him at a bar. This man did not like Frederick and considered him an unnecessary inconvenience in his home. For a time, Frederick wanted to live with his father, but the courts would not permit it. This only served to fuel Frederick's growing anger.

Around age thirteen Frederick was introduced to pornography at school. At first he was ashamed but quickly realized that the other guys whom he respected liked it, so he decided to indulge his curiosity. He discovered his stepfather's stash of porn magazines at home. He learned that he could take several copies and return them later without his stepfather or mother knowing. Frederick returned to his closet and secretly shut off the outside world while immersing himself in a growing imagination of sexual eroticism. It was not long before he was practicing his sinful habit. This outlet for his arousal seemed the most satisfying. He did not indulge himself all the time, but he did confess to a growing habit of it through his high school years. Furthermore, he consciously recognized that the frequency of this habituation increased when he was upset, stressed-out, or under a lot of pressure at home or in school. By now his body was well accustomed to this habit, so much so that life was not normal without it. As time went on his sexual fantasies included erotic thoughts about the girls at school, after hearing some of the sexual exploits of the other guys. One day, he even overheard the teacher in health class say that masturbation was a legitimate means of releasing sexual tension and frustration. "People who say masturbation is wrong are pietistic prudes," she said. "It is the normal function of adolescent sexuality as long as you do not hurt anyone." That sounded reasonable to him. It is just a simple biological function. How could it be wrong if God created it? Whatever guilt he felt was lifted.

Frederick not only had a seriously ingrained habituation of sexual self-satisfaction but also had developed numerous heart idols that fed this practice, going back into his childhood responses to his dreadful home life. Even though he had responded to the gospel of Jesus Christ in college through the faithful witness of Robin, he retained the same fleshly idols he had formed when he was a young child. Frederick realized that he had been lied to in his high school health class. His sexual fantasies and self-indulgence were taking a toll on his marriage. Robin could tell he did not want to have sex with her because of the infrequency of their intimacy. She did not believe that she was desirable to him. Actually, Robin would never be able to fulfill him the way he could fulfill himself, because she did not possess the immediate bio-feedback that he had. As you would expect, the greater the tension in their marriage, the more frequently he indulged himself.

The covetous sinfulness of Frederick's heart yearned for some type of reconciliation with the injustices of his past. His lost childhood, what he believed he deserved, could never be recovered. His anger had not been settled, and it continued to energize his sinful practices. Not only had he not learned how to handle stress and hardship God's way, turning to the Savior who is the Refuge and God of Comfort (2 Sam. 22:3; Pss. 2:12; 5:11; 7:1; 11:1; 14:6; 16:1; Isa. 51:12; 2 Cor. 1:3), he had not realized his anger was ultimately against God. He might have been able to stop his sinful practice, but this frustration and anger at life would manifest itself in another way. As his counselor, it was my duty to help Frederick unplug the extension cord of anger that energized his sexual escapism.

As we saw in figure 4.2, covetousness reigns in all sexual sins and enslavement. From there, the self-gratification of the heart will take one of two routes of justification, depending on the counselee's perception of life. It will want either solace for some perceived hurt or satisfaction for some inordinate craving. Each of these idols is further refined into four axes. On the one hand, a lustful person may hurt because of anger, self-pity, fear, or discontentment. On the other, the lustful person may crave flattery, power/control, self-reward, or comfort. The first is a more positive emotional desire and the second is more negative. Both categories are sinfully engendered. We will explore this more in the next chapter.

KEY CONCEPTS

habituation
muscle memory
endorphins
euphoria
greed
enslavement of greed
enslaving habits of self-gratification
heart context
experience-prompted questions
active ministry involvement
motivations that predispose
covetousness
comfort idolatry
layers of motivations
ripe for adultery
god of ease
personal satisfaction
materialistic cosmology
myopic
personal resistance fails
false memory
genuine painful memory
compensation for loss

STUDY QUESTIONS

1. "Masturbation is one sexual act that is an expression of pure greed." Define greed as it relates to sexual sin. Then explain how this was true in the example of the counselee Frederick.

2. "A heart problem of idolatry without a context is a formula for continuing idolatry." Based on this insight, answer the following questions:
   - Frederick's anger formed the context for his sexual sin of masturbation. What was Frederick angry about? How did he justify his indulgence in sexual sin?
   - The context for King David's sin with Bathsheba was not anger. Explain his context. Although we do not have a record of his inner thoughts, how did he seem to justify his indulgence in lustful adultery and murder? Study the relevant text of 2 Samuel 11.
   - What do you think was the context for King Solomon's sexual sin of polygamy? What seems to have been his justification? Study 1 Kings 11:1–8 and Ecclesiastes 2:1–11.

3. Since covetousness is at the root of all sexual sin, and serving and gratifying self is its core expectation, what do these passages of Scripture say the Christian ought to be wary of?
   - Matthew 23:25–28
   - Mark 7:21–23
   - Luke 20:46–47
   - Romans 1:24–32
   - Ephesians 4:17–24
   - Ephesians 5:1–4

4. "Asking experience-prompted questions of Scripture can help us see things in the text that *are* there but have been ignored or misread because of a lack of engaging in a strategic battle for holiness." Read through Psalm 51, David's repentance of his sin with Bathsheba. How do you think you would look at this passage differently if you did not know that it came from the experience of one who had committed adultery and murder?

How would you look at it differently if you did not consider your own sin? What does this say about how important it is to come to God's Word in order for our lives to be changed?

5. "In this case, it is clear that [the Israelites'] sexual immorality had a context and was fed by cravings for comfort and easy living, which they believed had been denied them in Egypt." Explain how the human heart can start with a desire for comfort and progress to craving and demanding that comfort, eventually ending up in sexual immorality. Write a conceivable mental dialogue that could have taken place to rationalize sexual sin. (This exercise will help you look for motivations and desires of the heart that predispose it to sexual sin.)

FOR FURTHER READING

Kruger, Melissa. *The Envy of Eve: Finding Contentment in a Covetous World.* Focus for Women. Scotland, UK: Christian Focus Publications, 2012.

Piper, John, and Justin Taylor, eds. *Sex and the Supremacy of Christ.* Wheaton, IL: Crossway, 2005.

Powlison, David. *Making All Things New: Restoring Joy to the Sexually Broken.* Wheaton, IL: Crossway, 2017.

Priolo, Lou. *Discontentment: Why Am I So Unhappy?* Phillipsburg, NJ: P&R Publishing, 2012.

PART 2

THE MOTIVATIONS OF
SEXUAL IDOLATRY

5

CONSOLING THE HURTING IDOLS OF PASSION

Scientists tell us that the human brain is the most sophisticated and complicated mechanism in the known universe. At best, the most renowned neuroscientists understand only a small percentage of how the brain actually functions. But, complex as it is, even more elusive is the knowledge of how the human soul interacts with the biological functions of the body. If we did not have divine revelation from God, we would be in complete darkness as to the nature of this association.

We know that the soul continues to think and ponder even after the physical brain is dead. As we discussed in chapter 2, the apostle Paul spoke of the fact that even when he is absent from the body he still has intentionality to please God (2 Cor. 5:9). Your soul does not need a physical brain to think. Nevertheless, while your soul and body are still united, whatever affects the body's biological functioning likewise impacts your ability to think and process information. This applies to the nature of sexual sin in this way: the habituations of the body (physical) will prompt your mind (soul) to think often in very ungodly ways. And as we've noted previously, the Bible says your heart is responsible for your thinking, planning, and purposing. There is an undeniable connection between the physical body and the heart.

Just as the brain is complex, so is your heart. Scripture says, "Many are the plans in the mind of a man" (Prov. 19:21). It is not just one thought or desire that leads you into sin. Why do you commit the sexual sins you do? It is a simple question, and you might long for a simple solution, but the answer may be more complicated than you ever conceived. Why is this so? Because your heart has *many* plans and purposes for doing what you do, thinking what you think, or reacting to temptation.

Your heart is not only complex but clever. It will deceive you into believing that you are better off than you are. It devises ways to appear free from sin, all the while indulging its lusts. It crafts various ways to avoid detection. Truly, your heart views enslaving sin as simple—a mere violation of God's law, a harmless infraction of the rules, a sin easily committed with very little forethought and just as effortlessly stopped. Little attention is given to competing lusts and ambitions that bring you to the acting out of sexual lust. As we discovered in our last chapter, sexual desires are mapped onto a variety of heart motivations, plans, and purposes. In this chapter and the next we will examine eight that are especially prominent in ungodly sexuality.

At the core of all sexual sin is a covetous heart—one ruled by sensual, self-seeking greed (Ex. 20:17; Deut. 5:21; Rom. 1:28–29; Eph. 5:3; Col. 3:5). This expression of greed can manifest itself in negative and affirmative motivations, both of which produce sinful sexual thoughts and behaviors. Negative motivations correspond to the circumstances of your life when your heart is hurting—when you have suffered. When you hurt, you are running from something you believe you do not deserve. Sexual pleasure is used as a way to compensate for difficulties or to lessen the pain and suffering. Greed will direct your heart to covet a sexual "pain reliever" in the search for solace. In effect, your heart says, "I do not want to suffer anymore; and the way I will escape my pain is through personal self-indulgence in sexual pleasure."

This chapter will describe four of these negative ruling desires of the heart in more detail:

- Anger
- Self-pity
- Discontentment
- Fear

On the other hand, more affirmative motivations correspond to circumstances in your life when you believe you are entitled and deserving. When your heart hungers, you are running toward something you believe you do deserve. Again, greed directs the heart, but in this case it is to find satisfaction through sinful sexual imagination and behaviors. Chapter 6 will examine four of these affirmative desires:

- Self-reward
- Flattery
- Power/Control
- Comfort

Sexual lust is fueled through these eight refined desires (see fig. 4.2, "Pantheon of Heart Idols"). Although these eight axes do not represent all possible conditions of the heart that precipitate sexual lust, they do represent significant influential cravings that my experience has found to be especially prominent through biblical study and years of counseling. Furthermore, it would be wrong to assume that these eight are isolated categories, unaffected by the others. Indeed, they can and often do overlap. Because the heart and its ruling motivations are so complex, it stands to reason that multiple overlapping desires could be at work at the same time. For example, the young woman who involved herself in premarital sex with her boyfriend because it was simultaneously a pleasing experience and a way to get back at her strict parents displayed two overlapping desires: pleasure and vengeance. Below is a description of how the first four of these axes from a hurting perspective can occasion and feed sexual lust from the heart.

ANGER THAT LEADS TO LUSTFUL FANTASY AND ACTIVITY

Sinful anger is a product of the covetous thought life of a person; for example, someone believes they have been denied something that is their right; this loss has caused some type of hurt—whether real or imagined. The resulting angry response is fueled by the emotional energy born of denied expectations. These unfulfilled desires give way to an ungodly rationalization of filling the "void" or "hurt" through self-gratifying activity (in much the same way that a dieter, out of frustration and anger for not losing the expected weight, will binge on chocolate cake). In this case, however, the fleshly nature of craving is sexual in nature. Indulging the sex drive becomes compensation for perceived loss. It brings temporary consolation to the hurt, which is often combined with the sweet feeling of revenge.

God is the ultimate target of this anger. "I'll tell you why I seek to satisfy myself," Frederick interjected (the counselee mentioned in chapter 4). "Every time bad things occur, it reminds me of all those awful childhood memories of my parents fighting that I want to forget." His hurt and anger found its source in his belief that he deserved to grow up in a more peaceful, emotionally stable home. Later in life, when he and his wife, Robin, would argue, his childhood memories were triggered and this belief would intensify. His chosen means of escape was habitual sexual sin, hoping to find the emotional solace he longed for. Frederick's sexual expression of anger was simultaneously therapeutic and malicious. Whether he realized it or not, it was ultimately directed at the Lord he claimed to love. It was the Lord who had designed the path of his life (Lam. 3:32–33, 37–40).

It was imperative for Frederick to understand the implications of God's salvific grace in relation to his latent anger. No solution for his masturbation or his anger could be found outside of a transformed heart that would embrace the truth of his own undeserving character and the true solace of God's gracious provision. God had allowed the hardships of his past to shape him into a better man as a believer (Heb. 12:10–11). Even the memories of deprivation and adversity could be graciously instructive. F. F. Bruce speaks to the heart of this issue in commenting on Hebrews 12:11: "The man who accepts discipline [hardship] at the hand of God as something designed by his heavenly Father for his good will *cease to feel resentful and rebellious*; he has 'stilled and quieted' his soul, which thus provides fertile soil for the cultivation of a righteous life, responsive to the will of God."[1] Instead of fueling unholy rebellious passion, hardship can be used to feed a righteous life of holy passion. As Frederick's counselor, I knew it was important to neutralize the octane of anger fueling his self-indulgent sin with an abundant reminder of God's neutralizing grace.

Self-satisfying sex is only one of many different types of sexual expression anger may take. One of the most notorious is rape. Women who give off the vibe that they are superior open themselves up to the likelihood of sexual violence at the hands of men who have been taught from a young age that *they* are superior and thus are given to angrily challenging that assumption. Roy F. Baumeister and his colleagues at Case Western Reserve University documented a thorough study of violent criminals. "One study of more than 100 rapists, for example, confirms that rapists sometimes choose a particular victim in order 'to disabuse her of her sense of superiority.' That is, the woman gave the man the impression she thought she was better than he and so he raped her as a way of proving her wrong. . . . 'The societal pursuit of high self-esteem for everyone may literally end up doing considerable harm.'"[2] Once a person with an elevated view of self encounters another person who calls into question his self-opinion, violent anger is often the result. This anger springs from covetous desires that long to be compensated for perceived injustice. In some kind of twisted, sinful logic, rapists persuade themselves that if others make them hurt, then they too will make others hurt. Baumeister also says,

Psychopaths are exceptionally prone to aggressive and criminal conduct, and they have very favorable opinions of themselves. Evidence about the self-images of specific murderers, rapists and other criminals tends to be more anecdotal than systematic, but the pattern

1. F. F. Bruce, *The Epistle to the Hebrews*, New International Commentary on the New Testament (Grand Rapids: Eerdmans, 1964), 361 (emphasis added).
2. Roy Baumeister, as quoted by Linda Chavez, "Self-Esteem's Dark Side Emerges," *USA Today*, February 21, 1996.

is clear. Violent criminals often describe themselves as superior to others—as special, elite persons who deserve preferential treatment.[3]

According to Scripture, this high view of self is a fundamental element of the sinful human heart. The elevated self is greedy and inordinately demanding. When anger is denied something believed to be deserved (respect, preferential treatment, sex with a beautiful woman, etc.), it can grow into sexually aggressive acts like exhibitionism, frotteurism, pedophilia, rape, or sex-murder. High self-esteem is formative for anger, and anger is formative for sexual sin.

A simple but ugly form of this anger is sexual jealousy. One man may see another man's fiancée or wife, be filled with covetous envy because he cannot have her, and rape her as a way of seeking vengeance. God warns of this: "But if in the open country a man meets a young woman who is betrothed, and the man seizes her and lies with her, then only the man who lay with her shall die. But you shall do nothing to the young woman; she has committed no offense punishable by death" (Deut. 22:25–26). This type of covetous desire can manifest itself in numerous sexual ways.

Sexual aggression that intends harm most often finds its source in vengeful anger. A man who is angered that one of his lovers has communicated AIDS, which is potentially fatal, may turn in anger against all the members of the opposite sex in order to give them the same deadly disease he has acquired. This perverse form of pleasure goes beyond sensual enjoyment. Its malicious intent is to do another permanent harm.

Romantic rejection is another example of the stirring of sexual anger that can result in the violence of rape. Amnon, the firstborn son of King David, was the heir-apparent to the throne of Israel (2 Sam. 3:2). Next to his father, he was the leading man of the household, accustomed to getting what he wanted in the royal residence. The account says that he loved his half-sister, Tamar, and was attracted

3. Roy F. Baumeister, "Violent Pride: Do People Turn Violent Because of Self-Hate, or Self-Love?," *Scientific American* 284, 4 (April 2001): 99.

to her obvious beauty (2 Sam. 13:1). Like his father, Amnon had an eye for beautiful women and was willing to do sinful things to acquire what he wanted once lust had conceived in his heart. "And Amnon was so tormented that he made himself ill because of his sister Tamar, for she was a virgin, and it seemed impossible to Amnon to do anything to her" (2 Sam. 13:2). His love for her was not a familial brotherly love; he was consumed with sexual lust toward her. This verse says he was "tormented." The Hebrew means "it was narrow for him, he was in straits, distress."[4] Amnon was frustrated, which is a type of anger. What made it hard for Amnon in Old Testament Israel was that virgins (unmarried daughters of marriageable age) were often kept in isolation from men and could not be seen privately. Here is an obvious example of what happens when the covetous heart is denied something that it yearns for deeply: it only serves to make that object even more desirable. Amnon wanted Tamar badly, and, like a spoiled child, he was angry that he could not have her. With the help of his cousin Jonadab, he staged an illness, which he knew would put him into personal contact with her.

His plan worked. Tamar had mercy on her sick stepbrother, "but when she brought [the cakes] near him to eat, he took hold of her and said to her, 'Come, lie with me, my sister'" (2 Sam. 13:11). She resisted him and used four arguments to attempt to dissuade him. First, this was a violation of what was accepted as proper conduct in Israel. As the people of God, this was an infringement of God's Word because it uncovered his sister's nakedness (Lev. 18:11). The consequences of this sin could bring the loss of the throne, bloodshed, and eventual death. Second, she appealed to his sense of honor and love for her by reminding him that such an act would permanently make her an object of scorn in Israel, even though she had resisted him. Third, if the appeal to common decency and love for his sister was not convincing, she told him that he would be "as one of the outrageous fools in Israel" (2 Sam. 13:13). In other words, he would share her disgrace. Perhaps

---

4. Francis Brown, S. R. Driver, and Charles A. Briggs, eds., *A Hebrew and English Lexicon of the Old Testament* (Oxford: Clarendon Press, 1978), 864.

she hoped his own self-dignity and self-love would stop this terrible act. Finally, in desperation, Tamar tried to get him to wait for permission from their father to have a legitimate marriage, even though this was forbidden in the Mosaic law (Lev. 18:9, 11; 20:17; Deut. 27:22). Amnon, knowing that their father David's permission was unlikely, was not persuaded. He would not deny his lust: "But he would not listen to her, and being stronger than she, he violated her and lay with her" (2 Sam. 13:14). His anger resulted in her brutal rape, and after his conjugal relations with her, his lust turned to hate. Now he despised her. Rapists commonly hate their victims after they have violated them. Hatred is a focused aspect of anger (Matt. 5:22).

Sinful anger does not always end in violent sexual behavior. It may also assume less obvious forms of imaginary immorality. One single woman in her early sixties came to receive counseling with a female counselor. She described her problems of depression, repeated difficulties at work with her male bosses, and immoral imaginations. After a few sessions of counseling she was willing to admit even entertaining sexual thoughts of other women. This placed the female counselor in an uncomfortable position, and she brought in another godly woman as a co-counselor.

This counselee had been a Christian for years and had even served full-time for many of those years in Christian organizations. Her confusion as to why she was being plagued with these sinful imaginations of lesbianism led her to conclude that she was probably demon oppressed. Being well acquainted with the biblical prohibitions concerning homosexuality, she could not imagine why her mind would keep drifting into these sexual encounters with other women. It bothered her deeply.

Eventually, the true hurts and disappointments of her heart came to the forefront. For years she had intensely longed for a husband, but it was not in God's plan for her life. As the years passed, her anger toward men grew. In her self-righteous thinking, she was angry not only with men but also with God. Any sexual thought of a man now disgusted her. In her mind, men were superficial scum. Years of increasing anger had redirected the course of her sexual passions to the gender that had shown her the love and acceptance she believed she rightfully deserved:

other females. Repeated conflicts with male bosses were a reflection of the same anger and bitterness that had been fermenting for years. In due course, she even admitted to gossip concerning the elders of her church and a very critical spirit toward *any* man in leadership. When she was able to see the long-standing anger in her heart, her depression, problems at work, and immoral imaginations began to make sense to her. Her covetous desire for a husband had concocted a wicked stew of anger and misery for many years as this idol lay hidden in her heart.

SELF-PITY AS THE FEEDER FOR LUSTFUL DESIRES AND DEEDS

Closely associated with anger is the pitfall of self-pity. This heart too operates from the notion that it has been denied something it deserves or has suffered something it did not deserve. Pity is understood as sorrow for some trouble or distress of another. It is often synonymous with sympathy or compassion over a hurt or injury. Self-pity's role in sexual sin is extreme and unabated sympathy for oneself because of a hurt that has been experienced. Self-pity becomes the rationalization for the expectation of special treatment or compensation for a perceived loss. The search for some kind of compensation can lead to the person granting himself special liberties to enjoy normally forbidden sexual pleasures. The heart rationalizes that under these unique circumstances, God will understand and overlook sensual indiscretions.

Sexual sin is easy to excuse as long as the hurt suffered seems to justify the indulgence. The human heart seems to have an infinite ability to justify almost anything it really wants. Jay Adams gives a typical case scenario:

Brad is the Christian husband of a hateful and unbelieving wife. . . . Ever since Brad became a Christian and altered much of his lifestyle to accord with his faith, Sally (his wife) has not only continually made fun of him, embarrassing him before all their friends, but has also worked hard at making life as miserable as possible for him.

Indeed, to top it all off, over a year ago she even stopped having sexual relations with him. Not only was that bad enough in itself, but during that time she has made a point of titillating him and then refusing to satisfy him.

Brad knows what he must do as a Christian. He must continue to hold up his part of the marriage vows as fully as possible, because he made a promise before God. God has not failed him; it is his wife who has. And since she is not a Christian, it is only to be expected that she would disapprove of his newfound faith. After all, he is no longer the man she married. If he lives as God requires—to please him—and seeks to obey and honor God in the relationship, he will succeed whether Sally becomes a Christian or not, because he has pleased God. And he knows that this is the prime thing. His peace and happiness do not depend on Sally and her moods but on the faithfulness of God.

"But it's so hard," he tells himself. "If only I had some encouragement from her! If only I could see some inkling of a change in her. But day after day, week after week she is the same, except that she seems to be getting worse. I'm having a terrible time keeping my thoughts and actions pure!" That's his battle. Inside, though down deep he knows God's answer, he asks, "Would God deny me a little sexual release on the side? Doesn't he want me to be normal, like all the rest of the believers at church? He knows that my capacity for self-control is small. And what harm would it do, anyway?"

There are several women at work with whom Brad is sure he could have an affair. Indeed, one of them, a fairly attractive secretary down the hall in another office, has often made what could only be understood as suggestive remarks. Until now Brad has let them fall flat, simply not taking them up. Should he grab hold of the next remark and see where it might lead? Or should he even initiate something? Such thoughts, and dozens like them, continually surge through his mind.[5]

5. Jay Adams, *Winning the War Within* (Woodruff, SC: Timeless Texts, 1996), 45–46.

If Brad is not careful, his self-pity will lead him into adultery. The fact that there are several women in the office who are available to him is not an indication of God's tacit approval for illicit fulfillment. Many people rationalize their sin by saying, "If it is an open door, then it must be all right with God." But the world and Satan are providing this "open door" for sin, not God. They are stirring the sinful heart to act on temptation. Brad's self-pity makes his heart fertile for such a sin to conceive.

Commonly, lustful thoughts gain the advantage when self-pity is permitted free reign in the heart. The real pain of disappointment or sacrifice is so unpleasant or unbearable that a counselee will escape into an unreal world of voyeurism, and then self-satisfying, before including others in his sinful sex. In this unreal world, Brad may find a make-believe kingdom of pleasant experiences that seduce his senses instead of exciting them and letting him down. Through his escape, he can imagine women who are perfectly happy with his overtures of intimacy and who favorably respond to him in every way, instead of a wife who is a tease and then vengefully withholds all sexual favors.

Some who struggle with self-pity as their excuse for sexual deviancy have discovered that self-pity was already a habit of thought from childhood. Perhaps even prior to adolescence and the onslaught of sexual arousal, a pattern of self-pity has become the justification and ritualistic way to relieve "emotional pain." Later, sexual drives are overlaid on top of this pattern, becoming the life-dominating outlet for self-pity. Even from a tender age, the sinful heart is clever in forming idols of attitudes and desires that become the landscape on which sexual impulses are mapped into intricate erotic escapes.

Jackie was a twenty-eight-year-old counselee who had been saved out of a fairly sordid sexual past. Her father had died in a tragic automobile accident when she was just two years old. Her mother had remarried two years later to a man who became her sexually abusive stepfather. Within a year of the second marriage, he was already regularly fondling Jackie when her mother was gone. He told her that it was a secret game just between the two of them, and she should never tell her mother. Jackie could remember sensing it was not right, but trusting her stepfather, she permitted the game to go on without saying a word. As time passed, she confessed that she began to accept it as a normal part of her life and even confessed that she enjoyed his attention and derived a little bit of pleasure from his caresses. Since this was the only father she knew, she desperately wanted to please him.

By the time Jackie was eight years old, her stepfather was beginning to penetrate her. She did not enjoy this at all and even complained of the pain. One Sunday she went to church with her mother and was overwhelmed with the emotion of what had happened. Her Sunday school teacher noticed that Jackie was not herself and after class asked her what was wrong. At first, Jackie was very shy and would not speak, but then she began to sob, telling her teacher everything her stepfather was doing. The teacher immediately contacted her mother and the pastor of the church who, in turn, contacted local authorities. After a physical examination, it was proven that Jackie was telling the truth. Her stepfather was put into prison, where he remains to this day.

Jackie was devastated by this outcome. As a young girl, Jackie had no idea that her confession would cause the only dad she knew to be thrown into prison. In the simple thinking of a child she blamed her Sunday school teacher and her church for taking away her father. Sure, he had hurt her, but the majority of her memories of him were pleasant. Furthermore, she had always wanted to please him as if he were her biological father, and by telling their secret, she had made him very angry at her. Now she would never be able to have a father who was pleased with her. She was angry because of what had happened. Jackie stopped going to church altogether. Her mother could not make her return.

Jackie began to have problems in school. Court-ordered counseling instilled in her mind that she was the wounded victim who would require years of therapy before she could function normally again. "The main thing I remember about the counseling I received," she recalled, "was the idea that there were still things buried in my subconscious that would make me different from everyone else. It would take many years of therapy and therapists, peeling back several layers of consciousness, before I would be normal again, they told me." Her whole view

126

of life changed. She became demanding and rude. Her grades in school dropped dramatically, and she started running with the boys who paid attention to her. Since Jackie's body developed early, she had her first volitional intercourse experience with a fifteen-year-old boy when she was twelve. She confessed, "My mother lost total control of me. It is a wonder I ever graduated from high school." Her mother never remarried, fearing that she would marry another man who would do the same thing to her daughter. Throughout high school, Jackie had several sexual experiences with guys at after-school parties.

Her anger had turned from open rebellion to wallowing in self-pity as she grew older. Her psychologist had spent a lot of time trying to dig into her memories of her biological father, which only served to deepen her self-pity and victimization. Being a fairly attractive young woman, Jackie had no problem with potential suitors. Her problem was that she wanted to receive from these young men the approval and acceptance she had missed as a little girl from her father. She recalled the traumatic events with her stepfather with a mixture of anger and self-pity for how these had robbed her of her childhood. Jackie believed this had forced her to grow up too quickly, and she was never able to enjoy the fun of being a kid. Her main memories of childhood were her knowledge of her father's death, her stepdad's abuse, and lengthy therapy sessions. She hated what she had become.

That was the reason she had come to a pastoral counselor. She had heard that biblical counsel was different from therapy, and as a Christian, she was interested in finding out if the Bible had anything to say about her life and experiences. Not long into the session, she confessed that she was serious about a Christian young man in the church, and he was serious about her. She also confessed that her desire to please him had been a real source of temptation for her. She wanted him to replace the love she had missed from her father. Now, for the first time in her life, she was feeling guilty for the thoughts of having sex with him, but she still believed that he was exactly what she needed to fill this "empty void" in her life.

Like Brad in the previous scenario, Jackie was walking a very dangerous line. If she were not careful, self-pity from the past would be the rationalization for additional sexual sin. This idolized motivation that had ruled her heart through her high school sexual exploits was still plaguing her as a new Christian. The desire of the flesh came from a heart filled with self-pity and seeking solace in love relationships with men.

In her childhood, Jackie's heart had formed an idol of a father's approval that was carried into puberty. As she grew older, her desire morphed into a demand for it, or something like it as a replacement. When she could not find what she was looking for, she fell headlong into the pit of self-pity. Sexual drives were laminated on top of this idol, becoming its chief expression. Being an attractive young woman, she soon learned that she could use her feminine attributes to obtain the love and acceptance from guys that she so desperately desired. Self-pity waylaid her guilt and encouraged her continual search for genuine love.

A drunk who tries to drown his sorrow in alcohol experiences a similar situation. The preferred elixir, whether sex or alcohol, is used to counterbalance the seeming disproportion of personal hurt and pain. The difference between sex motivated by anger and sex motivated by self-pity is the rationale. Anger carries a strong sense of settling the score or exacting revenge through sexual indulgence, like the woman who commits adultery because her husband had an affair. Self-pity is much more introspective, focusing on soothing the hurt of loss through sexual self-gratification. It views sex medicinally instead of as a weapon. For some counselees, like Frederick, there can be a mixture of both self-pity and anger in their improper sexual activity.

You can see the interplay between sexual self-pity and anger in the account of Judah and Tamar in Genesis 38.[6] Many theologians have wondered why this immoral story interrupts the story of Joseph and his captivity in Egypt. The best explanation is that after the disgraceful incest and deceitfulness of his brothers Reuben, Simeon, and Levi, and Joseph's seemingly permanent removal from the scene, Judah

---

6. This is the same Hebrew and English name as David's daughter, Tamar (תָּמָר), but in this case she is a Canaanite woman who preceded David's Tamar by over eight hundred years. She became Judah's daughter-in-law.

was naturally in line to receive the rights of the firstborn son from his father, Israel. This story reveals why he did not deserve such a status. In fact, this story serves as a vivid contrast between the wickedness of Judah, living in comparative luxury among the Canaanites, and the virtuous life of Joseph living in slavery in Egypt. By living among the Canaanites and marrying their women, Judah imperiled the Abrahamic line. The Canaanite religions threatened to absorb the descendants of Abraham and obliterate the lineage of the Messiah. God's design of sending Joseph to Egypt and putting him into slavery was an act of preservation.

Judah married a woman (daughter of a Canaanite man, Shua) who bore him three sons: Er, Onan, and Shelah. As he had done in marrying his wife, Judah chose a Canaanite wife for his son Er. Her name was Tamar. In due course, God struck down Er for committing an unspecified sin, and it became the responsibility of the second son, Onan, to take Tamar under his roof. Now as his wife, he had to care for her so that she would be able to bear children and continue his brother's family. This form of levirate marriage was commonly practiced among the Canaanites and was also later commanded in the Mosaic law (Deut. 25:5–10). "But Onan knew that the offspring would not be his. So whenever he went in to his brother's wife he would waste [spill] the semen on the ground, so as not to give offspring to his brother" (Gen. 38:9). Onan refused to impregnate his brother's wife and continue his line.[7] For this God judged him and took his life.

At this point, the practice of levirate marriage would have necessitated that Tamar become the wife of Judah's third son, Shelah, but for some reason Judah did not make it happen. He gave Tamar the rationale that Shelah was still too young for marriage at the time and

---

7. It is possible that Onan feared his brother's descendent would be a rival to his as heir and therefore refused full conjugal relations with Tamar. God takes refusing proper sexual relationship in a marriage just as seriously as the sin of improper sexual conduct. This text is not teaching that God is displeased with prophylactic sex in a marriage (e.g., the rhythm method, condoms, diaphragms, or the non-abortifacient pill) by the spilling of Onan's seed on the ground, but he is displeased with the failure to fulfill the vows and duty of marriage through monogamous coitus.

returned her to the household of her father, Shua. But all along he was afraid that Tamar carried some curse, and he did not want to lose a third son with her as his wife. Then Judah said to Tamar his daughter-in-law, "'Remain a widow in your father's house, till Shelah my son grows up'—for he feared that he would die, like his brothers. So Tamar went and remained in her father's house" (Gen. 38:11).

After a considerable amount of time, a third tragedy struck the household of Judah: his wife died. Thus far, his life among the Canaanites had been hard. Judah had suffered the loss of his two oldest sons and now his wife. Shortly after the customary period of mourning, Judah planned to visit his friend, Hirah, in the same town where he had met his wife. When Tamar received word that her father-in-law was coming, she changed her outfit from one of mourning to one of a harlot and covered her face. Perhaps she knew her father-in-law's way with women and understood that he would come looking for a woman as he had done before. After all, this is how he had acquired his own wife and Tamar herself as a wife for his firstborn son, Er. She undoubtedly knew that he had recently lost his wife and was hungry for some female companionship, so she contrived a scheme to trap him. Although we are not told explicitly, the text does suggests that Judah, after experiencing the loss of most of his family, decided to indulge his self-pity sexually. He eventually saw Tamar's attractive appearance near a gateway where prostitutes would wait, and not knowing that she was his daughter-in-law, he propositioned her.

This was easy to rationalize for Judah. He had lost some of the most precious things in his life, and they would never be returned. He had suffered far more than most men. Since he already had a penchant for Canaanite women in this part of the country and was away from home on a business trip to see his friend, no one would ever know. Judah solicited a harlot because of his need to be comforted.

Tamar's idol was different. She coveted something and wanted solace, but she also had a strong desire to make things right by forcing the hand of her father-in-law. Anger motivated her deception of harlotry. Her father-in-law had dealt with her unjustly. A good explanation is made by G. Charles Aalders:

Although Tamar's actions in this regard may seem strange to us, there is evidence that among ancient Assyrian and Hittite peoples, part of the custom was that the levirate responsibility could pass to the father of the widow's husband if there were no brothers to fulfill it. Thus Tamar was only trying to acquire that to which she had legal right.[8]

When she and Judah discussed the payment for her services, she would not accept the promise of a young goat as a future payment without some surety as a temporary down payment. At her request, Judah gave her the signet he wore around his neck, the cord that held it, and his personal staff. Later, he was to send the kid goat and redeem his personal items. Tamar slept with Judah and became pregnant. Tamar was not seeking some kind of personal approval, like Jackie in our previous case study. She was seeking to right a wrong that she had experienced, and she was using sex as her main tool to do so.

Judah's self-righteous piety reveals itself in the final verses of Genesis 38. Three months after their rendezvous, when it became publicly apparent that Tamar was pregnant without having a husband, Judah was told of her indiscretion.[9] Still technically being a member of his household, she was subject to his authority, and he ordered that she be destroyed by fire because of her disgrace. At that point, she revealed that she was pregnant with the child conceived by the man who had given her his signet, cord, and staff. Judah's sexual sin was now publicly exposed. "Then Judah identified them and said, 'She is more righteous than I, since I did not give her to my son Shelah.' And he did not know her again" (Gen. 38:26). In recording these words, Scripture is

---

8. G. Charles Aalders, *Bible Student's Commentary: Genesis*, trans. William Heynen (Grand Rapids: Zondervan, 1981), 2:194.

9. In the accusation against Tamar, it is interesting that Judah's friend Hirah refers to her as a *temple prostitute* "who was at Enaim at the roadside" (Gen. 38:21). It does reinforce the notion that Judah had fully endorsed the cultic practices of prostitution in Canaanite worship. It also underscores the ancient historical ties between cultic religions and illicit sexual practices like prostitution. Idolatrous worship and sex have ancient roots.

not condoning the deceptive sin of Tamar, but it is a recognition that she had more integrity in obeying the laws of inheritance rights than Judah had as her father-in-law. The death sentence that Judah had pronounced was fully rescinded.

Judah covetously desired to be comforted from his hardships, and Tamar covetously desired to be righted for the wrong she had suffered. Both motivations underlay the sexual means by which they were finally expressed. Each of these desires met in an unholy union of cultic prostitution and incest. Yet, in God's gracious design, this wickedness became a link in the chain of the messianic lineage through Boaz and Ruth, to King David, and ultimately to Jesus Christ the Redeemer (Ruth 4:18–22; Matt. 1:3). It was the Lord God of his father, Abraham, to whom Judah should have run for comfort instead of to cultic prostitution. To Israel the Lord says, "I, I am he who comforts you; who are you that you are afraid of man who dies, of the son of man who is made like grass" (Isa. 51:12). In the New Testament, Paul describes God as the One who comforts: "Blessed be the God and Father of our Lord Jesus Christ, the Father of mercies and God of all comfort" (2 Cor. 1:3). As a Canaanite, Tamar probably worshiped her cultic idols and did not know better, but Judah should have known and returned to the God of his family. There he would have found grace and provision for every need.

An abundance of counselees like Brad, Jackie, and Judah wallow in self-pity and seek sexual compensation for what has been deprived them in life. One soft-spoken married woman justified her daily consumption of romance novels and eventual affair because her husband was a "foul-tempered man who did not love her the way Christ loved the church." In fact, she rationalized, no one had ever loved her the way she should have been loved—not her parents who always fought, or grandparents who were never around, or her extended family and siblings who did not treat her well. Her attitude was, "I have loved so much but have received so little in return. I am running on empty with nothing more to give. How could God deny me a little romance in my life when my past is so full of hurt? My parents did not love me properly, and I doubt that I can love my husband anymore, because there is nothing left. In fact, I think I've become slavishly codependent on him anyhow, and my love tank is on 'E.'" Then she pulled out a book and read,

> So what if the parents are at odds, you say, as long as they can ade-
> quately love the child? The point is, unless they are keeping each
> other's tanks replenished, they cannot adequately pass a filled tank
> to their child. In fact, parental friction often endangers a particularly
> sad situation. . . . If we were to coin another definition for code-
> pendency, we might say, "It's the condition when the love tanks are
> running on empty."[10]

Empty "love tanks" have become another way to wallow in self-pity and rationalize all types of sin, especially sexual ones. As long as this woman continues to blame her misbehavior on other people, she will always be enslaved spiritually, if not bodily, to erotic fantasies and practices. She will never understand the comfort and help of the gracious gospel of Jesus Christ until she draws on the fullness of Christ and learns the practice of unmerited love with her husband and others.[11] Her "empty love tank" analysis only serves to magnify her self-pity and excuse her preoccupation with sex.

A middle-aged single man, somewhat pudgy and shy, believed his fixation with pornography on the internet was justified since no woman had ever really expressed an interest in a serious relationship with him. His habit had grown over a ten-year period, supplying his mind with endless images for his sexual fantasy world and self-gratification. Why did he need a woman now since he could adequately satisfy himself? This man had kept a mental list of all the girls and women to whom he had reached out over the years, from elementary school to college and beyond, hoping to have a girlfriend but ending in rejection. "Doesn't the Bible say somewhere, 'It is better to marry than to burn,'?" he

10. Robert Hemfelt, Frank Minirth, and Paul Meier, *Love Is a Choice* (Nashville, TN: Thomas Nelson, 1989), 38.
11. Matt. 5:43–48; John 13:1–35.

asked hesitantly. "But no one will marry me. So what choice do I have?" "Yes," I said, "the Bible does say that in 1 Corinthians 7, verse 9. But Paul was saying that by way of concession, not command. The contextual argument is for widows and singles. He was saying, 'Don't get married' during the early days of the Nerodian persecution (1 Cor. 7:26) of Christians in order to spare them additional trouble. But in this verse, he says that if they are in a relationship already and are strongly attracted to each other, it is better to marry. This verse does not teach that marriage cures lust. It does not. There are plenty of married people who have the same problem as you." This man's idol of self-pity would be carried into marriage, and if his wife did not respond to him in the same self-pleasing way, he would likely revert to the same self-stimulation he had practiced before marriage.

Another man who was married had the same problem. He believed his erotic escapes with R-rated videos were appropriate because his wife showed little interest in sex after ten years of marriage. His thinking ran something like this: "If my wife will not fulfill me, then I have to find some other means to find fulfillment. As a Christian, adultery is not an option; there is too much disgrace in that, but lustful escapes are face-saving ways of getting what I need." He was not angry, but he was certainly disappointed and full of self-pity like the previous man and Brad. These men believed that "rejection by women" and the associated emotional letdowns were adequate excuses for feeding the sensual slide shows of their minds. All three cases supposed there was sufficient hurt to demand some kind of sexual reparation. You must guard your heart from the self-justifying attitude of self-pity because it will become your excuse for sin.

DISCONTENTMENT AS FERTILE GROUND FOR SEXUAL LUST

Dissatisfaction with life is rooted in unrealized expectations. When life falls short of long-held hopes and dreams, discontentment often takes over, leading many to reach out for someone or something better to bring the satisfaction so desperately sought. Why is this so? It is because discontentment always seeks diversion or variety to fill its void. Discontented people seek new thrills and experiences that they hope will far surpass their previous experiences in life. When you map sexual lust on top of a discontented heart, you have a recipe for all types of sexual experimentation and perversion.

This was true of the men of biblical Sodom. No longer satisfied with their wives and sex partners within their own city, they longed for someone new—in this case the angelic guests visiting Lot's home. Jude, in his epistle, says "just as Sodom and Gomorrah and the surrounding cities, which likewise indulged in sexual immorality and pursued *unnatural* desire, serve as an example by undergoing a punishment of eternal fire" (Jude 7). The Greek term of special interest is deliberately translated "unnatural" (ἑτέρας) and "denotes the new member of a series distinct from those which preceded and either carrying the series forward . . . or concluding it."[12] These bisexual[13] men were seeking variety, something distinct and new for their sexual gratification, and these two foreign visitors presented them a new opportunity.

The thrill of the new and unfamiliar may be part of the connotation behind the word for "unnatural" or "strange" (i.e., "forbidden woman") in the book of Proverbs as well (2:16; 5:3, 20; 7:5). You have probably heard the saying, "Forbidden fruit is sweeter," meaning that the forbidden might offer you a surprising sweetness if you follow your curiosity and indulge yourself. Perhaps this is what Solomon had in mind when speaking of the adulterous woman in Proverbs 2:16 and 22:14. Sometimes the wife of another man is strangely inviting. She represents the unknown, and there is something exciting in her secrecy that is attractive to the discontent man. In these two verses, the same

12. Gerhard Kittel, ed., *Theological Dictionary of the New Testament*, trans. Geoffrey W. Bromiley (Grand Rapids: Eerdmans, 1965), 2:702.
13. Gen. 19:6–8. We assume they were bisexual, and not just homosexual, since Lot undoubtedly believed that offering his virgin daughters would satisfy their sexual desires. His daughters carried some of this sexual perversion away from Sodom, where Jewish tradition says they were reared to marital age and committed incest with their father in order to bear children (Gen. 19:30–38).

Hebrew word draws one's attention to the enticement of an unknown woman belonging to another man. Here she is "a woman who seems to be less the ethnic stranger or the devotee of an Astarte cult . . . than the (Israelite) wife of another, a lascivious wife against whom the wise warns students."[14] The fact that she is strange involves a sense of mystery that needs to be explored. Disenchantment with one's spouse may come from seeming familiarity and sameness, which causes the heart to crave for another who appears to be more enticing.

Also, what is forbidden takes on the aura of being even more alluring. Possessing the prohibited property of another man's wife adds to the thrill. Discontentment in the human heart will say, "Stolen water is sweet, and bread eaten in secret is pleasant" (Prov. 9:17). Consuming water and bread contextually can be understood to be Hebraic metaphors of having intercourse with another man's wife (i.e., accepting the invitation of the woman of folly). The fact that it is stolen and done in secret multiplies the attraction. When the heart is discontent, it searches into the unknown to see if it can find what is exciting and will awaken apathetic passions. For some, the greater the risk, the greater the intensity of attraction. Part of the allure of the strange woman to a discontented man is her distance and obscurity.

Jered felt himself strangely drawn to a new woman who had been hired in his office. Her European accent revealed that she was from another country and had only recently immigrated to the United States. Her name was Maria, and English was not her first language. With her dark enchanting eyes, she was one of the most beautiful brunettes he had ever seen. He had been married to his wife, Elizabeth, for fifteen years, but she had contracted a chronic disease early in their marriage that made her sickly most of the time. Her illness kept them at home and inhibited her desire for a regular intimate relationship. Jered was a committed Christian man but confessed in counseling to being on the edge of depression most of the time. He said the one word that summed up his attitude over the last ten years was *restlessness*.

14. Ernst Jenni and Claus Westermann, eds., *Theological Lexicon of the Old Testament*, trans. Mark E. Biddle (Peabody, MA: Hendrickson, 1997), 1:391.

When Maria came to his office, he realized he was in trouble. They were forced to work together and seemed to really enjoy one another's company. He could tell she had a good time flirting with him throughout the day. "I thought about changing jobs," he revealed, "but our medical insurance for Elizabeth would end, and a new company would be reluctant to bring her on without a heavy monthly premium. Besides, I am not even sure I could get another job that pays as well as the one I have now." Jered said that he would never cheat on Elizabeth, but he admitted to having an imaginary world of sexual fantasies that revolved around Maria. She had become his imaginary mistress.

Withdrawal from reality into an exciting world of heart-racing fantasies soon became Jered's pastime. His general unhappiness at home, and discontentment with what God had ordained for his life and marriage, reinforced the wearisome monotony of his real life. The longer he permitted his discontentment to grow, the more critical he became of Elizabeth. She was no longer attractive to him. Her many hours of sitting at home and lying in bed had made her overweight and disproportioned for his taste. He said that in recent years he had begun to satisfy himself on a regular basis. Now that Maria was a daily part of his life, this had accelerated in frequency. Mental images of Maria seemed to be the only bright spot in his day.

Jered is playing with fire. He cannot continue to feed this idol of discontentment and expect to maintain his marriage, much less restore purity to his heart. "For the lips of a forbidden woman drip honey, and her speech is smoother than oil, but in the end she is bitter as wormwood, sharp as a two-edged sword. Her feet go down to death; her steps follow the path to Sheol" (Prov. 5:3–5). His mental escape with his imaginary lover will only further embitter his life. He will grow to hate his wife and view her as a "ball and chain" with whom he is sentenced to live for the rest of his life if he does not confront his unhappy heart. The human heart, irritated by discontentment, is defiled enough to discolor all his life, and eventually Jered will turn around and blame God.

Discontentment is an idol that demands increasing worship. It is a god that is never satisfied. Jered's expectations will never be met, not by

Maria or by Elizabeth, because they are not God's expectations for his life. He must learn to want what God wants and nothing more. If he is willing to adopt God's desires, he will learn contentment and happiness in his marriage to Elizabeth. In the meantime, he must learn not to escape to his mental fantasies when his heart becomes restless. Solomon warns about the adulteress, both real and imagined: "Keep your way far from her, and do not go near the door of her house" (Prov. 5:8). The apostle Paul informs the young pastor Timothy, "There is great gain in godliness with contentment" (1 Tim. 6:6); this is after he has encouraged Timothy to treat "older women as mothers, younger women as sisters, in all purity" (1 Tim. 5:2). When your heart is discontent, it is not pure. Jered can be a godly husband, cleansed from the sexual impurities of his heart, if he pursues godliness. Godliness begins by repenting of the discontentment that has plagued his life and marriage for such a long time.

Another form of serious discontentment is seen in the desire by some to change their birth-given gender. This recent trend is derived from an ungodly sociology that originated with Alfred Schütz, who believed that people in a social system create their own mental representations and roles.[15] When these roles become "institutionalized," believing you are a male or a female becomes embedded in a child's thinking and eventually in society's fabric. The transgender person is told that male and female roles are a socially constructed reality and that you can choose to be any gender you wish regardless of your chromosomes at conception or genitalia at birth. Bringing up the case of intersex (older term: hermaphrodites) children who are born with multiple genitalia is not a valid argument for a transgender person because of the unique skeletal structure of males and females as well as strong distinctive chromosomal bisexual markers.[16] No matter how elaborate the sex reassignment surgery (removing and/or addition of soft tissue) or dedicated the regimen for taking hormones of the

15. P. L. Berger and T. Luckmann, *The Social Construction of Reality* (Garden City, NY: Anchor Books, 1966).

16. Intersex or hermaphrodites born atypically with ambiguous genitalia is very rare and estimated to be approximately 1 in 1,500 to 1 in 2,000 births and

opposite sex, the skeletal structure and God-given chromosomes of female (XX) and male (XY) remain constant. When a person ceases taking the hormones of the opposite sex, the body will eventually return to the natural state in which it was born. Transgender people have to constantly fight the way God designed them.

One's desire to become a person of the opposite sex demonstrates a significant discontentment with the way God has made that person. It is true that the transgender person does not necessarily have a problem with sexual lust. Although there is evidence to show that some transgender people have homosexual or lesbian orientations, not all do. Numerous reasons are given for why a female would want to be a male, and vice versa. But what is most common is the notion that they feel trapped in a body of the opposite sex. For some females, they believe that males have more opportunities in life and they like to do things that men do, so they want to be a male. For some males, they enjoy the things women traditionally do, so they want to be a female. Therefore, their body becomes the prison of their soul.

This is very similar to Docetism (a form of Gnosticism) in the first century A.D. Docetists believed that physical reality was essentially evil but spiritual reality was the world of perfection and goodness.[17] Their goal was to escape the trappings and limitations of their physical body and embrace the essence of spiritual reality. Transgender people are not Docetic, because they do not believe all physical reality is evil. But, like the Docetists, they do believe their soul is trapped in an evil physical body they do not want. To agree with the transgender mind-set, you

---

is nonsupportive of transgenderism. Furthermore, an infant may have the chromosomes of a female but have external genitals of a male (46, XX intersex) or the chromosomes of a male but the external genitals of a female (46, XY intersex). Legitimate corrective surgery can be assigned to infants with the chromosomes of one gender and external genitalia of another (disorder of sex development, DSD). Extremely rare is undetermined intersex disorders (45, XO—only one X chromosome; 47, XXY or 47 XXX—an extra sex chromosome), but these conditions do not cause external and internal genitalia disparities.

17. Joel R. Breidenbaugh, "Docetism," in *The Popular Encyclopedia of Apologetics: Surveying the Evidence for the Truth of Christianity*, ed. Ed Hindson, Ergun Caner, and Edward J. Verstraete (Eugene, OR: Harvest House Publishers, 2008), 186–93.

would have to believe that even though God may do some things well, he has made a terrible mistake in giving them the body they possess. But God is not like man. He does not make mistakes (Num. 23:19). "For everything created by God is good, and nothing is to be rejected if it is received with thanksgiving" (1 Tim. 4:4). To reject God's creation is to reject the Creator himself.

The moral imperative of earlier generations has always been "Do your duty!" With recent generations this has dramatically changed. Now the moral imperative is "Be true to your self!" The tragic result is that transgender people begin to live purely on the basis of inclinations and feelings instead of truth. For the transgender person, the self determines what is true, and external influences in society and religion are untrustworthy. However, God makes it clear that you cannot trust yourself. Your feelings and inclinations will lead you astray (Gen. 6:5; Pss. 14:1–3; 36:1–12; Prov. 6:18; 16:2; 21:2; Matt. 15:19; Rom. 1:28–32). The person who follows self has a fool for a guide. This will lead only to greater misery and despair. Such an approach to life nurtures unhappiness and serious depression for the person who is rebelling against the way God has created him.

FEAR THAT FEEDS SEXUAL LUST

Fear is a powerful emotion that channels thoughts and actions in certain predetermined directions. Fear comes from a heart that desires some kind of reassurance for its panic. There is a certain agitation or vexation of spirit that comes from fear, and it demands some resolution. It can often express itself in sexual ways. Fear can both instigate and feed a habit of sexual lust in a person's life. For example, fear of loneliness can compel a person to seek the companionship of an unmarried partner, prostitute, or pretend lover. Fear of an untimely marriage (too late to be a mother) can motivate some women to seduce their reluctant boyfriends into bed in order to get pregnant and possibly trap them into marriage. Fear of rejection can coerce a young man or woman to give in to the sexual pressure of a girlfriend or boyfriend before marriage. Fear of public scorn can force a fraternity plebe to secretly administer a date-rape drug to his girlfriend and rape her in order to complete his initiation. Behind each of these illicit desires is a covetous heart with selfish motivations that seeks some sort of self-gratification, whether physical or emotional.

Fear can be the motivational drive behind adultery. Sarah convinced Abram to commit adultery with her personal servant, Hagar, because she was fearful of being childless.[18] Abram's consent demonstrated that he was just as fearful that God somehow had changed his mind or forgotten the promise of an heir. "And behold, the word of the Lord came to him: 'This man [Eliezer] shall not be your heir; your very own son shall be your heir'" (Gen. 15:4). So they conspired together to help God out with their own plan to have a child. This is the child, Ishmael, born to Abram and Hagar, who Paul says "was born according to the flesh" (Gal. 4:23). By this Paul meant that Ishmael was a child born by human sinful means; he was born out of fear. Many Bible scholars believe Sarah was in her mid-seventies, well past the age to bear children. Abram was even older. From a human perspective, this adultery seemed the reasonable thing to do. It was certainly the custom of the day if a wife was barren. "To be a wife without motherhood has always been regarded in the East not merely a matter of regret, but also a matter of reproach and despair. . . . The wives of the patriarchs, in order to avoid the disgrace of barrenness, gave their handmaidens to their husbands, regarding the children born under such circumstances as their own."[19] The great sin here is that they disregarded the clear promise of God and proceeded to resort to pagan custom rather than trusting him to keep his covenant with them. You too will frequently have convincing human reasons for your sexual sin, but it is your fear and distrust of God's promises that feed your sexual thoughts and behavior.

Despite the patriarch's sin, God fulfilled the promise he had made to Abram. Sarah gave birth to Isaac, about whom Paul later said, "the son of the free woman was born through promise" (Gal. 4:23). While

---

18. Gen. 16:2.
19. *The Zondervan Pictorial Encyclopedia of the Bible*, ed. Merrill C. Tenney and Steven Barabas (Grand Rapids: Zondervan, 1975), 1:479.

Ishmael became analogous to a covenant of natural means and born of fearful human effort, Isaac became analogous to a new covenant of supernatural means and birth by the Spirit. You need to understand that sex motivated by fear upstages God's supernatural work.

Under certain conditions, fear has resulted in deliberate incest as well. Lot's daughters are examples of young women who feared they would grow old beyond their ability to bear children before they would have husbands. They knew their "biological clocks" were ticking. As we have seen, being childless in those days was a disgrace that implied the curse of God. In order to save face, they got their father drunk and had sex with him (Gen. 19:30–36). They were not particularly fond of incest, but their father was the only male around after their family had fled the wickedness of Sodom. Their desperation to have a child underscores their fear. The sexual liberties of Sodom undoubtedly had also made a significant impact on these young girls as they were growing up.

Most Christians today do not fear the humiliation of childlessness to the same degree as men and women of the ancient Near East (1 Sam. 1:10–20). The difference between the source of fear that fed their sexual sin and the source of fear that feeds contemporary sexual sin is cultural, not attitudinal. Today's society and culture may be different from that of the past, but the hearts of people today have desires similar to those who lived in the patriarchal period. People still struggle with fear, anxiety, worry, and panic, just as people did then. The only difference is the setting or circumstances. Additionally, the way they chose to manifest that fear may be culturally different (e.g., your wife wants you to have sex with her handmaiden), but the fact that fear can have sexual expression is not.

Several years ago, a young woman explained away her promiscuity with the exasperated declaration, "He is the only young man who has ever really cared about me, or even showed any serious interest in me." Her dominating fear was growing up to be an unmarried woman, left alone and never having a husband. "I am sure God will understand," she reasoned. "After all, it was his desire for man and woman to enjoy companionship together." Her desire to have a man in her life was so strong that she believed it must be God's desire too. She thought she could suspend Christian morality in order to achieve her dream and that God would understand.

This young woman's fear was similar to the fear of the Israelite women during the days of the divided kingdom of Judah and Israel. Isaiah predicted that God would judge the attractiveness of Judah's women because of their wanton ways: "The LORD said: Because the daughters of Zion are haughty and walk with outstretched necks, glancing wantonly with their eyes, mincing along as they go, tinkling with their feet" (Isa. 3:16). He would take away their beauty, and few men would be around for potential husbands because most of them would die on the battlefield. Desperation and fear of being single would reign, Isaiah said, "and seven women shall take hold of one man in that day, saying, 'We will eat our own bread and wear our own clothes, only let us be called by your name; take away our reproach'" (Isa. 4:1). Fear would grip their hearts so that they would be willing to do almost anything for a man, if only he would be their husband. Immorality rules when fear takes idolatrous control of the heart.

A fraternity freshman revealed his fear of being rejected by fellow members when he agreed to hire a prostitute and forfeit his virginity in order to please his peers. He did not want his fraternity brothers to think he was not a man. Everybody had to pass this test to be a part of the fraternity. For him, this was the beginning of years of lustful practices and enslavement to strip bars, peep shows, and pornography. Once this line of fornication had been crossed and sin was conceived in his heart, rationalizing lesser sexual indulgences like self-gratifying behaviors was easy, even though he made a personal vow never to have sex with a prostitute again.

An aging woman who had been rather striking in her younger years bemoaned the fact that she was losing her beauty. During counseling, she confessed to having a one-night affair with an older man in order to prove to herself that she was still attractive to the opposite sex. Fear of the fading beauty of youth can be a breeding ground for immoral intentions. The thought of her granddaughters finding out horrified her, and shame sent her into deep depression. Fear had destroyed any hope of being an example and role model for her grandchildren.

You are the most susceptible to sexual sin when your heart is hurting and the emotional distress seems unbearable. Anger, self-pity, discontentment, and fear are four very powerful rationalizations. They will weaken your resolve to the point that you will eventually surrender your will to sensual indulgence. You must deal with these ruling desires in your heart that demand appeasement. You can do this through repenting and actively pursuing a life of purity.

KEY CONCEPTS

complex heart
competing lusts and ambitions
covetous heart
negative motivations
affirmative motivations
hurting idols of passion
solace
escape
satisfaction
high self-esteem
self-pity
perceived injustice
unrealized expectations
forbidden woman
transgender
Docetism
vexation of spirit
cultural differences

STUDY QUESTIONS

1. Define negative motivations (the search for solace) as it relates to indulging in sexual sin.
2. Define affirmative motivations (the search for satisfaction) as it relates to indulging in sexual sin.

3. Carefully read Hebrews 12:3–11. (Discipline in this context is not punishment but rather hardship or trials). Answer these questions:
   - What is the source of the hardship? Who brings it into our life (vv. 7–10a)?
   - What does he intend the hardship to do (v. 10b)?
   - What is the end goal of this discipline (v. 11)?
   - The person who responds to hardship by escaping into the pleasure of sexual sin shows that he either does not understand God's goal in the hardship or, understanding it, has rejected it. He has become weary and fainthearted (v. 3b). Write a plan to help the counselee Frederick deal with his anger against God based on this rich passage of Scripture. Include teaching about the suffering of Christ, teaching about the nature of God as our Father, submission to the Father, and the end goal of this discipline. Make use of Scripture memorization in your counseling homework.
4. "High self-esteem is formative for anger, and anger is formative for sexual sin."
   - Read 2 Chronicles 26 and describe this biblical example of pride leading to anger.
   - Read Isaiah 3:16–17 and describe the connection of high self-esteem (haughtiness) with sexual advances.
5. Self-pity can be described as extreme sympathy, distress, and sorrow for one's circumstances, leading to a perception of earned self-indulgence. Describe how pride, anger, and unmet expectations (crushed hope for something good) can lead a person to self-pity that ultimately results in committing sexual sin (Prov. 13:12; 16:18; 29:22, 23; Ps. 37:8).
6. Describe how you would use the entire chapter of Proverbs 5 to help the counselee Brad.
7. In reference to the woman in this chapter who attempted to justify her affair because her husband was an unloving, "foul-tempered man," discuss how you would counsel her. She has committed adultery, and that is the sin that has brought

her to counseling. What ruling idols can you identify that led her to adultery—that predisposed her to fall into this type of sin? What did she love and desire so much that she was willing to sin because she did not receive these things?

8. "Fear can be the motivational drive behind adultery [and other sexual sins]." Give five examples out of contemporary culture that demonstrate this truth and discuss what the person is afraid of (e.g., high school cheerleader follows through on a dare by her peers to engage in a lesbian act).

FOR FURTHER READING

Adams, Jay E. *The Biblical View of Self-Esteem, Self-Love and Self-Image*. Eugene, OR: Harvest House, 1986.

Beeke, Joel R. *Living for God's Glory: An Introduction to Calvinism*. Lake Mary, FL: Reformation Trust, 2009.

Lambert, Heath. *A Theology of Biblical Counseling: The Doctrinal Foundations of Counseling Ministry*. Grand Rapids: Zondervan, 2016.

MacArthur, John. *How to Live for God's Glory*. Wheaton, IL: Good News Publishers, 2003.

6

FEEDING THE HUNGERING
IDOLS OF PASSION

The hurting heart not only aches but also has an insatiable appetite that demands satisfaction. Whether openly acknowledged or quietly disguised, most people march to the motto "I live my life for my own self-satisfaction and needs, not for others to judge!" But when you follow the demands of your heart for a fulfilling experience, you are surrendering yourself to a life of desperation and despair. Consider the words of Ecclesiastes: "And whatever my eyes desired I did not keep from them. I kept my heart from no pleasure, for my heart found pleasure in all my toil, and this was my reward for all my toil" (Eccl. 2:10). Only a few verses later the author concludes, "For all his days are full of sorrow, and his work is a vexation. Even in the night his heart does not rest. This also is vanity" (Eccl. 2:23).

The Hebrew term for *vanity* means "breath" or "vapor" and is often used to express emptiness, nothingness, or something very temporary, similar to the momentarily visible moisture of your breath on a cold day.[1] It is seen for a short time, then it is gone. So is the gleam of an iridescent soap bubble that commands your attention with its swirling

---

1. "Vapour, breath . . . fig. of what is evanescent, unsubstantial, worthless . . . fruit-lessness of all human enterprise and endeavor . . . a lifeless existence." Francis Brown, S. R. Driver, and Charles A. Briggs, eds., *A Hebrew and English Lexicon of the Old Testament* (Oxford: Clarendon Press, 1978), 210.

and shimmering but bursts after only a few seconds. When your hungering heart clamors for sinful sexual satisfaction, it is grasping at empty soap bubbles. The quest to fulfill ungodly sexual desires results in dissatisfaction and an insatiable hunger for more. Instead of producing the expected happiness, it brings instead an empty feeling, which ultimately leads to slavery as you seek to feed your ever-increasing appetite. Again, the wisdom of Ecclesiastes reveals the despair of sexual enslavement: "And I find something more bitter than death: the woman whose heart is snares and nets, and whose hands are fetters. He who pleases God escapes her, but the sinner is taken by her" (Eccl. 7:26). What was once a search for joy becomes a bitter and lifeless existence as you constantly pursue another sexual fix but are never truly satisfied.

As we learned in chapter 5, rarely will the heart of a believer yield to sexual sin without a preconditioning rationale contributing to the motivations to sin. These motivations help to anesthetize the pain of a guilty conscience while surrendering to sexual allurement. Four of the most common negative motivations that tend to rule the *hurting* heart are anger, self-pity, discontentment, and fear. This chapter describes four affirmative motivations that tend to rule the *hungering* heart: self-reward, flattery, power/control, and comfort. Each provides a spiritual cardiogram by which you can identify the rationales your heart uses to justify your lustful indulgence.

SELF-REWARD FOR EXTRAORDINARY DEDICATION

Unusual dedication to work and extended periods of personal self-denial are often reasons that underlie sensual fantasies and adventures. Unbelievers are not the only ones who use this excuse for indulging sexual lust. In a twisted form of reasoning, Christians will often use their extreme dedication and faithfulness to God or their spouses as justification for taking certain sexual liberties. While this is closely related to the motivations of anger and self-pity, it is much more positive. Instead of growing out of injury or hurt, it is coming from a sense of recompense. This person reasons from God's perceived bigness and fairness—"God is big enough to understand that I deserve a brief escape because of all the sacrifices I have made for him." Or the person might say, "God understands how hard I've worked and all I've sacrificed. What I'm about to do may seem wrong, but it's not as bad when you consider all the other good things I've done. My extreme faithfulness to my duties gives me the right to have a little fun." Righteous behavior becomes viewed like a bank account that grows until there are sufficient funds to make an occasional sexual withdrawal. Once the withdrawal has been made, out of guilt and a desire to recoup the account, the person retreats to greater efforts of self-sacrifice to pay penance for sexual escapades.

One such counselee was a young man who attended a Christian university noted for its rigid student code of conduct. On campus he was a respected leader among his peers and had even been placed into a position of student leadership, where he had the reputation of being strict with the rules. During counseling, in spite of the fact that he was a handsome young man, he admitted to not dating much because his standards for the young woman he would marry were too high for most Christian girls to meet. He was extremely picky about his future mate and wanted the girl he dated to meet that extraordinary standard. In fact, he explained that he himself lived by this standard, and he expected the girl he married to perfectly agree to live by it as well. But this same young man, who prided himself in his high standards for courting and marriage, also admitted to a vivid sensual thought life. This thought life, in time, gave birth to fondling young children and all the legal consequences. Somehow, in his thinking, his extreme dedication to the maintenance of his personal external purity justified his private sin. It also justified his critical judgment of others, especially young women whom he sought to court. "To the pure, all things are pure, but to the defiled and unbelieving, nothing is pure; but both their minds and their consciences are defiled" (Titus 1:15).

Another man who came for counsel was a very busy senior pastor of a large multistaffed church who had been arrested in a police sting for soliciting prostitutes. He disclosed one of the busiest schedules of ministry any pastor could have: he preached three weekly services, performed funerals and weddings, made house and hospital calls, counseled, took an active role in administrative duties, and was a frequent special speaker at conferences, camps, and Bible schools. His staff assisted him in the details, but he was the main person who kept his hands in all the business of his very active church. As his story unfolded, he revealed that his sexual escapes had been going on intermittently for years. For months he would faithfully maintain his heavy schedule at church and home without any moral failure, until fatigue would overwhelm him. Then, in physical and moral exhaustion, he would seek out a prostitute for some diversionary sexual fulfillment. This cyclical pattern had gone on for several years without the knowledge of either the church or his wife. "After pouring myself out for months on end," he confessed, "I needed a diversion, and it was my way of momentary escape from my responsibilities and duties." This practice soon became a habit, and the habit turned into a life-dominating routine. Prostitution became the only way he could really enjoy life. He did not hate his wife or find her unattractive, but she represented another responsibility to him. A prostitute was no responsibility. He could pay her and be done with her. This was his reward for service to the Lord above and beyond the call of duty. He knew his Bible and realized that it was wrong, but his performance-based self-righteousness justified his ongoing indulgence.

Self-reward seeks satisfaction for personal choices of sacrifice beyond the ordinary. While those who struggle with anger and self-pity tend to believe they are helpless victims, that victim mentality is lacking in the motivation of self-reward. The self-rewarders believe they have suffered, but they know it has been because of purposeful choice, while those who are filled with anger or self-pity have experienced suffering outside of their control—hence their victim identity. Victims seek redress for personal damage, while the self-rewarders seek accolades for personal achievement. This compensation takes the form of sexual gratification ranging from private forms of self-stimulation to illegal practices such as rape, incest, and pedophilia. Since these people are involved in diligent, honorable, and worthwhile work, it is not as common to counsel self-rewarders who choose to find their sexual expression with nonconsenting victims (e.g., rape, pedophilia). More often than not, they are more prone to using consenting human

participants with practices like immorality, fornication, adultery, prostitution, and homosexual practices.

Certainly one of the most difficult and demanding jobs in the
world is being a foot soldier. Historically, coming from a hard-fought
victory in ancient warfare was a time of rejoicing and celebration in
which certain liberties were taken with prisoners of war. Beautiful
female slaves were often raped and abused. Common practice decreed
that these captive women became the property of the victors.

> Throughout antiquity, war was one of the chief sources of supply for
> the slave-market, for captured prisoners were generally sold as slaves.
> The custom obtained in Palestine, too. In the days of the Judges,
> Sisera's army, had it been victorious, would have shared out the spoil:
> "a damsel, two damsels, to every warrior" (Jg 5:30) . . . the Chroni-
> cler records that Peqah, king of Israel, in his war against Judah, took
> 200,000 prisoners, women, boys and girls, who were set free at the
> protest of a prophet (2 Ch 28:8–15). . . . Strictly speaking, the slave
> is a chattel, belonging to his master by right of conquest, purchase
> or inheritance; the master makes use of him as he wills and can sell
> him again.[2]

Soldiers in Israel often indulged themselves according to cultural tradition. They would sexually use these women as their personal reward,
reckoning that they earned the right when they won the battle for the
Lord. The early Israelite soldier could easily rationalize his sexual reck-
lessness: "I have fought long and hard. I have often been injured and
seen my buddies fall on my right and left. Look what I have sacrificed
for this victory! Don't I deserve a little bonus? I captured this girl from
our enemy. She's my slave now, and she is really beautiful. All the other
armies do it. It is part of our payment for winning the war. Don't I get
to enjoy some reward for my life on the front line?"

However, God did not consider these captive women as mere chat-
tel that a hard-working soldier could use at his discretion. If a soldier

---

2. Roland de Vaux, *Ancient Israel* (New York: McGraw-Hill, 1965), 1:80–81, 84.

thought she was an attractive woman, he had to take her as his wife, but only after a period of time had lapsed. He could not treat her as a mere slave, indulging his raging hormones for momentary reward, but he must enter into a marriage relationship with her after she had mourned for an entire month:

> When you go out to war against your enemies, and the LORD your God gives them into your hand and you take them captive, and you see among the captives a beautiful woman, and you desire to take her to be your wife, and you bring her home to your house, she shall shave her head and pare her nails. And she shall take off the clothes in which she was captured and shall remain in your house and lament her father and her mother a full month. After that you may go in to her and be her husband, and she shall be your wife. But if you no longer delight in her, you shall let her go where she wants. But you shall not sell her for money, nor shall you treat her as a slave, since you have humiliated her. (Deut. 21:10–14)

Even though mistreatment of these captive women was common in the ancient Near East, it was not to be the practice of God's soldier. Hard work and sustained personal sacrifice for God were no excuse for indulging sensual pleasures for immediate gratification. The Israeli soldier had to practice sexual self-discipline and control after a victorious battle and wait for a proper marriage union. He could not use a woman sexually as a bounty payment for the suffering he endured in battle.

Indeed, faithfulness of the greatest degree is not a merit that can be accumulated for the payment of sin. No matter how abundant, faithfulness will never counterbalance the foolishness, or even wickedness, of indulging sensuality in God's economy. The author of Ecclesiastes has a memorable analogy to the destructiveness of a little stupidity. "Dead flies make the perfumer's ointment give off a stench; so a little folly outweighs wisdom and honor" (Eccl. 10:1). "A little folly"—not much is needed to destroy character. The self-rewarder is always proud of the fact that his good deeds far outweigh his bad ones. Would you drink from a gallon of milk, no matter how wholesome, if you knew someone had added a single drop of arsenic to it? No one in their right mind would. Sexual sins, no matter how intermittent, are just as harmful. One sexually foolish act can ruin a lifetime of faithfulness.

Christ's parable of the hardworking servant is an apt reminder (Luke 17:7–10). Above all, it reveals that faithful labor does not entitle God's people to unique and special privileges. The slave in this story spends his day plowing and tending sheep—both tiring and dirty labors. After spending a hot day in the fields he returns, sweaty and hungry, and must prepare his master's dinner. But he must first clean himself and put on the proper attire. Only after the master has eaten can this ravenous and exhausted servant eat his dinner. Jesus goes on to add that the master does not owe the servant any special thanks because he did his job. Likewise, Jesus pressed the parable home: "So you also, when you have done all that you were commanded, say, 'We are unworthy servants; we have only done what was our duty'" (Luke 17:10). The self-rewarder idolizes his occasional sexual voyeurism and diversion because he is self-deceived. He has deluded himself into believing he really deserves these infrequent sexual pursuits because of his past extraordinary endeavors. Like the dieter who loses a couple of pounds and then rewards himself with a hot fudge sundae, such a person is not living with altruistic motives. His faithfulness is not motivated by loving service to God. Rather, his greedy heart believes that he deserves some additional reward or payment for his faithfulness.

All the work in the world will not replace the lustful ways of a hardworking person, because the weariness of the flesh will soon prevail. Moral fortitude fails when fatigue sets in; the flesh is weak (Rom. 6:19; 7:18). Knowing this about themselves, many self-rewarders have tried to break their sexual routines by substituting additional honest work to their already busy schedule. They try to crowd out any opportunity for their promiscuous escapades with this new self-made law—an extreme form of the Puritan work ethic. The result is usually more failure because their bodily weariness is even greater than before. Mere behaviorism will always fail the person in bondage to lust because it relies on the frailty of the body: "Those who are in the flesh cannot please God" (Rom. 8:8). There must be an internal heart change that learns reliance on the Spirit of God through the grace found in Jesus Christ. Think carefully about this: "For God has done what the law, weakened by the flesh, could not do. By sending his own Son in the likeness of sinful flesh and for sin, he condemned sin in the flesh, in order that the righteous requirement of the law might be fulfilled in us, who walk not according to the flesh but according to the Spirit. . . . For if you live according to the flesh you will die, but if by the Spirit you put to death the deeds of the body, you will live" (Rom. 8:3–4, 13). Because of the sinful corruption of the self-rewarder's heart and weakness of his body, a new law or standard of strict performance cannot produce righteousness. Self-righteousness always succumbs to the feebleness of the flesh.

Those who reward themselves with lustful voyeurism are guilty of self-righteousness and greed. You have already seen how greed is at the core of every sexual sin. If you are a self-rewarder, you are nurturing a mentality of self-merited virtue that provokes in you a spirit of discontent and ungratefulness for God's gracious love and provision. You have come to believe that God owes you special favors for your sacrificial service and faithfulness in the other areas of your life. You likely see your accomplishments as largely a product of your own endeavors, not God's enablement. Therefore, like the Pharisees of the first century, you carry about a form of self-righteousness which cannot conceive that God would judge you for an occasional indulgence.

"Pharisee-type believers unconsciously think they have earned God's blessing through their behavior. Guilt-laden believers are quite sure they have forfeited God's blessing through their lack of discipline or their disobedience."[3] God's expectation for the believer is not to be mostly righteous, but to be perfectly righteous (Deut. 18:13; Matt. 5:48). Since no one has ever been able to achieve that standard except Jesus Christ, it is imperative that you repent of your *self*-righteousness and cling to Christ and his righteousness by grace. As a joint-heir with Jesus Christ and a recipient of all the promises of God, you possess

---

3. Jerry Bridges, *The Discipline of Grace* (Colorado Springs, CO: NavPress, 1994), 22.

the ability to clean up your life from the inside out with the Lord's enablement: "Since we have these promises, beloved, let us cleanse ourselves from every defilement of body and spirit, bringing holiness to completion in the fear of God" (2 Cor. 7:1). Just as an athlete does not go into a game intending to get hurt, so you must not go through your Christian life intending to sin—even just a little—because the Lord expects absolute holiness (Lev. 11:44; 19:2; 20:7; 1 Peter 1:16). Jesus Christ is both our holiness and our goal in sanctification.

FLATTERY AND PRAISE THAT NOURISH SEXUAL LUST

Sexual sin will often be the fruit of a search for personal approval. All people have a desire to be loved and adored, but believers who have an unusually demanding appetite for approval are special prey to the flattery of the sexually attractive. The central motivation in their relationships is attention and approval from those who are charming and captivating, which in turn makes these approval junkies foolishly vulnerable to sexual sin. Psychologized Christians will tell you that you suffer from a "wounded heart" due to low self-esteem and that you require immense amounts of praise and encouragement heaped on you from others to overcome your sexual compulsions. For example, in listing causes of sexual addiction, one source says, "Other factors that contribute to sexual addiction include low self-esteem."[4] Do not listen to this foolish counsel! While it is true that you have a "needy" heart, your need is not for self-esteem. Humans are already engaged in a high view of self, leading to a heart that fundamentally believes it deserves special flattery and praise. To indulge a sexual sin presumes a fundamental truth about your nature: it believes you deserve the indulgence! This comes not from a low view of self but from an uncommonly high view.

If your heart is starved for admiration, covetous desire will make praise from an attractive person particularly disarming and seductive.

4. Frank Minirth, Paul Meier, Stephen Arterburn, *The Complete Life Encyclopedia* (Nashville, TN: Thomas Nelson, 1995), 507.

When strong sexual drives are added to this mix, the result is an over-whelming yearning for some type of sexual convergence. If perhaps you are unable to find an actual cooperative partner, your creative mind will substitute an imaginary admirer. The dreamer who desires to be adored can spin intricate, erotic daydreams of make-believe lovers who shower all types of respect and praise. At times these dreams may be imposed on real people in your life, who are unaware they are the objects of your sexual fantasy. When these naive subjects of your day-dreams do have occasion to speak favorably to you, the approval-seeker in you may be surprised by your own clumsy response, never imagining that this lofty, idyllic person would even notice you.

Fantasy worlds of the mind have the capacity to create perfectly appealing men and women who captivate your imagination and feed your longing for some expression of appreciation and love. In your mind, these people will be instantly adoring, while you look on the real people around you with a fault-finding attitude of superiority. Once this imaginary world of your mind is fully functioning, the stage is set; you have been weakened and made ripe for a free fall into fornication or adultery when the right person comes along with flattering words.

Solomon cautions his son about another source of flattery, say-ing that married women who leave their husbands are the ones "who forsake the paths of uprightness to walk in the ways of darkness, who rejoice in doing evil and delight in the perverseness of evil, men whose paths are crooked, and who are devious in their ways" (Prov. 2:13–15). A naive young man can be easy prey for such wily women, especially older married women, because his heart's desire is to have a woman tell him he is strong and sexy. Solomon instructed his son to follow the ways of wisdom, knowing that in doing so he will be delivered from "the forbidden woman, from the adulteress with her smooth words, who forsakes the companion of her youth and forgets the covenant of her God" (Prov. 2:16–17).

This temptation of deceiving women is especially true in today's culture, in which a flood of provocative material continually beckons young men and appeals to their developing manhood. Steve Gallagher describes well the condition in which today's young men grow up:

Take the life of an average twelve-year old boy. He gets up in the morning and goes to school. In health class he is taught sex education that refuses to take a moral stand against pre-marital sex or even homosexuality. Often, while with his schoolmates, he overhears the popular, and often precocious, boys talk about their sexual escapades. On the way home from school, he stops in the local convenience store and sees magazine covers behind the counter or on the stands with nude women plastered on the front of them. At home he listens to the popular groups on the radio sing about sex. After dinner he watches a movie on television in which the characters are engaged in various sexual scenarios. The hero is almost always a womanizer—the "Casanova" type. Then there are the commercials that showcase beautiful women in bathing suits to sell anything from sports magazines to automobiles. With such overwhelming exposure as this, why should anyone be surprised that a young teenager turns into a sex addict?[5]

This paragraph was written in the year 2000. Eighteen years later, not only do sex education classes refuse to take a stand on sexual immorality but our children are openly taught that no one should repress their sexuality. Young people of all ages are told that they have the right to act on their sexual urges and that if anyone tells them otherwise, these "prudes" are the immoral ones. Indeed, the temptations facing our youth are greater than ever.

Women and men presented in licentious propaganda (on billboards and the internet) are always portrayed as inviting and flattering, and it is not long before a young man has built an image of the perfect young woman in his imagination who will be the same for him. Her sweet talk appeals to his longing heart. This seduction is complete and goes beyond simple physical attraction. He is convinced that he needs her because she touches something deep inside his hungering heart.

This seduction is sinister; it is truly a fatal attraction. Solomon says, "for her house sinks down to death, and her paths to the departed;

---

5. Steve Gallagher, *At the Altar of Sexual Idolatry* (Dry Ridge, KY: Pure Life Ministries, 2000), 157–58.

none who go to her come back, nor do they regain the paths of life" (Prov. 2:18–19). The young man who falls prey to her inviting form and flattery is the ultimate fool because her duplicity puts him on an irreversible course of destruction. Life does not get better from here; it gets worse. He thinks she is his personal source of gratification, but he finds that he is the one who is trapped and at the mercy of *her* desires. She consumes his life, rendering him useless and unproductive. Initially he was drawn to her because of her praise of his manly attributes, but ultimately she leaves him stripped of all respect.

Such was the case of an eighteen-year-old Christian man who came for counseling. He had been an excellent athlete and student with a four-point grade average in high school until the beginning of his senior year. His parents came with him to counseling, looking devastated and grieved. At the beginning of his final year of high school he had taken an English literature course taught by an attractive young teacher who was two years out of college, six years his senior, and married for less than a year. Everyone in class could tell that he was her favorite student. She openly praised his work, along with his athletic accomplishments, and would often ask him to stay after the bell for a little discussion of the assignment that day. He was completely drawn to her and spent all his limited study time preparing for her class, until his other classes began to suffer. By Christmas break, he had dropped out of school. She quit her job, left her husband, and left the state with this student. Despite the best efforts of his family, the school, and a detective agency, they could not be found. Almost two months later he showed up at his parents' home one night looking rather disheveled. He had hitchhiked across two states in order to get home.

His teacher had used him to get away from an unhappy marriage. Her heart excused her sexual sin because she was discontent and angry with her husband. Once in another state, she left this student within five weeks for an older pro golfer at the local country club. This young man, who had formerly been a respected leader on his campus, now sat in counseling with an ashen complexion and a venereal disease. All the bogus respect and praise that she had showered on him, and that had drawn his heart away from his high school life, had turned and robbed him of whatever honor and dignity he previously possessed. Since his return, it was rumored that the teacher's unbelieving husband had threatened vengeance as well. Thankfully, both he and his parents were more than willing to follow biblical counsel in order to grow from this experience and repair the situation as best they could.

Following the warnings of Scripture and godly parents is critical for susceptible young men. Solomon says these exhortations are given "to preserve you from the evil woman, from the smooth tongue of the adulteress" (Prov. 6:24). Pride of intelligence in some young men works against them by making them gullible. They *think they know* when a woman is trying to seduce them, but some women are experts at the deceptive aspects of seduction. Their appeal is persuasive and convincing. Like this literature teacher, a seductive woman understands the right words that appeal to a young man's heart as it searches for affirmation and praise. She can reduce him to a "loaf of bread" (Prov. 6:26) with her smooth tongue. A loaf of bread offers no resistance to someone who wants to tear it apart and consume it. Bread is not like an iron pipe that is strong and puts up solid resistance, requiring special tools to cut it in two. Our young man is reduced to the helplessness of a loaf of bread, offering little or no resistance. He is a pitiful sight because he is convinced not only that he wants her but also that she desires him just as much (Ps. 36:2). That is the deceitfulness of this wicked seduction. "But a married woman hunts down a precious life" (Prov. 6:26). Like a wild animal, she will track down and devour the tender heart that longs for approval.

The wisdom of Proverbs goes further by explaining that a person who is willing to take another person's wife will find no mercy. The teacher's husband was jealously angry and seeking some type of revenge. People may forgive a robber who steals in order to avoid starvation. Even if that thief has to repay seven times what he stole, he is still better off than the man who steals another man's wife (Prov. 6:30–33). The man who takes another man's woman will not be shown leniency: "For jealousy makes a man furious, and he will not spare when he takes revenge. He will accept no compensation; he will refuse though you multiply gifts" (Prov. 6:34–35). Stealing bread is forgivable under most conditions because it is necessary for life, but taking another man's wife is not as easily forgivable since everyone understands it is not necessary for life. When the heart begins to listen to the seductive talk of a beautiful woman, it needs to remember the devastating consequences that await. As Solomon says, "He who commits adultery lacks sense; he who does it destroys himself" (Prov. 6:32). It is a form of self-destruction or suicide.

In Proverbs 7, Solomon gives a case study of a naive young man who falls prey to a similar situation. His temptress is described as an adulteress: "with her smooth words. . . . She is loud and wayward . . . . With much seductive speech she persuades him; with her smooth talk she compels him" (Prov. 7:5, 11, 21). This woman is self-confident, assertive, and knows how to stroke a young man's ego. His "needy" heart, hungry for some female admiration, immediately resonates with her clear message. She tells him she purposely and "eagerly" came out to meet him (Prov. 7:15). In this way, she implies that he is the only person she really desires. Then she proceeds to describe the sensual furnishings of her bedroom—her imported linens, perfumed bed, and scented spices providing an alluring aroma (Prov. 7:16–17). Her husband is away, presumably on a long journey since he has taken a large sum of money, so she invites the young fool into her home. "Come, let us take our fill of love till morning; let us delight ourselves with love" (Prov. 7:18). He finds his heart in full agreement with her proposal, and he suddenly follows her into her house and to her bedroom.

Solomon compares him to a dumb ox that puts up no fight and is led to the slaughterhouse, or like a deer that throws caution to the wind and purposely puts its hooves in a noose. The young fool is captured by her seduction until an arrow pierces his body and it is too late. All of this figurative language builds a vivid picture of the tragedy of a young man who is deceived by the alluring words and appeal of a female admirer before he realizes that his inability to resist this temptation will be fatal. What appears to offer life, because of its exhilarating thrill, in reality robs him of it. Consequently, notice how Solomon addresses the heart of man: "Let not your heart turn aside to her ways; do not stray into her paths" (Prov. 7:25). Later in Proverbs, Solomon warns men to beware of the talker who seduces with her words; she entraps men with whom the Lord is angry. "The mouth of forbidden women is a deep pit; he with whom the LORD is angry will fall into it" (Prov. 22:14). Men who lust after praise from a harlot's mouth have angered the Lord. A smooth talker can easily seduce a heart hungry for praise and admiration.

Men are not the only ones susceptible to seductive speech. Both genders must be alert to their own covetous hunger for the admiration of an attractive flatterer. A thirty-year-old Christian nurse fell prey to a charming single male doctor at the hospital where she worked. She had married her husband following a whirlwind romance, only to find herself on her fourth anniversary bound to a man who was hypercritical and jealous of her poise and practical intelligence. What complicated matters was his lack of employment. He had lost his job as a computer specialist two years into their marriage, and the economic downturn had kept him out of work for almost two full years since that time. They made do on her salary, but as his unemployment prolonged, he became increasingly derogatory of her. His judgmental attitude had set up her heart for this enchanting doctor. The single doctor praised her work, and not a day went by when he did not speak of how attractive she looked. He invited her to what he called a "business" lunch to discuss their patients, but he spent most of the time complimenting the kindness and grace of her bedside manner. "I have never seen a nurse work so well and be so uncomplaining with such difficult patients. You have a tenderness that most women lack today," he told her. More than anything else, she wanted her husband to see in her the things this doctor saw. In due course, the entire staff of her hospital wing attended a three-day medical conference in Hawaii, doctors and nurses together. The complimentary doctor did not take long to make his move. The nurse said she never intended to commit adultery but admitted she had often imagined what it would be like to have a sordid affair and sleep with such a kind and caring man. Her imaginary dreams were fulfilled.

From that point on, everything in her life changed. Through one of her "friends," word of her one-night-stand spread rapidly through the medical staff and eventually to her husband. Of course, this confirmed in his mind his suspicious and critical spirit toward her. Although he did not become physically violent, things got ugly at home. She also noticed a radical change in the attitude of the doctor with whom she had had the affair. He avoided her, and their conversations became terse and stilted. In fact, the doctor grew increasingly critical of her performance. It dawned on her that a "Casanova" womanizer had seduced her. She was just another notch on his sexual gun belt, and this made her angry for being such a fool. He had preyed on her "needy" heart, and she had allowed his seductive words to stir deep passions within her. Her lust gave birth to adultery and proceeded to end her marriage as well as her job at the hospital.

Manipulative flattery has an element of enchantment to it. It charms the receiver like a magical spell. God's judgment on and eventual exile of ancient Israel included putting an end to flattery: "For there shall be no more any false vision or flattering divination within the house of Israel" (Ezek. 12:24). Flattery is the deceiver's tool. The people of Israel loved the seers who spread flattering fortunes concerning their lives. These soothsayers made them feel good about themselves when they should have repented of their wickedness. God hated the soothsayers' flattering ways because they fed the corrupt desires of Israel's hearts, and so he brought these false prophets to a tragic end through his judgment.

Though many would lay all the blame on the flatterer, the real power of the spell is not in the flattery itself; it is in the heart of the receiver. An unwilling quarry cannot be put under the flatterer's enchanting spell if there is no covetous idol of desire present. Seductive words, no matter how enticing, cannot charm the disinclined heart. Seductions are like radio frequencies: if the receiver is not on the same frequency as the sender, no transmission will take place. The flirtatious flatteries of many attractive charmers fall on unresponsive hearts, not because they are unappealing but because the receivers' hearts are pure. They have made their hearts free of the kinds of covetous cravings that remain unsatisfied until they hear praise and admiration. But the heart yearning for approval and admiration is easy prey for seduction. If a smooth-talking charmer finds an impure heart as he goes about with empty compliments, then the enchantment begins. When this is the case, "a flattering mouth works ruin" (Prov. 26:28). If the radar of your heart is attuned to praise and flattery, eventually it will find a seductive signal.

Flattery is also a form of favoritism—a way in which one person seeks to be partial to another, usually for some ulterior motive. The doctor favored the nurse because he wanted her to favor him with sex. Therefore, flattery must be seen as a type of manipulation that seeks to gain advantage over another who is searching for favorable treatment in return. Elihu was one of Job's younger counselors, and even though his statements were not always wise, he acknowledges, "I will not show partiality to any man or use flattery toward any person. For I do not know how to flatter, else my Maker would soon take me away" (Job 32:21–22). While it's doubtful that Elihu lacked the ability to flatter, he did realize that if he resorted to flattery in order to please people, it would be a form of partiality and God would be displeased. The apostle Paul and his companions acknowledged their innocent motives to the Thessalonian Christians: "For we never came with words of flattery, as you know, nor with a pretext for greed—God is witness" (1 Thess. 2:5). King David calls manipulative flatterers liars: "Everyone utters lies to his neighbor; with flattering lips and a double heart they speak. May the LORD cut off all flattering lips, the tongue that makes great boasts" (Ps. 12:2–3). People often tried to manipulate David with flattery and praise, and he saw them as treacherous deceivers with double hearts. On the one hand, they do acknowledge and highlight positive attributes in another person, but on the other hand, they use it for their own selfish advantage. David's prayer was that the Lord would judge and cut them off from his covenantal blessing. Flattery is a form of false praise that God hates.

THE DESIRE FOR POWER AND CONTROL NOURISHES SEXUAL LUST

Seduction often involves a type of control over another person. Some men and women relish this control over another person's sexual responses. Do you take special delight in using your sex appeal to flirt

163

with or seduce another person? If so, like many others, it is possible that, for you, there is more to a sexual experience than the goal of a climax or orgasm. Eroticism lurks in the thought or idea that you have power to control another person using your sexuality.

Earlier it was stated that the women of Judah were proud of their seductive abilities. Isaiah gives a vivid description of their adornment in the practice of seduction:

> The LORD said: Because the daughters of Zion are haughty and walk with outstretched necks, glancing wantonly with their eyes, mincing along as they go, tinkling with their feet, therefore the Lord will strike with a scab the heads of the daughters of Zion, and the LORD will lay bare their secret parts. In that day the Lord will take away the finery of the anklets, the headbands, and the crescents; the pendants, the bracelets, and the scarves; the headdresses, the armlets, the sashes, the perfume boxes, and the amulets; the signet rings and nose rings; the festal robes, the mantles, the cloaks, and the handbags; the mirrors, the linen garments, the turbans, and the veils. Instead of perfume there will be rottenness; and instead of a belt, a rope; and instead of well-set hair, baldness; and instead of a rich robe, a skirt of sackcloth; and branding instead of beauty. (Isa. 3:16–24)

This is a description of how the women of Judah would dress in order to seduce men. They were proud of their seduction and strutted around, knowing they had the power to lure men into relationships with them. They could turn heads, and they knew how to dress to do it. These women possessed a form of power or control through attractiveness. God hated their seductive methods. They lost their power because in his judgment he afflicted their heads with scabs, causing them to go bald. He also took away their fine jewelry and clothes, and he afflicted their bodies with a revolting smell. Then he sent their men to die in battle. Now there were few men around, and the ones who were left did not want to be with these women.

Women enjoy the power and control of sexuality as much as men. In Proverbs, the seductress lures her man with her tongue, eyes, and beauty (Prov. 6:24–25)—like a helpless lamb—into her trap where "she seizes him and kisses him" (Prov. 7:13). Potiphar's wife, a woman whom most Egyptian men would never refuse because of her position and power, tried to force Joseph to sleep with her (Gen. 39:10–12). She had the power to back her words with action if he failed to obey, and she did when he refused. This is lustful power to gain sexual gratification.

An important distinction needs to be made between someone using power or authority over another person to gain sexual favors and someone gaining sexual pleasure from the distinctive position itself. As has been illustrated, people in authority, such as presidents, pastors, politicians, and police officers (e.g., King David, Herod), have been known to use their positions of authority to gain sexual advantage over others. In these cases, eroticism is not derived directly from the control over another; rather, the position of power is used to exact the desired pleasure. The power and control of their position are only means to an end. However, in sexual sadism, sensual excitement is derived from the perception of another person being at one's mercy. Watching a victim's humiliation and suffering causes sexual arousal in some, as does seeing the victim's terror at the prospect of this sadistic act happening to him or her. The suffering of the victim under control produces the arousal. This is an awful wickedness.

Conversely, being controlled and overpowered by another person can also be sexually exciting to some. Sexual masochism involves the behavior of being humiliated, bound, and/or beaten by another person because it stimulates an erotic experience. This can often come in various forms, from the less hurtful but humiliating experience of being forced to cross-dress in clothing of the opposite sex or in baby clothing and diapers, to the more painful method of being beaten, whipped, shocked by electric probes, spanked, pierced (infibulation), and so on. In the more popular cases it is described as "leather, whips, and chains." Some women have admitted that the fantasy of being raped is erotic. These are women who have never been raped. Some men speak of the arousing experience of being tied and whipped by a dominatrix. Of course, most of this is said to be done playfully, and there is usually a signal to end when the subject is finished. Regardless, these practices stem from a heart saturated with sinful self-gratification and are expressed through perverted desires that focus on dominance or being dominated.

Even though Scripture does not speak specifically to these practices, the guidelines given for sex are general enough to cover these practices and particular enough to reveal their sinful incentives. Broad biblical terms like *lust, lasciviousness, dissipations, immoral imaginations,* and *sexual greed* provide ample clues for instruction in dealing with these self-centered sexual practices of power and control. Most of these refined sexual practices are, in reality, variations of the same theme of selfish sexual desires that have been focused on specific types of preferential erotica. Such people are never satisfied with normal sexual relations with their spouses; like the nomadic Israelites who grew tired of the manna and quail given them by God, they crave the fish, cucumbers, melons, leeks, onions, and garlic of Egypt (Num. 11:5). Of course, fish, cucumbers, and melons are not sinful in themselves, but they do serve to illustrate that greedy hearts are never fully satisfied with God's provisions, no matter how good and abundant they may be. "The righteous has enough to satisfy his appetite, but the belly of the wicked suffers want" (Prov. 13:25; cf. Eccl. 6:7).

Scripture often uses the metaphor of the grave to describe the appetite that is never satisfied. The grave is an apt analogy because it continues to claim more and more people as the years go by; it has an appetite that is never fulfilled. The Old Testament prophet Habakkuk speaks of those who try to gain control over their neighbors by getting them drunk. "Woe to him who makes his neighbors drink—you pour out your wrath and make them drunk, in order to gaze at their nakedness!" (Hab. 2:15). To uncover nakedness was a Hebraism that meant to expose another indecently in order to satisfy a sinful sexual desire (Gen. 19:33–35; Lev. 18:6–19; 20:11–21; Deut. 22:30; 24:1). This is the same person of whom Habakkuk says, "His greed is as wide as Sheol [grave]; like death he has never enough" (Hab. 2:5). A person who is willing to gain control over another person, whether it be by alcohol or some other sedative-like chemical (i.e., date-rape drugs), has permitted his sexual appetite to grow to the point that it is worshiped as a god. This person takes control of others, even if it means that the victims are hurt, in order to find selfish gratification. Has a deep desire for power and control fueled your sinful sexual demands?

THE DESIRE FOR COMFORT NOURISHES SEXUAL LUST

Sexual desires are powerful drives because they offer a considerable amount of bodily pleasure. They are pleasing to the flesh. Anything that appeals to somatic pleasure centers of the brain has the potential to be a powerful agent in activating the covetousness of the sinful heart, which is why it is so important for you to know your own heart. Aside from the chemical processes of your brain, your mind (a part of the biblical concept of heart) decides to channel these drives into sexual practices and patterns of thinking and behavior that bring about the soothing relief of physical tension. When your hormones are heightened to a passionate peak and then released, the physiological result is a relaxing calm that settles across your body. This easing of intense physical strain and the resulting pleasurable sensation of climaxed desire becomes enslaving as your heart lusts for more and more.

In the earlier illustration of Frederick, anger, reinforced by the comforting sensation of masturbation, conspired to make masturbation an undeniable habituation for him. Helping Frederick solve his problem meant more than addressing the act and thought of masturbation. It involved speaking to incentives of both anger and comfort that energized his sinful desire for imaginary fornication. He had become a type of religious zealot, paying regular homage to his idols of anger and comfort. Instead of using his sexual energy to please his wife, he was using it for personal solace and satisfaction. The God-given sense of sexual pleasure is distorted into a grotesque monster of comfort or ease; it rules ruthlessly by feeding self-centeredness, deceit, anger, and greed in the life of the one whom it rules. Frederick could see these sins in his own life. Life gets ugly when holy lust is replaced by unholy lust.

Another way to describe the lust for comfort is to speak of it in terms of a love for pleasure. You have no doubt discovered that pleasurable experiences also bring an abundant measure of temporary comfort.

Comfort can become your lover—your idol—that brings you the most pleasure. You desire her company more than anyone else. You find yourself escaping with her to imaginary places of your mind as she rewards you with erotic pleasures. Paul warns that men in the last days will be "lovers of pleasure rather than lovers of God" (2 Tim. 3:4). Pleasurable things that bring comfort will replace God as your greatest love.

The comfort of sexual pleasure is the harlot that seduces you away from your love for God. At this juncture you must beware of being "slaves to various passions and pleasures" (Titus 3:3). Pleasure in the sexual experience is not sinful or forbidden in Scripture, but it was never intended to rule a man or woman and become one's primary lover. It is a holy lust when it is channeled toward one's spouse in a monogamous marriage of heterosexuals: "Let marriage be held in honor among all, and let the marriage bed be undefiled, for God will judge the sexually immoral and adulterous" (Heb. 13:4). But when all the thoughts, energies, and passions of the body are channeled by the drive for comfort into self-gratifying imaginations and activities, they have replaced God as the central passions of the heart. This dishonors marriage and defiles the marriage bed.

If you have made such an idol of comfort, you must be aware that you have a new religious idol in your heart—a new romantic lover, real or imagined, that you make love to through masturbation or actual fornication. If you are married, your new religious god of comfort directs your sexual energies away from your spouse. Solomon metaphorically inquires, "Should your springs be scattered abroad, streams of water in the streets?" (Prov. 5:16). The obvious answer is no! Misdirected sexual energy is useless and destructive.

Often in the Old Testament, adultery is used figuratively to speak of how the Israelites left the worship of Yahweh and turned to worshiping idols of wood and stone common among neighboring nations. The prophet Jeremiah turns the analogy around to speak of the idol of adultery or harlotry: "How can I pardon you? Your children have forsaken me and have sworn by those who are no gods. When I fed them to the full, they committed adultery and trooped to the houses of whores. They were well-fed, lusty stallions, each neighing for his neighbor's wife" (Jer. 5:7–8).

Sexual lust is a captivating type of idolatry. It is idolatry not of wood or stone but of the heart. Along with worshiping Baal (Jer. 7:9), the Israelites craved indulgent sex with their neighbors' wives. The comfort of self-gratifying sexual pleasure took the place of honor at the altars of their hearts. Even though the covenant God of Israel had fed them well, their hearts were turned aside to worship the comfort of sensual indulgence. Like lusty stallions, they pawed the ground and whinnied, prancing around God's stable while craving another stallion's mare in the pasture nearby. Frequently they would jump the fence (marriage boundaries) and copulate with that mare. For that, God's whip of judgment was heavy on them.

Living to satisfy the lust for sexual pleasure is not only a male problem. Charlotte was a counselee who had been married twice. Prior to salvation at the age of twenty-four, she had been the party girl in college. Mercifully, God had preserved her from most sexually transmitted diseases and AIDS. Now she was forty-two years of age and no longer had any feelings for her second husband, Bob. She confided that she did not enjoy their times of intimacy together; she agreed to participate only because she saw it as an obligation. During her sex with Bob, she even confessed to reminiscing about exciting sex parties of her college days as well as sex times with her previous husband. He had run off with another woman two years into their marriage. She longed for the days when she could again feel the excitement and thrill she enjoyed before. In fact, she could not remember the last time she had experienced enjoyment with Bob. All the pleasure was gone, and she really pined for a return of those party days of the past.

There was a woman described in the Bible, much like Charlotte, whose name was Gomer. Her sexual unfaithfulness was so notorious that her harlotry is used as an analogy for the unfaithfulness of Israel as it prostituted itself with the idolatrous worship of Baal.[6] The prophet

6. I realize the debate between some Bible scholars of whether Gomer was a literal woman or just a symbolic literary device who demonstrates God's disapproval of

Hosea was commanded by God to "Go, take to yourself a wife of whoredom" (Hos. 1:2),[7] so he married Gomer. Their marriage was tumultuous because of the sexual adventurousness of Gomer. She eventually became a prostitute. With resolution in her heart, she said, "I will go after my lovers" (Hos. 2:5). She was a "kept woman." Her statement is one of strong, lustful desire. Why does she want to go after other men? She says they are the ones "who give me my bread and my water, my wool and my flax, my oil and my drink" (2:5). She believed they offered her the enjoyment and comfort of sex and security. Just as Gomer would not be deterred from pursuing her lovers and attributing her prosperity to them, Israel would not be deterred from Baal or attributing her prosperity to him. Again, idolatry and intense sexual lust are equated. Yet, somehow, God never allowed Gomer to find the satisfaction she sought through her illicit encounters with these men. She was never fulfilled, because her sexual yearning was unappeasable. She said, "I will go and return to my first husband, for it was better for me then than now" (Hos. 2:7). Her change of mind occurred, however, only after God hedged her around with thorns in his judgment (Hos. 2:6). This woman had an intense desire for sexual pleasure and comfort, but such a ravenous sexual appetite bore only the fruit of misery.

In a similar way, Charlotte's past sexual experiences had sown an idolatrous craving for the comfort of sex. She had become enslaved to its desires to the point that sex with one man was not normal. Her body craved for more. Like Gomer, she believed she needed the comforting pleasures of many men (even her previous husband began to look appealing) before she could find satisfaction for her erotic desires.

Israel's unfaithfulness. If she is a literary device, the marriage scenes of Hosea 1–3 are to be taken allegorically. I prefer the position that she is an actual person used as an analogy. But even if she is not, it is still possible to use her hypothetical personage to illustrate how God views those who are controlled by the pleasurable idols of sexuality.

7. I take this to be a proleptical command, which means Gomer would be this way in the future. Hosea undoubtedly chose a wife who was already flirtatious and made her way around among the men.

The comforting sensation of sexual behavior, or even the thought of sexual arousal, rewards the enslaved with pleasurable experiences. Yet these sensations have been mapped on a heart that has already idolized comfort. Long before puberty, a child may grow to love comfort more than God. Lasting help for Frederick and Charlotte can come about when the counselor addresses the issue of living for comfort rather than living for God. If the idol of comfort is demolished in the heart, it will cease to fuel the sexual practices.

This is true of each of the eight axes in the "Pantheon of Heart Idols" (see fig. 4.2). Anger, self-pity, discontentment, fear, self-reward, flattery, power/control, and comfort are common examples of a variety of latent desires that characteristically manifest themselves in sexual enslavement. Patterns and themes of these idols run deep in the past and in the heart. When the sex drive is superimposed on top of them, they turn the purity of proper sexual desire into unholy and demanding lust. Competent biblical counsel is the only answer to eradicate these roots.

Importantly, after the apostle Paul describes people of the last days as being "lovers of pleasure rather than lovers of God" (2 Tim. 3:4), he proceeds to say, "For among them are those who creep into households and capture weak women, burdened with sins and led astray by various passions" (2 Tim. 3:6). Although the context suggests that these women were weak in their understanding of the truth of Scripture and were easily misled by false teachers, the term *passions* (ἐπιθυμία) is used to describe their desire, and the adjective *various* (ποικίλος) is used to refer to the diversity of their lusts. This terminology suggests that these women were weak in virtue as well. Whether or not sexual lusts are assumed as part of this diversity (though I think they are), this verse shows that the human heart can have a variety of wicked desires. These desires can easily be led astray and captivated—if not by the persuasive appeals of false teachers, then by the sexual appeal of lustful gratification. Your job is to identify these various desires in your heart and repent of them in order to achieve biblical purification.

KEY CONCEPTS

insatiable appetite

vanity

hungering heart

affirmative motivations

self-denial

recompense

self-sacrifice as penance

diversionary sexual fulfillment

self-rewarders

self-esteem

starved for admiration

fantasy worlds

manipulative flattery

seductive nature of power

lust for comfort

comforting sensation of sexual behavior

STUDY QUESTIONS

1. Before a person commits sexual sin, what *one common sin* is the hungering heart guilty of? You can discover this by answering these questions:
   - How does the self-rewarder rationalize his sin?
   - What does the heart that longs for flattery think of itself?
   - What does the person who exerts power and control think of himself in comparison to others?
   - Who is the one lusting for comfort always thinking of first?
2. Based on your answer to the first question, plan how you will give counsel regarding this from the book of Proverbs. List at least six verses that will apply.
3. Read Proverbs 6:16–19. Based on each of the things that God hates, describe how the one who gives in to his insatiable

appetite for reward, flattery, power, and comfort is violating the very things that God hates most in the heart of man.

4. The previous questions have centered on what the godly person is *not* to be like. Now read Titus 2:11–14 and write instructions for the person enslaved to sexual sin as to how he is called to live as a Christian. Emphasize both the help provided by God himself as well as the responsibility of the Christian in response.

5. Explain what is so very evil about reveling in a fantasy world of sexual indulgence. Describe how it affects
   • the purity of your thought life
   • your spouse (or future spouse)
   • the person you are fantasizing about
   • your worship of a pure and holy God

FOR FURTHER READING

Jones, Peter. *The Pagan Heart of Today's Culture*. Phillipsburg, NJ: P&R Publishing, 2014.

Mack, Wayne, and Joshua Mack. *Courage: Fighting Fear with Fear*. Phillipsburg, NJ: P&R Publishing, 2014.

Priolo, Lou. *Pleasing People: How Not to Be an Approval Junkie*. Phillipsburg, NJ: P&R Publishing, 2007.

Welch, Edward T. *When People Are Big and God Is Small: Overcoming Peer Pressure, Codependency, and the Fear of Man*. Phillipsburg, NJ: P&R Publishing, 1997.

7

A BIBLICAL STRESS TEST

If you were to have chest pain, a heart attack, or some other physical cardiac episode, your doctor would likely order a stress test to diagnose any defects in the heart. Light to moderate exercise on a treadmill, along with an electrocardiogram, puts just enough stress on your heart to identify a defect. The purpose of this test is to preempt heart failure that could result in undesirable life changes or even death. You may have experienced no symptoms (chest pressure or pain) yet have an undetected heart problem. Some people seem to function well with their normal routines of life yet carry within them a cardiac time bomb waiting to explode in their chest—they are completely oblivious to the hidden danger. A similar principle is at work in you as you face your own sexual temptations and repeated failures.

Perhaps you are painfully aware of your struggle with sexual sin, and although you try to resist, you find yourself giving in repeatedly. What you may be *unaware* of are the specific preconditions of your heart that make you so vulnerable. You may not even know what a precondition of the heart is. Simply stated, this term refers to habitual, automatic, and unconscious patterns of thoughts and responses that result in sinful attitudes and behaviors.[1] When it comes to your war

---

1. More specifically, a preconditioning problem of the heart is often a trained and unconscious pattern of thought in automatic reaction to past circumstances or experiences of life (often unpleasant) that results in the present repeated sinful attitudes and behaviors.

with sexual sin, each temptation plays out on the battlefield of these patterns or, if you will, these preconditions.

In fact, the thought may have crossed your mind, "I can't believe I have surrendered to this awful temptation so many times!" You may have sincerely prayed about the problem, begging God to remove the temptation altogether, only to fail miserably once again. It is at this point that your understanding and application of the doctrine of sanctification becomes your greatest help. An accurate operation of sanctification in your life works as if spiritual "special forces" have joined ranks with you in this war of wars.

You may already know that justification in Christ is wholly a work of God, not based on any merit or action of your own. This is not so with sanctification. The work of sanctification is a dual process—one that requires both your work *and* God's work, based on the justification he secured for you (Heb. 10:10–14). He provides the enabling grace, and you must work hard at replacing old sinful habits of thoughts, desires, attitudes, words, and deeds with righteous ones (Rom. 6:5–7; Eph. 4:17–24; Col. 3:5–10). You can see this as the apostle Paul described how he progressed throughout his difficult ministry: "For this I toil, struggling with all his energy that he powerfully works within me" (Col. 1:29). The duality is clear: it was God's energy, but Paul had to toil. He used the word *toil* (the Greek term ἀγωνίζομαι, from which the English term *agonize* is derived) to indicate the struggle—a fierce fight, a striving—to please and honor God with his life. Real and lasting change is not going to come from some wishful identity focus (antinomianism), or waiting for some spiritual lightning strike from heaven (mysticism), or mere change in external behavior (behaviorism). God wants you to begin behaving as a redeemed saint now. It is not behaviorism or pharisaical to engage this fight with all your strength and his wisdom. You will have to make substantial changes to achieve a pure heart. These changes will not come easily, but they are necessary for the sake of your holiness.

Paul encourages the Roman Christians in their struggle with sin by assuring them of abounding grace: "Now the law came in to increase the trespass, but where sin increased, grace abounded all the more, so that, as sin reigned in death, grace also might reign through righteousness leading to eternal life through Jesus Christ our Lord" (Rom. 5:20–21). But he quickly admonishes believers to resist continuance in sin "that grace may abound" (Rom. 6:1). Instead, they are to engage in the hard work of sanctification.

> Let not sin therefore reign in your mortal body, to make you obey its passions. Do not present your members to sin as instruments for unrighteousness, but present yourselves to God as those who have been brought from death to life, and your members to God as instruments for righteousness. For sin will have no dominion over you, since you are not under law but under grace. (Rom. 6:12–14)

It is imperative that the reign of sin come to an end in your life. This sin comes from willfully yielding your obedience to your passions—obeying these rather than obeying God. These sinful passions come from your heart and stimulate your body to sin. For your change to be complete, you must deal with your passions at their source.

Understanding that you are in Christ, that you have been brought from death to life, is an important beginning as a redeemed believer, but you must go further. This understanding must also lead you to the full acknowledgment that the members of your body are to be used as instruments for the purpose of righteousness and no longer for unrighteousness. Your brain is a member of your body, and its mental processes (fueled by your heart's intentions) invite temptation, giving rise to the reign of sinful lust. This is the result of unconfessed preconditions that exist in your heart. Identifying these impure preconditions is the necessary step toward biblical repentance and living a life of purity. You cannot repent, you cannot change, until you know what these impurities are.

This chapter provides you with some diagnostic questions to help clearly identify the impurities that make your heart so vulnerable to sexual sin. As you attempt to answer these questions, they may moderately "exercise" your heart—a biblical "stress test" to detect weaknesses in the form of sinful intentionality still present in your heart, causing it to be susceptible to sexual sin. This test is not foolproof, because it requires absolute honesty before God, and your heart will fight truthful analysis. But when it is used properly, it can be a very effective tool.

As stated earlier in this book, the core of all sexual sin is a covetous desire for self-gratification (Eph. 5:3). However, this is difficult to identify when your heart is covered with layers of self-justifying intentions. First, you must discover and come clean about these intentions and motivations before you can replace them. Second, you must honestly acknowledge the grip that these influences have on your heart.

IDENTIFYING HEART MOTIVATIONS

Begin by writing your answers to the following questions. Be detailed and thorough in your responses. The more comprehensive your response, the more sure you can be that you are uncovering the real motivations that tend to rule your heart.

A. When I am tempted to sin sexually, am I seeking to redress a hurt in my life or to gratify a hunger for sexual satisfaction? Explain yourself with full-sentence answers. (If you say a hurt, then answer question 1. If you say a hunger, then answer question 2. If you say both, then answer both questions.)

  1. In what ways does your heart crave comfort or solace through your sexual sin? Consider the fact that your heart may be angry, full of self-pity, discontent, or fear. Explain how your heart has manifested this comforting desire in your choice of sexual sin. You may need to re-read chapter 5 in this book to be specific in your answer.

  2. In what ways does your heart crave satisfaction through your sexual sin? Is your heart seeking self-reward, flattery, power/control, or comfort? Explain how the heart has manifested this desire for satisfaction in your choice of sexual sin. You may need to re-read chapter 6 in this book to be specific in your answer.

B. What past experiences do you believe have contributed to your answer in question 1? What major events have helped mold your desire to sin in this way? (Remember, if another person[s] has sexually victimized you in your past, they have committed a horrible sin against you and God, which can be very influential in your life, but with God's help, it does not have to be determinative. You do not have to allow those events to define your life or who you are. Christ is the One who should define who you are! Gal. 2:20.) It is common for your specific expression of sinful sexual lust to be mapped on your past good and bad experiences.

C. In what ways have your past experiences warped your sexuality away from God's good and beautiful expression of sex in a monogamous heterosexual marriage? (Gen. 1:27, 31; 2:24–25). Sexual sin is fueled by the heart's greediness as it hurts or hungers, and it always destroys what is good and beautiful.

CLARIFYING HEART MOTIVATIONS

Once you have identified the craving(s) in your heart when you commit sexual sin, you need to clarify how these craving(s) have ruled your heart in controlling your thoughts, attitudes, and behavior. Write your answers as carefully and completely as possible. Based on your answer to the questions above, answer the appropriate questions below that address your particular motivation(s) dominating your sexual lust. If you have more than one ruling motivation, answer the questions for each one that tends to dominate your heart.

A. The Motivations of the Hurting Heart

1. Anger
   a. Describe your anger when you sexually sin. Explain the last five times you were angry and sinned sexually.
   b. What is it you want that you do not have which makes

you angry? Or, what do you possess that you do not want?

c. What denied expectations have prompted your anger?

d. Are there some perceived rights you believe you are being denied?

2. Self-pity

a. Describe your self-pity when you sexually sin. How often, and in what ways, does self-pity manifest itself in your sexual sins?

b. What do you want that God does not want or desire?

c. What are your chief expectations when you find yourself filled with self-pity?

d. In what ways do you express feeling sorry for yourself sexually?

3. Discontentment

a. Describe the discontentment in your heart. How often, and in what ways, does discontentment manifest itself in your sexual expression?

b. What you desire may be good, but is your desire so intense and demanding that you become ungodly, unhappy, and discontent when you cannot achieve it?

c. Are there rights you believe you have been denied that have contributed to your discontentment and your sexual sin? Describe each one in detail.

d. What has been the greatest contributor to your unhappiness and discontentment?

4. Fear

a. Describe the fear that overtakes your heart when you are tempted to sin sexually. How often, and in what ways, is fear evident in your sexual sin?

b. Are your fears linked to pleasing people so much that you are willing to sexually sin to keep them happy with you? Describe your thoughts when this is true.

c. In what ways do you see fear as being the dominant motivation in your heart when you are sexually tempted?

d. How are you using sex to extinguish the fearfulness of

your heart? Whose opinions rule you when governed by this fear?

B. The Motivations of the Hungering Heart

1. Self-reward
   a. Describe how sexual sin is used for self-reward in your life. How often, and in what ways, is self-reward connected to your sexuality?
   b. What is your heart saying when you are convinced you have a right to commit sexual sin as a self-reward?
   c. How is arrogance connected to your expectations of sexual self-reward in your heart?
   d. What are the ways your heart has convinced you that you are deserving of sexual self-reward?
2. Flattery
   a. Describe how flattery is demonstrated in your sinful expressions of sex. How often, and in what ways, is flattery connected to your sexuality?
   b. What are the ways you see sinful pride manifested in your willingness to commit sexual sin?
   c. What thoughts control your mind when you are indulging sexual sin for personal adulation?
   d. What sexual sins are you willing to commit in order to receive praise and excessive compliments from others?
3. Power/control
   a. Describe how you see power/control motivating your sexual sin. How often, and in what ways, is power/control involved in your sexual thoughts and behavior?
   b. Why, and in what ways, is your sexuality connected to the concept of sexual conquest?
   c. What thoughts mostly consume your thinking when you use your sexuality to dominate or control others?
   d. How is your desire for power/control linked to your earliest (childhood, adolescent) memories of sexual desire?

4. Comfort
   a. Describe how you see comfort as a chief motivation in your sexual sin. How often, and in what ways, is comfort ruling your sexuality?
   b. When your heart longs for comforting satisfaction through some sexual sin, what is your heart demanding?
   c. How is your desire for comfort in sex tied to your desire to be relieved of stress by surrendering to pleasurable sin?
   d. What thoughts dominate your mind when you are desiring comfort through sinful sex?

Keep in mind that the more diligent you are in giving careful answers to these questions, the more thorough you will be in digging out the deeply ingrained sinful motivations that rule your heart. There are no short-cuts to this process, but the spiritual benefits will be lasting. The value of a cleansed conscience, freed from sexual guilt, is beyond calculation.

A critical but often forgotten biblical principle is vital to this self-discovery process: "Cease to hear instruction, my son, and you will stray from the words of knowledge" (Prov. 19:27). Spiritual growth and change is a dynamic process—you are either moving forward or slipping backward. No one remains neutral! Answering these questions is one effective means of moving forward in dealing with stubborn sexual sins.

Thankfully, this is not the end of the story. You do not need to be overwhelmed with the sin you have uncovered in this diagnostic test. Now that you understand the specific controlling motivations behind your sinful sexuality, you can begin to repent and replace them with righteous desires and pure motivations. You will learn just how to accomplish this in the next chapter.

KEY CONCEPTS

precondition of the heart
justification vs. sanctification
enabling grace
hard work
antinomianism
mysticism
behaviorism
members of your body
redress a hurt
gratify a hunger
contributing past experiences
major life events
cravings that rule
pleasing people
arrogance of self-reward
sexual conquest
relief from stress

STUDY QUESTIONS

1. Explain why being justified in Christ is not enough to keep a Christian from becoming enslaved by sin. Is there an insufficiency in justification? If not, what should the Christian think about his justification?
2. Explain from Scripture why sanctification for the Christian is a process and not a one-time event that brings about instant perfection.
3. Explain the difference between
   - antinomianism and progressive sanctification
   - mysticism and progressive sanctification
   - behaviorism and progressive sanctification

FOR FURTHER READING

Lundgaard, Kris. *Through the Looking Glass*. Phillipsburg, NJ: P&R Publishing, 2000.

Sibbes, Richard. *The Tender Heart*. Carlisle, PA: Banner of Truth, 2011.

Viars, Steve. *Putting Your Past in Its Place*. Eugene, OR: Harvest House, 2011.

Wragg, Jerry, and Paul Shirley. *Free to Be Holy: Conference Edition with Selected Chapters*. CreateSpace, 2017.

STRESS TEST NOTES

STRESS TEST NOTES

PART 3

THE CHARACTERISTICS OF A PURE HEART

8

CRITICAL PREREQUISITES OF A PURE HEART

The first home my wife and I purchased was an older house with a nicely painted front porch. When our daughter was nine months old, my parents came to see their first grandchild, Krista. During the visit my mother came out to the front porch carrying our little girl. As she leaned against the porch railing, it collapsed underneath her. She and Krista fell backward off the porch three feet down onto a concrete walkway. With protective grandma love, my mother shifted the baby to the center of her chest, which meant that she bore all the impact of the fall. Krista was unharmed, but my mother had broken every rib in her body. It turned out that the previous owner had painted over rotten wood in order to sell us the house. This painful story illustrates what will happen to you if you carelessly jump to steps of purifying your heart without carefully identifying its rotten preconditioning issues. Much like my mother in this story, you will suffer greatly.

Up to this point, this book's focus has been understanding and identifying what is wrong in your heart when it comes to your indulgence of sexual sin. The stubbornness of your sin cannot be underestimated; this is why you must carefully identify it for what it is. Otherwise, the consequences of your wickedness will wreak havoc on your life and those who are close to you. Even more tragic is the shame you will bring on the Lord Jesus Christ, the One you profess to love. Skipping or cavalierly handling the previous chapters to recklessly jump to this one will lead to disastrous results.

PURITY STARTS WITH BIBLICAL HEART HERMENEUTICS

Careful and accurate biblical interpretation is essential to knowing what God's Word means. Likewise, knowing how to purify the lustful heart must include good interpretive principles and skills. Proper "heart hermeneutics" is the fMRI test of the wise Christian.[1] It is a set of biblical guidelines used in identifying and interpreting your inner man as it interacts with the various temptations and enslavements of your life. Essentially, it defines the parameters that help you make evaluations and decisions about your life as you seek to change and grow— What do I really think? How do I rationalize my worldview? What is my true motivation? What do I love and hate the most? Whom or what do I genuinely worship? Just as all Christians must rely on good interpretive principles in understanding the Bible, sound hermeneutics of the heart must underlie an understanding of your own thoughts and motivations. Sometimes a well-trained biblical counselor or pastor can help in this process.[2]

This type of interpretation can be extremely difficult. Consider, for example, that when a person studies the Bible, he has objective propositional statements with which to work, some easy and some more difficult, that require standard rules of grammar and syntax to aid in the proper understanding of its meaning. Even though the exegetical process may be tedious, depending on the difficulty of the terminology

---

1. Functional magnetic resonance imaging (fMRI) provides a computer-generated image of the brain and other nerve clusters of the body while they are active. It offers a means for improved diagnosis.

2. "It is here that pastoral counseling can have a sharpening influence on psychological practice. After all, this is where pastoral counselors make their living. We are avowed worldview specialists." Edward T. Welch, "A Discussion among Clergy: Pastoral Counseling Talks with Secular Psychology," *The Journal of Biblical Counseling* 13, 2 (Winter 1995): 25.

and genre, the interpreter is still working with an unchanging text. The Word of God is immutable.

Working with the human heart, however, is quite a different thing. As we have already noted, the heart is cunning, calculating, and constantly changing. It is often actively deceiving and self-deceived, not inert. In other words, the heart will vigorously resist "exegesis." Proper interpretations come only to those who are battle-wise in their application of biblical principles. Often a good counselor will find himself doing the job of interpretation in a war zone called the counseling session. The counselor not only fights the sinful tendencies of his own heart (e.g., frustration, impatience, anger, oversimplification, overidentification, excessive sympathy) but, in that interpretive moment, often faces considerable resistance from the counselee.

An exegetical tug-of-war goes on between the analysis of fact and the determination of meaning. Just as "each of us reads the Bible in a foxhole surrounded by the fire of cosmic war between evil and the Spirit," each of us reads our own hearts in the middle of a similar war.[3] In fact, in a counseling session, the battle is more immediate and fraught with emotion. The intense drama of a counseling session seldom affords the thoughtful withdrawal and reflection enjoyed when studying the Bible. This makes proper identification of the motivations underlying idolatrous lust more complicated but nonetheless imperative.

THE HOPE FOR PURITY IS FOUND IN GOD'S WORD

Death, and the subsequent perfect sanctification of heaven, is the only time that Christians will be freed once and for all from the impurities of lustful sin. Until then, it should be your goal to aggressively seek to live lust-free on this earth. If you have been stubbornly enslaved by sexual lusts for years, you may believe that this goal is unreasonable—unattainable. Your cynical hopelessness does not come from God. Rather, this futility comes from following the cursed feelings of

3. Richard L. Pratt Jr., *He Gave Us Stories: The Bible Student's Guide to Interpreting Old Testament Narratives* (Phillipsburg, NJ: P&R Publishing, 1993), 45.

the flesh, the residue of lust, and is being nourished by Satan and the world. Your despair reveals that you fundamentally believe God has no real answers. The great Puritan preacher Thomas Brooks explains what has happened to bring such a negative outlook on life:

> Ah! How many professors [of Christianity] in these days have for a time followed hard after God, Christ, and ordinances, till the devil hath set before them the world in all its beauty and bravery, which hath so bewitched their souls that they have grown to have low thoughts of holy things, and then to be cold in their affections to holy things, and then slight them, and at last, with the young man in the Gospel, to turn their backs upon them. Ah! The time, the thoughts, the spirits, the hearts, the souls, the duties, the services, that the inordinate love of this wicked world doth eat up and destroy, and hath ate up and destroyed.[4]

The job of Satan and the world is to convince you that there is no hope. Some of those who are so convinced were never believers to begin with; they are still part of the world. Yet some believers fall under the delusion that change and purity are hopeless endeavors; they have become persuaded that their pursuit of sanctification is useless. Even some who call themselves Christian counselors have been known to advocate this material/biological hopelessness, given that God made humans as sexual beings and that the hormonal and biological functions appear to color everything a person is and does. It is disheartening at the very least to hear Christians in positions of influence and authority conspire with Satan and the world to reinforce your cynicism; you begin to truly doubt that God has any permanent answers for change and purity.

In refreshing contrast, God's Word is full of optimism for overcoming the obstinate obsession of sexual lust. Hardly any group of Christians had better reason to be cynical than the recipients of

---

4. Thomas Brooks, *Precious Remedies against Satan's Devices* (1652; repr., Carlisle, PA: Banner of Truth, 1990), 102–3.

Peter's first epistle. After the burning of Rome, many Romans accused Emperor Nero of arson, believing that his zealousness to build a better city had propelled him to destroy many of the old shantytowns and slums that existed. To deflect their fury, Nero accused the Christians, an ideal group of people to blame: "The Scapegoats, however, were the Christians, whose withdrawal from the close-knit framework of pagan society had won them the animosity of the Roman mob."[5] Christians were despised both for their failure to join the Romans in their pagan festivals and for their close association with the Jews. Roman anger turned with fury on the Christians. Many died abominable deaths, and those left alive were forced to survive under the constant shadow of persecution and martyrdom. Yet Peter proceeded to give them positive counsel on how to deal with lustful temptations.

These Christians had to fight not only their own fleshly lust for sexual gratification (and all the associated sexual enticements that a cosmopolitan city like Rome brought with it) but also the powerful incentive for taking part in pagan promiscuity. For if they did not participate in the pagan festivals, along with the use of temple prostitutes who were associated with emperor worship, they would be accused of treason, convicted, and sentenced to death. Therefore, if the underpinnings of the idolatrous fear of man resided in their hearts, they would yield to the social pressure and give vent to their lustful ways. Fear and self-doubt became the true enemies of Christians in the Roman Empire.

Within this cauldron of trouble, the apostle Peter instructed the Christians by using the suffering of Jesus Christ as their encouragement. He admonished them to adopt the attitude of a soldier going to war: "Since therefore Christ suffered in the flesh, arm yourselves with the same way of thinking, for whoever has suffered in the flesh has ceased from sin" (1 Peter 4:1). The perfect tense of the term *ceased* (πέπαυται, perfect, middle, indicative) points to death. What is the worst that can happen to the Christian undergoing unjust suffering?

---

5. *The Zondervan Pictorial Encyclopedia of the Bible*, ed. Merrill C. Tenney and Steven Barabas (Grand Rapids: Zondervan, 1975), 4:411.

The answer is death. Once death is realized, the struggle with lustful sin has once and for all ceased. The worst weapon of the enemy is death. Ironically, death is a weapon that actually helps the believer rid himself of lustful sin. Death is not to be dreaded, because it marks liberation from the body of sin with all its lustful weaknesses (Rom. 7:5, 18; 8:8; 1 Cor. 15:42, 49).

However, Peter is not suggesting that Christians who are struggling with lustful sins should go out and get killed or even commit suicide to achieve their goal.[6] How, then, does a Christian continue to deal with lustful passions in the context of a world that will do all it can to drag him into its depravity? If his goal is to be completely rid of lust, and he knows this will be achieved at death, then it stands to reason he will spend the rest of his days with the determined attitude of a soldier seeking to live according to God's righteous standards. Peter says Christians facing the temptation of sexual sin, being fueled by fear of rejection and persecution, ought

> to live for the rest of the time in the flesh no longer for human passions but for the will of God. For the time that is past suffices for doing what the Gentiles want to do, living in sensuality, passions, drunkenness, orgies, drinking parties, and lawless idolatry. (1 Peter 4:2–3)

No longer living "in the flesh" parallels the idea of living "for the will of God." The word *suffices* means "sufficient" (ἀρκετός). Far too much time has gone by for these Christians to give in to their fears and follow lustful pagan practices. The meanings of each of the words associated with these emperor-worship festivals are significant:

- *Sensuality* (ἀσέλγεια) refers to unbridled and unrestrained living that usually involves sex.

---

6. Some Christians, burdened with guilt, have seriously thought of suicide to bring to an end their fierce battle with lust. Severe hopelessness and depression can set in for the believer who fails to find the answers he needs to bring about real change.

- *Passions* (ἐπιθυμία) is a general term for desires or passions, including sexual deeds in its somatic range.
- *Drunkenness* (οἰνοφλυγία) is used to refer to habitual drunkards.
- *Orgies* (κῶμος) are reveling through swaying and singing songs while drunk; *drinking parties* (πότος) are designed for the consumption of alcohol.
- *Lawless idolatries* (ἀθέμιτος εἰδωλολατρία) are the lawless worship of idols.

Fear of persecution, as well as the familiarity and comfort of their previous sinful practices as unbelievers, provided a temptation that was hard for these new Christians to resist. These well-intentioned believers were showing signs of returning to these drunken sex parties, which would be equivalent to accommodating idolatry. They would be surrendering not only to the worship of the emperor but to the worship of their own covetous desires.

HUNTING DOWN *ALL* YOUR IDOLS

This is a clear example of one important factor to consider in identifying and repenting of the idols of your heart: more than one idol may be operative at the same time. To stop searching for idols after discovering one that is ruling you could be counterproductive. What if you identify that one idol, and through repentance and faithfulness try to escape from your sexual enslavement, only to find that you are still entrapped by other less obvious yet powerful idols? You will likely despair when you repeatedly fail to put off your sexual sins. While it is true that for some there truly is only one idol, be diligent to prove this true in your case.

Multiple idols intensify the temptation. In the case of the persecuted Christians that Peter was teaching and encouraging, a combination of drunkenness, sexual gratification, and fear operated in their hearts, making the temptation to return to these pagan festivals real and powerful. In a previous chapter, this was illustrated in counselee Frederick's idols, which included anger and a desire for comfort and pleasure. The human heart is convoluted and cunning. Assuming that only one idol feeds your sexual problems is unwise. You must constantly be asking yourself, "What is feeding my sexual thoughts and behavior? What is it I crave the most in my sexual sin preference?" For example, when alcohol is mixed with sexual promiscuity, as it often is, your question should be, "What common desires of the heart are these two indulgences satisfying?"

For instance, a woman may fantasize about a relationship with a man other than her husband because she is attracted to his affirming ways. She enjoys his flattery. At the same time, she may daydream about an erotic affair with the same man as an escape from the monotony of the life she leads. Depending on the circumstance, she may call up the idol of either flattery or self-reward to find some type of satisfaction for which her adulterous heart hungers.

In a similar manner, a man may seek a means of sexual escape with his imaginary lover because he is angry with his wife over her lack of sexual interest. Furthermore, he also believes he deserves a bit of voyeurism given the fact that he works so hard with a demanding job and busy schedule. Added to these, since his wife is not very appreciative of his leadership and financial provision, his imaginary lover showers him with plenty of praise. This is a welcome relief from his demanding job and the unthankful wife to whom he comes home. In this man's heart, three idolatrous desires are collaborating to motivate his erotic indulgences. His heart wants to gratify the rage of anger, the hunger for praise, and the demand of self-reward.

Robert was a young man who was teased mercilessly during his boyhood and accused of being a homosexual because of his size and seemingly effeminate ways. During these early years of his life he was embarrassed and did his best to act like the other boys, but to no avail. No matter what he did, he could never please the guys whom he wanted as friends. His embarrassment in the long run turned to anger, and he gave up trying to please them. He became convinced that he was obviously an outcast and would never lose that status among his peers. He began to go on the offensive at school, defending the homosexuals who had become his only friends.

Yet for several years the thought of sex with another guy disgusted him; he was attracted only to girls. Despite this, and largely because of his outcast status, girls did not want to have much to do with him, and he found himself hanging around the "gay" group even more. This was when he began to entertain the subtle idea that maybe he was gay. At first, the idea was revolting; but as time went along he realized a certain platonic attraction to these guys who seemed to care for him more than anyone else did. Then, during an evening at the home of one of his gay friends, he got turned on to another guy, and he "explored" his new sexuality.

In this case study, Robert's desire to have people like and accept him is not sinful or idolatrous. This desire became sinful only when he was willing to allow it to become the central driving motivation of his life. In fact, when he did not receive the praise or acceptance of his peers, a deep anger—which could not be denied—formed in his heart. It drove him toward the "gay" gang, who gave him what he wanted— full nonjudgmental acceptance. He felt a close companionship with them. They were kind to him, and he did not feel the anger toward them that he did with the others. Layered on his desire for acceptance was a self-justified anger, both because of the rejection from his other male friends and the romantic rejection of the girls. This was the first time he had felt his anger directly connected to his sexual desires. When his romantic overtures to the girls were repeatedly rebuffed, he began to gradually lose interest in female attention. The realization that they did not want him stifled his sexual desires for any female, and a general distaste grew into anger toward the whole lot of them. When he came to counseling for help, his presentation problem was one of homosexual thoughts and tendencies that plagued him. He was disturbed because he caught himself lusting after other guys, and he confessed he even acted out his erotic imaginations at a recent party.

Robert's problem with homosexuality stems from a host of idolatrous desires that have been forming in his heart over the years. Initially, there was a desire for people's praise and approval, which he never addressed biblically. Then there was the anger toward the guys whom he wanted as friends and later the girls he wanted as girlfriends. When his sexual advances received constant rejection from females, he turned toward a rethinking of his own sexual identity. For the guys to reject him was one thing, but when the girls rejected his positive heterosexual overtures, his anger intensified. He desperately wanted the hurt from this rejection to be healed, and he wanted some type of outlet for his growing sexual desires. Since society rejected his attempts at heterosexual relationships, there was only one way that his sexual passions could be gratified—through homosexual relationships. This new idolatrous desire was fed by his anger and desire for people to accept him.

When confronting sexual lust, you must recognize the presence of multiple gods of desire that may lead to both the conception and feeding of sexual sin (see fig. 8.1). These gods of desire in the heart are not always initially or directly connected to sex and the driving hunger of sexual hormones, but they do serve to underlie, support, and nourish their sexual expressions.

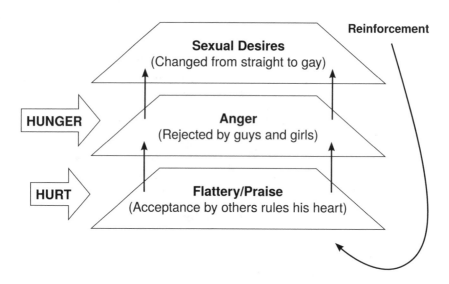

Fig. 8.1. Layered Reinforcement of Sexual Desires

To properly identify and interpret the lustful tendencies of your depraved heart, you must realize that your heart is a fertile womb, capable of multiple conceptions. The lustful heart not only contains a variety of idolatrous desires but greedily manufactures *more* idolatrous desires. Covetousness is at the core of its prolific depravity, and as long as you live life in the flesh, your sinful heart will fabricate and refine these desires. The Mosaic law confronts this covetous nature of sexual sin not once, but twice. "You shall not covet your neighbor's wife" (Ex. 20:17; Deut. 5:21). The apostle Paul attests to the reality that covetousness is involved with sexual lust when he warns the Ephesian Christians, "But *sexual immorality* and all impurity or *covetousness* must not even be named among you, as is proper among saints" (Eph. 5:3). To the Colossian church, Paul reinforces the concept of covetous sexual lust: "Put to death therefore what is earthly in you: *sexual immorality*, impurity, passion, evil desire, and *covetousness*, which is idolatry" (Col. 3:5).

The compounding problem of covetousness is this: a strong presumption of your own importance fills your covetous heart with demanding drives that seek sexual gratification. John Calvin exposes the covetous pride of the heart of man when he says, "But there is no one who does not cherish within himself some opinion of his own preeminence. Thus, each individual, by flattering himself, bears a kind of kingdom in his breast."[7] Calvin sees pride's greedy expectations as the mother of everything in the heart that rebels against God; she will coddle and nurse all sexual sins until they have established a ruling kingdom there. Unholy sexual desires often set up a kingdom in the heart that becomes the domain of idolatry.

Pride cultivates a sense of self-deserving expectation. It indulges the heart, which both hungers and hurts. As the heart hungers, it is prone to crave

- the praise of others (flattery),
- the possessiveness of others (control/power over),
- the prize of others (self-reward), and
- the pleasure of others (comfort).

7. John Calvin, *Institutes of the Christian Religion*, ed. John T. McNeill, trans. Ford Lewis Battles (Philadelphia: Westminster Press, 1960), 1:694.

The heart's self-deserving disposition makes it prone to avenge hurt as well. Therefore, it will crave solace for

- its fury at others (anger),
- the failure of others (self-pity),
- its fright of others (fear), and
- its familiarity of others (discontentment).

All these cravings have the potential to enslave a person to many different types of sins, especially the lustful sins of sex.

Calvin indicates the starting point for a remedy: "For when the Scripture bids us leave off self-concern, it not only erases from our minds the yearning to possess, the desire for power, and the favor of men, but it also uproots ambition and all craving for human glory and other more secret plagues."[8] The beginning point for dealing with your heart's ruling kingdom of lust does not involve Prozac or "power encounters" but rather the power of Scripture to overturn the reign of lust in your heart.

HEART CHANGE BEGINS AND CONTINUES WITH THE GOSPEL OF JESUS CHRIST

THE GOSPEL OF GRACE IN YOUR SALVATION

How does Scripture change your covetous heart that yearns for sexual gratification? All real change begins and ends with the gospel of Jesus Christ. As Jay Adams states, "The Christian counselor is to minister God's Word in a life-transforming way, such that God himself changes the counselee—from the heart outward. The counselor's is a ministry not of reformation but of the gospel, which is always a ministry of transformation. The change that he seeks must be substantial, in which God brings the counselee closer to himself."[9]

8. Ibid., 691.
9. Jay E. Adams, *How to Help People Change: The Four-Step Biblical Process* (Grand Rapids: Zondervan, 1986), 7.

The gospel is intended to be not only a message of salvation to the unbeliever but also an ongoing message of change for the believer. If the gospel of grace is the answer for the unbeliever who belongs to the first Adam, then it is also the answer for the believer who belongs to the second Adam (Christ) and finds himself still struggling with sinful cravings of the first Adam. Specifically, how does the gospel help the person who is in bondage to sexual cravings and practices?

THE GOSPEL OF BIBLICAL MOTIVATION

Interpreting the heart enslaved to sexual sin means that you must put into practice a biblical theology of motivation. People approach motivational desires in many ways; most of them are not God's way. In teaching this truth, Dr. David Powlison asked a series of questions that serve to address the various explanations for heart motivation:

> Why do people do what they do? Is it the alignment of the planets? Are people genetically hardwired towards aggression or depression? Is it uncontrollable raging hormones? Maybe their instinctual psychic impulses collide with the demands of society? Is it possible the behaviorists are right—your drives toward anti-social behavior have been rewarded with enough positive stimuli to cause you to continue to act the way you do? Is it possible that you have become fixated somewhere on the hierarchy of needs and you are conditioned to be obsessed with that one thing? Are you compensating for some perceived inferiority complex? Or could it be a demon of Addiction that has invaded a crevice of your personality? Maybe it is your personality—you are melancholic, sanguine, or phlegmatic, and you foresee no way of changing? Why do people do, think or form the attitudes they do?[10]

These suggested theories represent the world's feeble attempts to address the problem of motivation without taking seriously the desperate depravity of the human heart.

---

10. Dave Powlison, *Dynamics of Biblical Change Class Notebook* (Glenside, PA: Westminster Campus Bookstore special printing, 1997), 34.

Previously, it was demonstrated that James, in his epistle, identifies the central problem of the believer to be sinful lusts (i.e., cravings, desires, and longings) within the heart. The heart longs for many things it should not. This longing comes from the covetous desires that are at its core. The heart of man hungers for what it does not have, while selfishly believing it deserves it; and it hurts when it lacks something believed to be wrongfully denied. Self-gratification produces all these idolatrous longings, and they, in turn, fuel sexual sins as a means to satisfy the cravings or soothe the hurts.

THE GOSPEL AS A REVEALER OF HIDDEN SIN

Like many other sins, sexual sins have both private and public aspects. King David spoke of two broad categories of sin in his prayer: "Who can discern his errors? Declare me innocent from hidden faults. Keep back your servant also from presumptuous sins; let them not have dominion over me! Then I shall be blameless, and innocent of great transgression" (Ps. 19:12–13). The "hidden faults" were sins he committed of which he was not aware. "Presumptuous sins" were willful, deliberate sins (both private and public). You must be aware of both private and public sins in dealing with lust. Selfish sex is a good example of the former hidden sin, and adultery is a good example of the latter.

In this prayer it is also obvious that David did not believe man was capable of changing his own heart—"declare me innocent . . . . let them not have dominion over me." Only God can transform the sinful heart (Ps. 51:10). The author of Ecclesiastes adds a warning concerning these two types of sin at the conclusion of his book: "For God will bring every deed into judgment, with every secret thing, whether good or evil" (Eccl. 12:14).

Whatever the sexual sin, whether open or hidden, cravings that rule the heart both change and evade, maneuvering in and out of hiding. Figure 8.2 illustrates how these sexual desires and deeds orbit around the heart of greed with a cagey dynamic that can elude both counselee and counselor.

The shifting dynamic of heart idols became apparent when Roger sought counseling. The scenario he unfolded to me had happened

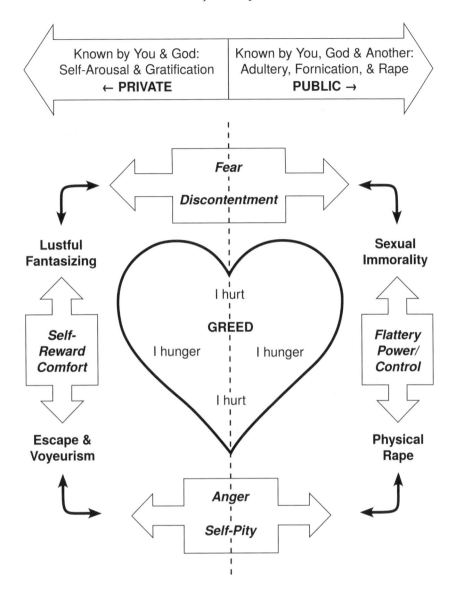

Fig. 8.2. The Evasive Dynamic of Heart Idolatry

more than once, and he was ready for help. Recently Roger experienced what you could call "bad" days: he yelled at his wife and subsequently felt guilty; he withdrew and became depressed; he masturbated and so got a late start, receiving a traffic ticket in his rush to be on time; he sat at work thoroughly frustrated and consequently did not get anything done; he left work early, purchasing a porn magazine on the way home, and finally arrived at his front door in a foul mood.

When Roger first came to counseling, he said he needed help with his "addiction to pornography." He confessed a rather vivid fantasy life and the fact that he had purchased several pornographic magazines recently. For the first time in his life, he was also struggling with the habit of masturbation. His guilty conscience led him to attempt to stop, but he could not.

What is wrong with Roger? Instructing him that his mind is like a computer (the old "GIGO" illustration—garbage in, garbage out)—is easy. He cannot expect his mind to be pure if he is regularly dumping sewage into it. Pinpointing his deception and the lies he has told his wife concerning his masturbation and money spent on porn would also be fairly straightforward. Several Scripture passages could be shown demonstrating that God expects Christians to be people of honesty and integrity. The problem of poor communication with his wife and his need to share the truth with her could be addressed. All these attempts, however, are reproving his behavior and not his heart.

The real question is, "What is ruling Roger?" When the counselor begins to think in terms of lustful themes in the heart, he then begins to see deeper heart problems that feed all the other behaviors. This is the beginning of heart hermeneutics. Roger was angry with his wife because she would not have sex with him that day, so he snapped at her before leaving for work. He withdrew and sulked in self-pity. Next, he decided that if she would not have sex with him that day, then, out of spite, he would take care of himself. So he masturbated. This made him late for work, and he raced down the freeway in order to make up for lost time. When he got the traffic ticket, Roger really became angry. Arriving at work late, he was reprimanded by his boss, which put him in a still worse mood for the day. His productivity for the day amounted to sitting at his desk and fuming.

Since everything that happened that day did nothing but displease him, Roger began looking for something that would be pleasurable and rewarding. When he left work, he stopped by a neighborhood park, browsed the magazines he had picked up, and found some more pornography on his smart phone. The females shown in these pictures served to create an imaginary harem in his mind. They were always erotic and inviting. They seemed to be beckoning to him personally—as though he were desirable and without any flaw. Unlike his wife, he could call for them any time he chose and they were right there, existing to respond to his every lustful whim.

What is ruling in Roger's heart? What idols have established a kingdom there? Masturbation and porn magazines are a problem, without a doubt, but they are the fruit of greater root issues of the heart. Roger is full of anger, self-pity, and a longing to be desired and satisfied. Roger has a "needy" heart because it is a "greedy" heart, not because others have not loved him. Roger loves himself so much that he is willing to do sinful, mean, God-dishonoring things to serve his idols. These idols are more important to him than God himself.

After three weeks of improvement in counseling, Roger's idolatry suddenly begins to cycle around the axis of greed. While Roger has learned about and repented of his anger, self-pity, and pleasure-seeking habits, he has begun to appear uncharacteristically anxious. Previously he had been quite sure of himself, full of self-confidence. Why would Roger succumb to timidity now? He had withdrawn from his wife before when she would not please him, but this was out of a vengeful anger to punish her, not out of fear.

Why was Roger now demonstrating fear? He was losing sales at work and showing signs of having panic attacks while driving on the freeway. Even though he had stopped his masturbation weeks before, he finally confessed that he was having impotency problems while trying to have sex with his wife. At first he thought it was a medical condition, so he went to his doctor for tests, but no physical problem was discovered. The longer this persisted, the greater his self-doubt grew. Loss of his masculine sexuality was draining his self-confidence.

This is where the counselor reminds himself that the human heart is convoluted and cunning. To assume that idols that have been identified and repented of are the *only* idols of Roger's heart is short-sighted. You must constantly be asking yourself, "What is feeding my counselee's sexual thoughts and behavior?" By using probing questions about Roger's thought life, other idolatrous cravings came to the surface.

Roger still harbored an elaborate imaginary harem of beautiful women in his mind whom he would use for personal arousal. He was beginning to understand this to be as much a sin of adultery as physically committing sexual sin with someone other than his wife (Job 31:9–12; Prov. 6:25; Matt. 5:27–28). As he repented, he was learning to focus his desires on his wife alone. But in doing so, he could not avoid her imperfections—being slightly overweight with a few unattractive moles and age spots. He was becoming fearful that she would never be attractive to him. He could not fake arousal without resorting to imagining the perfect women in his mind. Roger wanted to do right, but he found that his mind and body rebelled. For him to have sex without envisioning his virtual harem proved to be a battle that he was losing.

Furthermore, Roger always viewed himself as rather virile—a ladies' man. He never conceived that he could have any problems pleasing a woman. Now his inability to fulfill his manly duty was bothering him much more than it was bothering his wife. She loved the fact that he was more romantic now—more interested. But Roger was distressed, believing he was losing his masculinity. Fear had set up shop in his heart. The idols had changed, but the source was the same.

GOSPEL TRANSFORMATION IS GIVEN TO THE HUMBLE OF HEART

Even though his certainty had waned, Roger showed he still had strong confidence in his own ability to perform. In the attempt to abolish his former idols, he resorted to yet another idol as his confidence led him to presume that he could transform his own heart. Roger determined that *he* was going to maintain power and control over the change process. Though he was failing to perform sexually with his wife, he was convinced in his own ability to succeed. Roger thought he could please his wife. He thought he could please the counselor. He thought he could please God. He believed he could do it alone, yet he was failing miserably. For a while, he even tried masculine performance drugs, but these did not change his heart.

Roger had not seriously sought the help of God to bring about his change. Biblical transformation, which is true and lasting, begins by acknowledging our inability to please God. King David clearly realized this, as we saw earlier in Psalm 19:12–13 and also in Psalm 51:10, in which David cries out, "Create in me a clean heart, O God, and renew a right spirit within me." The apostle Paul relates a similar, agonizing struggle with sin in Romans 7:7–24. But he quickly reveals the transforming power of God in Christ: "For God has done what the law, weakened by the flesh, could not do. By sending his own Son in the likeness of sinful flesh and for sin, he condemned sin in the flesh, in order that the righteous requirement of the law might be fulfilled in us, who walk not according to the flesh but according to the Spirit" (Rom. 8:3–4).

While it is true that Roger had to do his part in the work of sanctification, he was failing because his work was fully vested in self-effort, implying that he had everything within himself to please God. To him, Jesus Christ was unnecessary to his struggle with lust. Roger could not articulate the role that Christ had in his transformation process because, in his mind, he had no essential role. Roger, like many other Christians, was missing a key component of sanctification.

We are told to "work out your own salvation with fear and trembling, for it is God who works in you, both to will and to work for his good pleasure" (Phil. 2:12–13). Roger was missing the "fear and trembling." In thinking he could handle his problem through his own efforts—believing he could change through self-righteous performance—he lacked the humility necessary for biblical change to occur. "Fear and trembling" represents the sinning Christian's attitude because he knows he cannot change on his own; therefore, he comes humbly to God in fear and trembling for the transformation that only he can give.

Roger had good news coming. If he were willing to see his idolatrous reliance on his own ability to control the outcome and repent of it, he would then begin to experience the blessing of God in his endeavors. Here is the good news for those pursuing biblical sanctification: "But he gives more grace [greater than Roger's lust and self-help ability]. Therefore it says, 'God opposes the proud, but gives grace to the humble'" (James 4:6). As Roger began to see and repent of his idol of control and self-confidence, God was introducing holy fear into his life and an utter reliance on him—quite a new experience for Roger. He was slowly coming to the end of himself. His self-confidence was eroding, and a genuine humbleness was taking its place.

But what if he fails again? For a time that may be the case. This is where the forgiveness of sins found in Christ comes in.[11] Ed Welch speaks well to this:

> Because an understanding of God's forgiving grace is so crucial to growth and change, you may find that this will be a fierce battleground. The fear of the Lord does not come naturally. It is here that Satan may want dominion, because if one-time addicts fail to grasp complete forgiveness, they can easily fall into despair and look to drugs as a temporary savior.[12]

Likewise, Roger may convince himself that his anxiety and panic attacks are organic (medical) rather than spiritual. However, if he trusts in the forgiveness of Christ, he will not resort to some psychotropic drug to relieve the symptoms. Undoubtedly, taking a drug might provide some help for Roger to regain personal control in overcoming his sexual problems. But if he relies on the medication rather than relying on Christ, he will never understand the power of God's grace, nor will he understand the importance of Jesus Christ in overcoming sexual bondage.

GOSPEL APPLICATION BRINGS DEATH TO SELF

For Roger to be released from this enslavement, something has to die. Death always precedes freedom. Just as in ancient times when a family slave often had to die to be released from his slavery, so Roger must die. He must die to himself. The Christian's union with Christ is so complete that everything that happened to him happens to us.

---

11. Ex. 34:7; Ps. 130:3–4; Col. 1:14; Heb. 10:18; 1 John 2:12.

12. Ed Welch, *Addictions: A Banquet in the Grave* (Phillipsburg, NJ: P&R Publishing, 2001), 169.

Paul explained it this way: "We know that our old self was crucified with him in order that the body of sin might be brought to nothing, so that we would no longer be enslaved to sin. . . . But now that you have been set free from sin and have become slaves of God, the fruit you get leads to sanctification and its end, eternal life" (Rom. 6:6, 22). When Roger dies to self in his heart, he will find the beginning of progressive sanctification.

Unregenerate men may acknowledge the miserable consequences of life-dominating lust, but no serious desire or ability to change will form without complete self-denial. Since unbelievers have only an "earthly nature" and not a "new nature," they remain in a permanent state of enslavement. Roger was a believer, but he had been trying to deal with the lustful idols of his heart as an unbeliever would and thus was still stuck in his sinful ways. Once he humbled and denied himself and began to rely on Christ, he began to see the fruit of sanctification at work in him.

What about professing Christians who persist in sin after knowing the truth? You will never be able to die to self—which is the key to being freed from enslavement—if you are making a continual practice of sin (Matt. 24:13; Heb. 3:14; 1 John 3:9). Your habitual sinning calls into question your faith; if you are not born of God, you will never be able to die to self. John Murray comments, "To say to the slave who has not been emancipated, 'Do not behave as a slave' is to mock his enslavement. But to say the same to the slave who has been set free is the necessary appeal to put into effect the privileges and rights of his liberation."[13] The Christian who has died with Christ can daily die to self and live in the freedom that righteousness brings (Matt. 16:24–25). Such freedom is a result of the grace found in Christ Jesus.

In summary, interpreting the idolatrous cravings of unholy lust in the counselee is difficult because the heart is so active and evasive. You must use hermeneutics that search for heart themes and sources,

---

13. John Murray, *The Epistle to the Romans*, New International Commentary on the New Testament (Grand Rapids: Eerdmans, 1968), 1:213; quoted in Jerry Bridges, *The Discipline of Grace* (Colorado Springs, CO: NavPress, 1994), 74.

relationships and commonality, loves and hates between its various sexual manifestations. Sexual lust is so elusive and unlike other sinful cravings like drunkenness because of its stealthy capacity to minimize outward consequences. You must use theological insight to discern the important themes from the more pressing and immediate expression. But for you who desire real transformation, the Word of God and the gospel is key. You must go to battle against sexual lust with the attitude of a soldier—but a soldier who recognizes his own inability to secure a victory. As a soldier, you must be willing to die to self to gain final freedom from sexual slavery. Only then will you realize the transforming grace of Jesus Christ that will bring the final conquest. In the meantime, you are in this battle, waging war against the flesh on the battlefield of the heart. The war is tough because the enemy is often varied, layered, and constantly reproducing. The enemy also knows the territory.

Paul entreats those who minister the Word of God to Christians with serious problems: "And we urge you, brothers, admonish the idle, encourage the fainthearted, help the weak, be patient with them all" (1 Thess. 5:14). The heart ruled by sexual lust must be ministered to in such a faithful and determined way that the Holy Spirit may use the gospel to transform the enslaved person by the power of God. This is the beginning of lasting change from stubborn and enslaving sexual sins.

KEY CONCEPTS

biblical heart hermeneutics
resistant heart
hope for purity
permanent answers for change
sensuality
passions
drunkenness
orgies
lawless idolatries
multiple idols

nonjudgmental acceptance
homosexuality
greed produces multiple idols
presumption of your own importance
biblical theology of motivation
private sins
fear and trembling
grace for the humble
death to self

STUDY QUESTIONS

1. What does the author mean by the statement, "Purity starts with biblical heart hermeneutics?"
2. The Christian who believes that there is no hope, that he will never be freed from his sexual enslavement, is making a statement about God. What is he saying about God? What Scriptures would you give him to show him the true nature of God?
3. "This futility comes from following the cursed feelings of the flesh." Discuss how living by strong impulses and overwhelming feelings can produce despair in the heart of the Christian. See Ecclesiastes 2:1–11.
4. "In this case study, Robert's desire to have people like and accept him is not sinful or idolatrous. This desire becomes sinful only when he was willing to allow it to become the central driving motivation of his life." Discuss how a simple desire to be liked by others turns into a sinful motivation. What does this say about a person's thought life—what and whom are they thinking about continually? What does this say about a person's devotion to Jesus Christ? How does this sinful motivation then turn into outward acts of sin?
5. Read Genesis 15:1–16:3. Describe how Abram moved from the desire for a son; to a sinful, controlling desire for a son; to sexual sin. Although we do not know what Abram was

thinking, use this passage as a case study to contemplate the various thought processes and feelings that Abram might have had—leading him to produce a child in a way that God had not established as right and good.

6. Explain what pride has to do with coveting.

7. "Instructing [Roger] that his mind is like a computer (the old 'GIGO' illustration—garbage in, garbage out)—is easy. He cannot expect his mind to be pure if he is regularly dumping sewage into it." Many Christians function with the assumption that as long as they keep their environment pure, they will have no problem with lust. These well-intentioned Christians do everything they can to keep evil out. Examples of their behavior include not going to public beaches, not driving on the boulevards where pornographic billboards are known to be displayed, and having no TV in their homes. While all these things are helpful and good, what crucial element of purity does this approach overlook? What happens in the heart of the person who successfully keeps all these evil influences away from him? Who does he become like?

8. Explain how the unpopular concepts of humility and death to self are in fact some of the strongest weapons that the believer has in fighting lust.

FOR FURTHER READING

Adams, Jay E. *How to Help People Change: The Four-Step Biblical Process*. Grand Rapids: Zondervan, 1986.

Ganschow, Julie, and Bruce Roeder. *The Process of Biblical Heart Change*. Kansas City, MO: Pure Water Press, 2013.

Lane, Timothy S., and Paul David Tripp. *How People Change*. Greensboro, NC: New Growth Press, 2008.

Murray, Andrew. *Humility: The Beauty of Holiness*. Pensacola, FL: Chapel Library, n.d.

Scott, Stuart. *From Pride to Humility*. Bemidji, MN: Focus Publishing, 2002.

9

THE SOURCES OF PURITY FOR THE PURE HEART

"My marriage is falling apart because of my sexual obsessions, and I need help," was Charles's desperate cry. "I need direction— real answers—and I need them now!" Sexual lust had so enslaved this man with rousing fantasies that he would peruse pornographic pictures while driving his car. He often stayed up all hours of the night surfing the internet. Sometimes he would slip away from church during the Sunday school hour to visit a magazine stand at the nearby shopping mall. In one counseling session, his wife complained that his mind seemed to be somewhere else when they were making love together.

What is the approach needed to purify Charles's heart and the behavior of this self-destructive obsession? This man is unquestionably in need of counsel to preserve his marriage. Will counsel from the local psychologist or psychiatrist help to lessen this man's sexual struggles? They may attempt to repair his marriage conflicts, but they would not view his pornographic practices as a serious problem. Unfortunately, pornographic material, whether real or imagined, is viewed as a healthy thing to most counseling professionals. In fact, the pornographic industry has a huge interest in influencing secular psychology's view of it as an innocent indulgence.

The American Psychiatric Association (APA) does not recognize sexual addiction as a disorder or a serious mental health problem, as observed by David Ley: "The American Psychiatric Association is updating their 'Bible' of diagnostic categories of mental health. Yet again, the sex addiction industry has been clamoring for creation of a disorder to support their work. And yet again, the APA has turned them down flat."[1] Apparently, the pornographic industry is far more influential than the sex addiction industry. As a biblical counselor, I would agree with the APA on one point: sexual addiction is not a mental illness. It is much worse—a serious sinful habituation that destroys lives and relationships.

Labeling chronic sexual indulgences outside of a monogamous heterosexual marriage as a serious disorder has been controversial since the 1980s. The APA usually will not recommend getting involved in counseling such a man unless his obsession becomes sociopathic.[2] When it does, the man is often labeled with obsessive-compulsive disorder (OCD), an underlying sexual disorder attributed to anxiety, or the more specific disorder, compulsive sexual behavior (CSB). These diagnoses care little for the purity of the individual's personal thought life unless it causes mental instability that adversely affects personal stability and/or the person's interpersonal relationships.

Some Christian psychologists will apply biblical passages like Matthew 5:28 in their counseling. "But I say to you that everyone who looks at a woman with lustful intent has already committed adultery with her in his heart." These counselors are much more likely to counsel the sexually enslaved person. Sadly, however, the focus of their counseling is not on the gospel and its solutions but on behavioral morality and ethics, with a combination of cognitive behavioral therapies. According to these well-intentioned counselors, to be competent to counsel the sexually "addicted," you must possess special psychological training. Two Christian psychologists explain,

1. David J. Ley, "Sex Addiction: Rejected Yet Again by the APA," *Psychology Today*, December 5, 2012, https://www.psychologytoday.com/intl/blog/women-who-stray /201212/sex-addiction-rejected-yet-again-apa.

2. This is an individual with a so-called personality disorder who demonstrates little or no regard for the laws, rules, ethics, and morals of society or for the rights of other individuals in that society.

"Competent sexual treatment includes both ethical and clinical dimensions. . . . Clinical sexual treatment includes proper training in sexual therapy, including earning specialized certification for some."[3] What is lacking here is the requirement for biblical training. These counselors do not believe the Bible is sufficiently exhaustive to deal with serious sexual compulsions.

Furthermore, most of these therapies are situation-determinative in their interpretation of causality. Psychology-based counselors, whether Christians or not, turn the sexually obsessed individual into a victim of past psychological trauma, which they see as the driving source of the subconscious for uncontrollable, erotic imagination. They are convinced that only a trained psychotherapist can peel back the layers of consciousness to uncover the "out-of-awareness mind" (subconscious) and bring its deep and disturbing thoughts to the surface in order to deal with them, which will require years of therapy.

Those who advocate clinical sex therapy believe that lustful thoughts and behaviors come from an internal struggle for intimacy. According to them, the source of lust is the individual's internal pain of alienation, loneliness, or poor self-image. Counselees who encounter this type of therapy will be led to adopt something like the following typical explanation for their sexual obsession: "My parents did not raise me with the proper love I should have had, and this has caused me to adopt destructive sexual attitudes and behaviors. It has damaged my love for myself, so I tend to avoid real intimacy and seek superficial relationships in my life, real or imaginative, that will keep me from getting close to others. Pornography and masturbation are not harmful; they are just helping me fulfill my need for intimacy."

Indeed, many of these individuals have suffered great abuses at the hands of others, and their memories of those are haunting. They have been caught up in the sinful tendency of the human heart to compensate for the past by indulging in the present. But God's Word is clear. People do not commit sexual sins because they fundamentally believe

3. George Ohlschlager and Peter Mosgogian, "Sex Therapy in the Body," *Christian Counseling Today* (Summer 1994): 13.

they are unworthy. Although they may have suffered greatly at the hands of others, they do not practice incest, voyeurism, exhibitionism, homosexuality, molestation, and rape out of a poor view of self. Nor do they become obsessed with pornography, fantasizing, and mastur- bation because they have low self-esteem. Christians do not disobey God out of a low view of self; they disobey God out of a high view of self. A false view of causation disseminated among the suffering does not give hope or God's answers to their difficulties, because it is not based in the truth.

Another common practice among psychology-based counselors is a referral to twelve-step programs such as Sex Addicts Anonymous. This is an international program built on the highly publicized Alcoholics Anonymous founded by Bill Wilson and Bob Smith.[4] In these pro- grams, the goal is to get a person out from under his "addictive" compulsions (e.g., alcohol, drugs, sex). The purpose is to stop the destructive behaviors. They even acknowledge a "god" in the process. This understanding of God was a compromise to avoid offending alcoholics who came into the program angry at God.

> Although the first AA workers themselves knew God intimately, they felt that in some way they had to sidestep this bitterness toward God by using the phrase "God as I understand him" in their now famous twelve steps. Their intention was to focus on the need for outside help. . . . Eating disorders (for example, anorexia, bulimia), sex addiction, rageaholism, workaholism, the compulsion to spend and spend, and extremely rigid and legalistic approach to living, the compulsion to wash one's hands fifty-five times a day—these and other addictions have been placed in the same class as alcoholism.[5]

In the program for so-called sexaholics, God is reduced to whatever you would like him to be. One man said, "My god is a light bulb."

4. *Pass It On: The Story of Bill Wilson and How the A.A. Message Reached the World* (New York: Alcoholics Anonymous World Services, 1984).
5. Robert Hemfelt, Frank Minirth, and Paul Meier, *Love Is a Choice* (Nashville, TN: Thomas Nelson, 1989), 12–13.

Another said, "Mine is a shoe." As long as you believe in a higher power, you are supposed to be able to progress toward the goal of sobriety or freedom from sexual compulsions.

These twelve-step programs ignore the God of Scripture and replace him with idolatry. For most participants, their sin is not really sin—it is simply an unwanted disease. Furthermore, they have latched on to the false teaching that self-hate and repressed memories are the root of all compulsive behaviors. A lustful person may enter into one of these twelve-step programs an angry, hedonistic, controlling sexaholic, and what happens? He comes out just as angry, hedonistic, and controlling as he went in, but now he is free of the external manifestations of sexual bondage. He goes in an enslaved sinner; he comes out a self-righteous pharisee.

Is there a biblical answer for the impure heart? Is there a strategy for the right kind of purification? Absolutely! Obsessions and compulsions are not anything new to God or the Bible. The Bible not only speaks of sexual enslavement but also provides insight into the core issues of the human heart that generate and feed these problems. Charles, the married man mentioned at the beginning of the chapter, can find real answers to purify his sexual obsession if he and his counselor are willing to follow biblical insight into both the source and remedy for the problem. A fivefold strategy will aid you in purifying the heart of sexual compulsions and all its associated ruling motivations.

BECOME A DISCIPLE OF THE GOSPEL OF GRACE

CONFESSION AND REPENTANCE

Once you have determined the extent of the idolatrous motivations ruling your heart, confession and repentance are necessary (Ezek. 14:6–7; 1 John 1:8–10). In the same way you began the Christian life, you must submit to God in calling your thoughts, behaviors, and idolatrous cravings what they are: sin. That is confession. Then you must repent by transforming your mind so completely that it leads to a permanent change of life. Repentance puts a plan into action that will guarantee permanent change and inhibit any return to that sin while also facilitating righteousness. Repentance is needed to renounce the worship of idolatrous sexual cravings and all associated desires that have become your substitute gods. This is always the beginning of internal purification. Repentance proves confession as genuine.

Prior to his third visit to the church at Corinth, Paul wrote, "I fear that when I come again my God may humble me before you, and I may have to mourn over many of those who sinned earlier and have not repented of the impurity, sexual immorality, and sensuality that they have practiced" (2 Cor. 12:21). As a caring pastor, Paul was concerned that they had not properly dealt with their sensual ways through repentance. He used the perfect tense of the participle for the word *sinned* (προημαρτηκότων, perfect active participle), which indicates they had participated in their sexual sins and persisted in them during some past extended period of time. Then for the word *repented* (μετανοησάντων, aorist active participle) he used the aorist tense to contrast their lack of change. The perfect tense followed by the aorist says that if the Corinthians had repented in the past, they would have stopped their sexual compulsions immediately. But they had not repented.

Paul proceeds to use three terms that describe their sin, undoubtedly indicating the diversity and obsession of their sexual habits:

- *impurity* (ἀκαθαρσία), all types of sexual uncleanness that includes impure thoughts;
- *sexual immorality* (πορνεία), fornication or any type of illicit sexual deeds; and
- *sensuality* (ἀσέλγεια), unrestrained animal-like lust.

If Paul had arrived on this third occasion and still found them in bondage to these sexual cravings, it would have been a humbling disgrace to the gospel.

WEAKNESS AND HUMILITY

The Corinthian believers were showing a continual proclivity toward sexual sin. They should have repented and begun to change during Paul's previous two visits, but he was concerned that they were still unrepentant. By this time they were weak, pathetic, and enslaved to their sensuality. That is why Paul used his own personal illustration of weakness earlier in the same chapter. He had struggled firsthand with a great difficulty: "So to keep me from becoming conceited because of the surpassing greatness of the revelations, *a thorn was given me in the flesh, a messenger of Satan to harass me*" (2 Cor. 12:7). We are not told exactly what it was that tormented him. We do know that he prayed on three occasions for its removal, but God denied his request. Instead, God reassured him: "But he said to me, 'My grace is sufficient for you, for my power is made perfect in weakness.' Therefore I will boast all the more gladly of my weaknesses, so that the power of Christ may rest upon me" (2 Cor. 12:9). From this, Paul understood a great lesson of the Christian life—human weakness provides the occasion for a grand display of God's power in grace. In fact, the weakness he experienced was "to keep me from becoming conceited" (2 Cor. 12:7). Part of the reason so many enslaved people sense the powerful irresistibility of sex is to teach them the powerful enablement of the grace of God.

Through his struggle with this thorn in the flesh, Paul also learned to be "content with weaknesses" (2 Cor. 12:10). Why? Because, he says, "Therefore I will boast all the more gladly of my weaknesses, so that the power of Christ may rest upon me" (2 Cor. 12:9). He learned that his own abilities to overcome weaknesses were not only insufficient but excluded the power of Christ. This specific weakness—whatever it was—had caused him to see two things. First, it showed him the importance of humility—that God would go to such lengths to see that Paul would not become conceited. Second, it also showed him weakness—his inability to overcome it and therefore his need to rely on the power of Christ. As a Christian, Paul desired to live to God's glory, yet, when it came to dealing with his weaknesses, he was tempted to act as if his Lord was not necessary. Now that he understood that, as long as he did not resort to human means like Abraham and Sarah had (Gen. 16:1–16), Christ would be magnified in a greater way *through* his weakness. In this way, Paul had to die to self for the glory of Christ to be manifested in him.

FREEDOM FROM SIN'S DOMINION

But how is this particular weakness, this struggle with sexual sin, to be overcome? Taking a closer look at Romans 6:8–10 gives the answer: "Now if we have died with Christ, we believe that we will also live with him. We know that Christ, being raised from the dead, will never die again; death no longer has dominion over him. For the death he died he died to sin, once for all, but the life he lives he lives to God." What does Paul mean when he says that Christ died to sin and that Christians died with him? Here Paul is referring to the fact that sin's *absolute domination* has ended for the Christian, although not the occasional desire or practice of sin. Of all people, Christians do not need to be in bondage to sexual desires. Jerry Bridges elaborates on this vital distinction.

> But the believer who has died to sin's reign and dominion delights in God's law. The believer approves of it as holy, righteous, and good (Romans 7:12), even though he or she may struggle to obey it. We must distinguish between the activity of sin, which is true in all believers, and the dominion of sin, which is true of all unbelievers. . . . We succumb to temptations, either from our own evil desires (James 1:13), or from the world or the Devil (Ephesians 2:1–3). Further, to paraphrase from [Sinclair B.] Ferguson on John Owen, our sin is a burden that afflicts us rather than a pleasure that delights us.[6]

Genuine believers will not be content to continually practice sexual sin. They will come to view it as a menacing misery that imposes a cruel and unwelcome tyranny. But liberation from sin's powerful influence is possible for the Christian. It is not a false hope; it is a reality.

LIVING IN GRACE

Since this liberation from sin's dominion is accomplished through the grace of salvation, grace also continues to benefit the Christian in

6. Jerry Bridges, *The Discipline of Grace* (Colorado Springs, CO: NavPress, 1994), 70–71.

his ongoing struggle with sin. It serves an instructional and strengthening function—grace is the counselee's best trainer. Paul explains this to Titus:

> For the grace of God has appeared, bringing salvation for all people, *training us to renounce ungodliness and worldly passions, and to live self-controlled, upright, and godly* lives in the present age, waiting for our blessed hope, the appearing of the glory of our great God and Savior Jesus Christ, who gave himself for us to redeem us from all lawlessness and to purify for himself a people for his own possession who are zealous for good works. (Titus 2:11–14)

Grace does more than impart knowledge. It serves to train the believer in godly living. The original word for *training* (παιδεύουσα) means to prepare by discipline, which carries four connotations: instruction, correction, training, and encouragement. Like a good parent, grace will discipline its children to deny the wrong lifestyle (ungodliness) and cravings (worldly desires), and it will strengthen its children to lead godly (self-controlled, upright) lives. When you fail to submit to the discipline of grace, you will assume that sexual purity is attained through personal effort, stubborn willpower, and dutiful performance. But when you learn by grace, your heart is instructed about your sinful motivations, corrected through confession and repentance, trained through renouncing sinful habits, and encouraged in new righteous habits of life.

As a parent, I have seen the discipline of grace work in my own home. When one of our children would disobey, my wife would often bring the child to me. Just the process of bringing him to Dad was often sufficient for humbling him. But having been brought, that child would be required to confess what sin had been committed and seek my forgiveness, if necessary. Based on his knowledge of me as his father, the child knew some form of punishment was deserved and imminent, and he was often fearful (reverent, not terrified) of what was to follow.

On certain occasions that warranted it, I would be merciful and relent from giving a just chastisement. At those times, I would extend grace and give certain undeserved privileges. The effects of such grace soon became apparent. For the remainder of the day, that child lived in Dad's grace, and he knew it. It resulted in the most well-behaved child you could ever want to meet! "Dad, can I get you anything?" "Dad, is my music too loud?" "Dad, I want to help mom do the dishes tonight." My child was living in grace, and it had a profound, positive effect on his conduct.

Lust-filled Christians can easily forget that they live in grace. Your conscience informs you that you are caught in your sin, yet you have forgotten the grace of Scripture's instruction about sinful motivations. You have ignored grace's call to confession and repentance. Because of this, you remain enslaved to your passions, becoming dissatisfied and unhappy with your present sex life. Your unrepentant, covetous heart demands something more or different. Tragically, you have convinced yourself that you really deserve this sexual amusement. Your hungering or hurting heart motivated by sexual greed craves something it does not have—and believes it is worthy of such an indulgence. You do not see yourself as an undeserving, corrupt sinner that already possesses more than it deserves. Instead, you exalt yourself in your thinking, convinced that you can keep the demanding desires of sex under control. You think sexual compulsions are corralled and managed by your sheer grit and willpower. This is a huge part of your self-deception. Whether you believe it or not, you are flirting with something bigger than yourself. You also presume on the enabling grace of Jesus Christ that promises to continually strengthen you throughout your Christian life.

What is this discipline of grace? Living in the discipline of grace means that you understand that the atonement of Jesus Christ has provided for the forgiveness of all your sins and your unqualified acceptance before God the Father. It is the daily reminder that God's wrath and judgment for your sin is fully deserved but that these have been remitted because of the sacrifice of Christ. When you finally realize the enormity of your canceled debt before God and that you are living in his grace, this becomes a great motivating factor for cleansing and develops in you a growing hunger for righteousness. A human heart filled with rationalizations has forgotten the position of grace in which it lives. But good conduct is always a by-product of good doctrine. Dr. Jay E. Adams continues this thought about the importance of grace-enabled change:

> All the stress that the Bible puts upon human effort must not be misunderstood; we are talking about grace-motivated effort, not the work of the flesh. It is not effort apart from the Holy Spirit that produces godliness. Rather, it is through the power of the Holy Spirit alone that one can endure. Of his own effort, a man may persist in learning to skate, but he will not persist in the pursuit of godliness. A Christian does good works because the Spirit works in him.[7]

In addition, the daily provision of an abundant supply of enabling grace empowers you "to renounce ungodliness and worldly passions, and to live self-controlled, upright, and godly lives in the present age" (Titus 2:12). This verse teaches that grace not only corrects your ungodliness but also instructs your godliness. It teaches you the importance of putting off the idolatrous desires of lust and replacing them with holy desires.

CLEAN UP YOUR LIFE THOROUGHLY AND BIBLICALLY

HOLINESS

This may come as a surprise to you, but your goal is not improvement—it is *holiness*. This is true of any type of sin that Christians struggle with, but it is especially important for you to understand in your sexual enslavement. Perhaps you have been so drawn into the powerful allurement of your sins that you believe even a little improvement will bring great relief. But the will of God for you is holiness.

> For this is the will of God, your sanctification: that you abstain from sexual immorality; that each one of you know how to control his

---

7. Jay E. Adams, *The Christian Counselor's Manual* (Grand Rapids: Zondervan, 1986), 186.

own body in *holiness* and honor, not in the passion of lust like the Gentiles who do not know God; that no one transgress and wrong his brother in this matter, because the Lord is an avenger in all these things, as we told you beforehand and solemnly warned you. For God has not called us for impurity, but in *holiness*. Therefore whoever disregards this, disregards not man but God, who gives his Holy Spirit to you. (1 Thess. 4:3–8)

In the self-deceit of sexual slavery, you may find that you are guilty of setting less than biblical objectives—falling far short of holiness. These may include stopping the bad behavior, minimizing the consequences, placating family and friends, covering the shame, gaining relief from the pressure, blame-shifting the responsibility, getting by, coping, improving the marriage, and similar aims. None of these goals is sufficient or honoring to the Lord when your ultimate purpose is to remove sexual idolatry from your heart and install holiness in its place. J. C. Ryle explains it well:

Holiness is the habit of being of one mind with God, according as we find His mind described in Scripture. It is the habit of agreeing in God's judgement, hating what he hates, loving what he loves, and measuring everything in this world by the standard of His Word. He who most entirely agrees with God, he is the most holy man. . . . A holy man will follow after purity of heart. He will dread all filthiness and uncleanness of spirit, and seek to avoid all things that might draw him into it. He knows his own heart is like tinder, and will diligently keep clear of the sparks of temptation. Who shall dare to talk of strength when David can fall? There is many a hint to be gleaned from the ceremonial law. Under it the man who only touched a bone or a dead body or a grave or a diseased person became at once unclean in the sight of God. And these things were emblems and figures. Few Christians are ever too watchful and too particular about this point.[8]

8. J. C. Ryle, *Holiness: Its Nature, Hindrances, Difficulties, and Roots*, 7th ed. (Durham, England: Evangelical Press, 1993), 34, 36.

As formerly discussed, any impurities of the heart (anger, self-pity, discontentment, fear, self-reward, flattery, power/control, and comfort) are sufficient to cause it to spontaneously combust with the fire of passionate lust if they are permitted safe haven. When you are sincere and diligent in your pursuit of purity, you will purpose to cease sinning instead of purposing to sin less. "You shall be holy, for I am holy" (1 Peter 1:16; cf. Lev. 11:44; 19:2; 20:7).

Because interpreting your heart idols requires patience, skill, and plenty of brutally hard work, you must examine yourself fully to identify any previous ungodly compromises that have set up your heart for failure. King David made several significant compromises in his life before his sin of adultery with Bathsheba. He clearly violated most of the commands God had given Israel's kings (Deut. 17:16–17). A well-established pattern of sexual compromise existed long before he committed sexual sin with Bathsheba. It is imperative that you meticulously investigate the hidden corners of the heart in order to clean up any hint of unholy sexual desire.

KILL SIN

Paul describes the transformation process in the third chapter of Colossians. It starts with putting sin to death. "Put to death therefore what is earthly in you: sexual immorality, impurity, passion, evil desire, and covetousness, which is idolatry. On account of these the wrath of God is coming. In these you too once walked, when you were living in them" (Col. 3:5–7).

In these verses, Paul lumps "sexual immorality, impurity, passion, evil desire, and covetousness" into the heart category of idolatry. For these passions to set up a kingdom, reign in the heart, and replace the Lord God as functional king is a cinch. This does not mean that God ceases to be the King. By the legal rights of Christ's atoning death, he is the sole King of the Christian's heart, but during this earthly time of enslavement he may not be the operative king. In similar fashion, Absalom replaced his father David for a time and ruled as king in Jerusalem, even though David was the official king (2 Sam. 16:16–19). For a time, "sexual immorality, impurity, passion, evil desire, and covetousness," along with their associated rationales, may assert a commanding presence as the "functional gods" in your heart. Their lustful presence may even grow in power to habituate and enslave your mind and body. Surrendering to their cravings and demands seems like normal living to you, and denying their pressure may seem abnormal and impossible. Therefore, you become a devoted idolater, performing acts of worship every time you surrender to erotic passions and lustful desires.

Paul says to you, "Put to death therefore what is earthly in you" (Col. 3:5). Your body's faculties are no longer under the legal rule of lust's authority. People who desire to be freed from lust must go through a death process. Death demands everything. When you die, you give up everything—not just *what you own* but *who you are*. Conquering sexual idolatry and its cravings requires giving over everything. You will never conquer lust with partial obedience to Jesus Christ or a partial purification of heart idols. You must hand over your entire life to righteousness and permit self-gratifying lust to die.

This is not a grim call for perpetual self-abasement, like some Tibetan monk. Paul warned against that when he said,

> If with Christ you died to the elemental spirits of the world, why, as if you were still alive in the world, do you submit to regulations—"Do not handle, Do not taste, Do not touch" (referring to things that all perish as they are used)—according to human precepts and teachings? *These have indeed an appearance of wisdom in promoting self-made religion and asceticism and severity to the body, but they are of no value in stopping the indulgence of the flesh.* (Col. 2:20–23)

Merely refusing yourself these pleasures will never purify your lust, because self has not died. But when you truly die to self and "to the elemental spirits of the world," Paul affirms that this is the right kind of death: "For you have died, and your life is hidden with Christ in God" (Col. 3:3). Mere behavioral modification and strict self-discipline without a death experience will never bring complete purification.

There is another dimension to this death experience. As mentioned previously, a dead slave is no longer a slave. As Roman 6:6 says, your "old self was crucified with [Christ]." Your old self that was enslaved to sin has died. Freedom from the tyranny of that idol is achieved because of the death and resurrection of Jesus Christ. Nevertheless, understand this: even though the legal war is won, there may be intense daily skirmishes, which of necessity must take place. You must be willing to deny yourself and take up your cross daily—die to yourself *daily*—and follow Christ (Luke 9:23). Purification from lust requires nothing less.

You may think you have a reasonable objection: "If I have to daily fight lustful temptations, then the fact that I am legally free in Christ means nothing to me in my struggle!" In this you are seriously mistaken. It means everything! If someone stole your car and drove it to his house to keep it, suddenly the legal issue of ownership becomes important to you. You are not in control of your car; the thief controls it, but you own it. In fact, you have the full weight of the law behind you to recover it. So you call the police and show them the title, and they go with you to pick up the car. Likewise, a Christian under the tyranny of lust and its idolatrous co-conspirators may, for a time, have lost control of his heart and body, but he is still owned by Jesus Christ. You have the full force of God's covenant behind you, and you must reclaim your heart by force if necessary. It should anger you that your lust has been a dishonest thief, attempting to gain idolatrous possession of your heart and body that do not rightfully belong to it. You should hate what it has done to you and the testimony of Jesus Christ.

Paul proceeds to say in Colossians 3:6 that God's wrath is coming because of the earthly idolatry that resides in you. He reminds Colossian Christians in verse 7 that prior to their salvation, they, too, lived under the dominion of these idolatrous sins. At that time, they had no legal right or godly authority to deny these sins, but now they do. Paul continues to explain how they can reclaim their own hearts and bodies from lust's oppression. "But now you must put them all away: anger, wrath, malice, slander, and obscene talk from your mouth. Do not lie to one another, seeing that you have put off the old self with its practices" (Col. 3:8–9).

Notice that Paul lists some of the idolatrous co-conspirators with lust in the heart—anger, wrath, malice, slander, and abusive speech. Each of these is a passion that is nurtured by greed and issues forth from the heart (Matt. 12:34–36; 15:19; Mark 7:21–23; Luke 6:45). He counsels the Christian to use justified force and "put them all away" (ἀποτίθημι). Cast them off like the uniform of an enemy. If they are sinful sexual behaviors, throw them by the wayside. If they are erotic thoughts and imaginations, dismiss them. If they are idolatrous cravings of greed, expel them. They are no longer welcome, because they are trying to rule in a heart that belongs to the King of Life. In casting these aside, there is a death experience—death to the emptiness of a self-centered life, death to personal rights, and death to covetous cravings and selfish pleasures. Self must die for Christ to have functional reign within. Now you are ready for the next step in housecleaning.

ENLIVEN RIGHTEOUSNESS

Permanent change has another factor, which is the important principle of replacement. Real change comprises more than simply stopping the bad desires and behaviors, which is mere behaviorism. If you *only* put the ungodly passions and sinful sexual behaviors aside, that leaves a vacuum in your heart. You cannot expect lasting transformation until unholy lusts are replaced with holy desires. As J. C. Ryle said, "Holiness is a habit of being of one mind with God . . . hating what he hates, loving what he loves."[9] You may need to do a concordance study of the hates and loves of God and then thoughtfully fashion this examination to the specifics of your own heart. If you discover an appetite in your heart for something more, it should be filled with holy things that God loves and a greater love and worship of Christ.

This is not just an effort to fill some "psychological void"; it is the biblical process of replacing evil desires with ones that the heart was originally designed to possess. The biblical course of action for this is to "put on the new self, which is being renewed in knowledge after the

9. Ryle, *Holiness*, 34.

image of its creator" (Col. 3:10). The lustful person must first die to self, casting off all its vestiges, *and begin anew living for Christ.* This is accomplished by thoughtful replacement.

When it comes to behaviors, you must replace selfish sexual activities with God-honoring activities—pastimes centered on loving and helping others. When it comes to thoughts, you must replace erotic fantasies with pure, mind-engaging thoughts that tap just as much creative imagination as the ungodly thoughts once did. One counselee could not conquer his erotic imagination until he found replacement thoughts that tapped his creativity. His counselor assigned some Scripture memorization to call to mind when tempting thoughts would surface and also taught him to seek other pure thoughts that demanded much of his already creative mind (Phil. 4:8). For instance, building model trains was his hobby and passion. Every time an impure sexual thought surfaced, he would purposely turn his creative thoughts to building model train sets for his grandchildren instead of building lurid stories for gratifying himself. He continued to do this until his new mental adventure became automatic, unconscious, and comfortable. He also found that if his creative thoughts included doing helpful acts of love for others, the flow of thought was more easily reversed. God-given creative energy can be turned from selfish endeavors to beneficial ones.

Your heart will never be fully transformed and freed from the susceptibility to lustful temptation until it is filled with passions that are pure—free from sexual lusts. Your new godly desires, thoughts, and attitudes will become habitual when you practice them long enough to become automatic, unconscious, and comfortable. They must become the new norm of your heart. Only then will your heart be holy.

DO NOT TRUST THE WEATHERVANE OF YOUR FEELINGS

FEELINGS DECEIVE

Giving in to the feeling of lustful enslavement will lead to hopelessness and despair. When you believe you cannot enjoy a good rest until indulging in sin, you are being deceived by your feelings. When a nymphomaniac believes she must give her body away in order to be loved, she is being deceived by her feelings. When a pedophile believes he cannot really enjoy sex until it involves the exhilaration of violating a child, one of society's most precious treasures, he is deceived by his feelings. When an exhibitionist believes he must expose himself to an unsuspecting victim in order to find fulfillment, he is deceived by his feelings. When a sexually enslaved Christian believes he cannot change, he is being deceived by his feelings.

FEELINGS OF HOPELESSNESS

Solomon explains in Proverbs 5:22 how feelings take over the sexual sinner. "The iniquities of the wicked ensnare him, and he is held fast in the cords of his sin." Within the immediate context of this verse, his captivity is to sexual enslavement, and the cords are those of sexual bondage. They are not actual leg irons or handcuffs or ropes. The phrase "held fast in the cords" refers to being bound figuratively by feelings of helplessness. Sexual desire and compulsion *feel* irresistible. Some outside force seems to draw the sexual sinner into full indulgence. Paul calls your feeling of helplessness "bondage to corruption" (Rom. 8:20–23). The psalmist speaks of the imprisonment of the righteous in a similar manner: "Some sat in darkness and in the shadow of death, prisoners in affliction and in irons" (Ps. 107:10). This may be your experience with sexual enslavement. Jesus also described this condition: "Truly, truly, I say to you, everyone who commits [continually practices] sin is a slave to sin" (John 8:34).[10] When you are in bondage to sexual lusts you know all too well the weak sense or feeling of being out of control and helpless. Many like you have falsely concluded that sensual desires are irresistible and cannot be denied.

All of this is part of the curse of God on the human sinner. God's misery index on sin causes the sinner to conclude that it is impossible to change. From one perspective, as discussed previously, God determines ultimate transformation and change. It is also true that God

---

10. In John 8:34, "commits" (ποιῶν) is a present participle meaning a continual practice of sin. The tense of the verb indicates this is a habitual practice of sin.

wants you to be involved in the process of change (Phil. 2:12–13; Col. 1:29).

Solomon warns the sexual sinner who does not do his part: "He dies for lack of discipline, and because of his great folly he is led astray" (Prov. 5:23). The Hebrew term translated *discipline* (מוּסָר) literally means "discipline, chastening, correction."[11] Solomon says that the enslavement of sexual lust will eventually cause actual death, figurative death, or both. Why? The sinner's folly of believing his feelings of helplessness will lead him astray.[12] These are the feelings of being held captive with cords, as described in Proverbs 5:22 previously. He is a fool because he believes what his helpless feelings tell him more than what Scripture says about his capacity for discipline. Proverbs 5:23 says that he has more self-discipline than he feels. Therefore, because he believes the sensations of irresistible passion over what God says about his own self-control, he will die. Believing feelings over God will always result in trouble.

BE VIGILANT ABOUT OCCASIONS OF TEMPTATION

Vigilance is an important characteristic of a soldier in battle. In the battle against sexual enslavement, heart idolatry wins every time a person heeds the body's prompting. But a true soldier of Jesus Christ has hope of a strong victory if he persists in vigilantly guarding against temptation's corrupting influence. Likewise, as J. C. Ryle mentioned earlier, your heart is a tinderbox that must be kept away from every spark of temptation. Such an attitude in your heart views temptation as deadly.

Any thing or occasion that would stir and feed these desires should be radically removed from your life if it proves to be a source of temptation. This includes friends, magazines, business trips, hotel rooms,

---

11. Francis Brown, S. R. Driver, and Charles A. Briggs, eds., *A Hebrew and English Lexicon of the Old Testament* (Oxford: Clarendon Press, 1978), 416.

12. "Go astray" is from the same Hebrew word (שָׁגָה) as the word *exhilarated* (lit. intoxicated or to stagger) in verses 19–20. A person enslaved to sexual feelings is a fool who will stagger like a drunk while he indulges his craving.

videos, movies, TV, internet, and even smart phones. Of course, removing these will not accomplish much if heart motivations are not sufficiently addressed. But once heart idols are confessed and genuine repentance has occurred, removing various external sources of temptation from your life will help you keep your heart clean. Paul says in Galatians, "For you were called to freedom, brothers. Only do not use your freedom as an opportunity for the flesh, but through love serve one another" (Gal. 5:13). Jesus said that no matter how precious things might have become to us (like a right eye or right hand), if they cause us to sin, we must radically remove them (Matt. 5:29–30). It is imperative that you purge from your life anything that could inadvertently lead you back into sin. If they lead you into sin, they must be disposed of forever.

LEARN TO TRUST THE BIBLE-TEACHING CHURCH

Jet pilots are taught that when they are visually impaired during storms, they must trust their instruments. Similarly, you cannot trust your feelings when going through the storms of sexual lust, but you can trust the Bible-teaching church. The church is part of the gracious provision of God for every Christian who is struggling with debilitating sin. It provides positive examples to follow as well as authoritative, loving accountability. The writer of Hebrews instructs Christians, "Remember your leaders, those who spoke to you the word of God. Consider the outcome of their way of life, and imitate their faith" (Heb. 13:7). Godly examples are not just a part of the contemporary church; many of God's people throughout church history provide inspirational examples of resisting sexual sin (e.g., Joseph in Gen. 39:7–10; Tamar in 2 Sam. 13:12–14; Moses in Heb. 11:24–26).

Furthermore, since the flesh is weak and prone to disobedience, the church is an excellent environment for personal accountability. The church's elders are responsible for overseeing the personal development and growth of its members. Hebrews goes on to say, "Obey your leaders and submit to them, for they are keeping watch over your souls, as those who will have to give an account. Let them do this with joy and not with groaning, for that would be of no advantage to you" (Heb.

13:17). When you are in an active church with a very high view of the authority, inspiration, inerrancy, and sufficiency of Scripture—one that takes seriously the godly oversight of its members—its fellowship will be one of the greatest sources of strength and encouragement when you are at your weakest. When an errant professing Christian fails and persists in sexual sin, a truly loving church will take that person through loving church discipline, not to remove him but in the hope that he will repent and purify his heart (1 Cor. 5:5–13). When this happened among the Corinthian believers, the brother who was disciplined out of the church for unrepentant sexual sin with his stepmother eventually repented and was restored to the church (2 Cor. 2:5–11). Accountability to a godly fellowship of believers who genuinely care for one another's righteous welfare is invaluable to your liberation from this slavery (Heb. 10:23–25). The right church—one that is strong in biblical doctrine and practice—can be one of your greatest sources of hope and help when you are sexually enslaved.

KEY CONCEPTS

self-destructive obsession
pornography as an innocent indulgence
American Psychiatric Association (APA)
behavioral modality and ethics
cognitive behavior therapy
past psychological trauma
"out-of-awareness" mind
struggle for intimacy
Sex Addicts Anonymous
confession
repentance
weakness and humility
overcoming sin's struggle
discipline of grace
goal of holiness
put sin to death

put on the new self
distrust feelings
vigilance
Bible-teaching church

STUDY QUESTIONS

1. Many Christians seek out a biblical counselor only after years of sitting under the counsel of psychologists or psychiatrists. Why does psychology ultimately fail the Christian counselee?
2. "People do not commit sexual sins because they fundamentally believe they are unworthy." Another way of saying this is that people commit sexual sins because they fundamentally believe they are worthy (deserving). Explain from Scripture how this statement is true.
3. Give a biblical rationale for *not* sending a Christian to Sex Addicts Anonymous.
4. "From this, Paul understood a great lesson of the Christian life—human weakness provides the occasion for a grand display of God's power in grace. In fact, the weakness he experienced was 'to keep me from becoming conceited' (2 Cor. 12:7). Part of the reason so many enslaved people sense the powerful irresistibility of sex is to teach them the powerful enablement of the grace of God." If God had removed Paul's "thorn in the flesh," he would have been tempted to become conceited and not seen the power of God at work in his weakness. Please finish the following sentence, explaining what would be the result of this removal: It follows, then, that if God instantly removed our weakness for the irresistibility of sexual sin . . .
5. Explain how living in God's grace enables a person to overcome sexual enslavement.
6. "Your goal is not improvement—it is *holiness*." Discuss the difference between mere improvement and actual holiness. What would be the characteristics of one who had simply improved a little in the areas of sexual lust? What characteristics would

you expect to see of someone who is continually growing in holiness?

7. How does worshiping God as *King* aid the Christian in putting sexual sin to death in his life?

8. Explain how involvement in a strong, Bible-teaching church will be a great help to the Christian who is sexually enslaved as well as for the Christian who has repented of sexual sin and is seeking to live a life of godliness.

FOR FURTHER READING

Challies, Tim. *Sexual Detox: A Guide for Guys Who Are Sick of Porn.* Adelphi, MD: Cruciform Press, 2010.

Coyle, Rachel. *Help! She's Struggling with Pornography.* Wapwallopen, PA: Shepherd Press, 2017.

Jones, Peter. *The Other Worldview.* Bellingham, WA: Kirkdale Press, 2015.

Mack, Wayne, and Joshua Mack. *A Fight to the Death.* Phillipsburg, NJ: P&R Publishing, 2006.

10

THE SEXUAL DESIRE
OF THE PURE HEART

In 1993, Hollywood released *Indecent Proposal*, a movie that effectively illustrated the vacuum of virtue that exists in contemporary marriage and family. In this fictional story, an enormously rich man desires sex with another man's beautiful wife. He craved this woman so much that he offered the couple one million dollars to fulfill his fantasy. Most husbands jealously protect their wives from such men. But as this tale unfolds, the couple found the huge sum of money so tempting that they began to entertain the prospect of accepting the proposal. As they bantered the idea about, they began to rationalize accepting such a potential threat to their marriage. The thought of that much money and the lifetime of dreams it could fulfill was more than they could resist. Resolving to love each other and keep their marriage strong through the affair, they consented. Instead of refusing, they rationalized.

The millionaire was lust-driven by his sexual desires, but the husband and wife were just as lust-driven by the comforting prospect of having lots of money and living in ease for the rest of their lives. Wealth provided the millionaire the opportunity to indulge his lust for sexual fulfillment, and the attractiveness of the man's wife provided the couple with the opportunity to indulge their lust for riches. Both sides had a craving that demanded satisfaction.

Long before the opportunity presented itself to the rich man and the wannabe-rich couple, idolatrous cravings existed in all their hearts, providing the perfect preconditions for adultery. Prior to the offer, the only things lacking were opportunity and resources. Many Christian husbands and wives have similar desires—latent idols of the heart that lack only opportunity and resources. But given the right circumstances, they would commit adultery if they could minimize the consequences and maximize the benefits. Similarly, few prostitutes are in the business because they enjoy gratuitous sex. They continue to "turn tricks" because their lust for money outweighs their virtue. Men want sex; hookers want money. Sometimes the roles are switched between the sexes. And sometimes these things occur between people of the same sex. Without exception, all are driven by preexistent idolatrous desires in the heart.

Many people will recall the notorious adulterer Joey Buttafuoco, who made national news for having sex with Amy Fisher when she was sixteen years old. Buttafuoco claimed that it was not a serious affair and that his actions were motivated by "strictly lustful sex. . . . Sometimes lust takes me over. It's very painful."[1] Apparently, Fisher did not see it that way and believed there was much more to the relationship, so she shot Buttafuoco's wife, Mary Jo, in the face. Mrs. Buttafuoco survived, a bullet lodged near her brain. According to news reports, Fisher testified in court, "I know with all my heart that if Mr. Buttafuoco had permitted me to cross the bridge between adolescence and adulthood unmolested, I would not be where I am today. This man took me to expensive restaurants and cheap motels. I am sad to say that he taught me well. He taught me to disrespect myself and to deceive my parents. Unfortunately, these were lessons that I learned too quickly."[2] The passion of lust stirs covetous jealously in people's hearts to the point that there is a driving desire to murder a rival. In a jealous rage, husbands have killed their wives and lovers; wives have killed their husbands and

---

1. "Buttafuoco Blames His Crime on Lust," *Dayton Daily News*, November 17, 1993.
2. Ibid.

lovers; and, as in this case, lovers have attempted to remove a spouse. Solomon explains how this works:

> He who commits adultery lacks sense; he who does it destroys himself. He will get wounds and dishonor, and his disgrace will not be wiped away. For jealousy makes a man furious, and he will not spare when he takes revenge. He will accept no compensation; he will refuse though you multiply gifts. (Prov. 6:32–35)

Sexual lust takes a heavy toll on both marriage and the family. A lustful, idolatrous heart not only gives birth to sexual sin but also stirs strong passions in others. When these lusts are permitted to thrive, they result in self-destruction as well as the devastation of marriage and family relationships. Solomon describes it as a form of suicide: "he who does it destroys himself." Even the most basic insight into human nature reveals that when someone has violated a man's wife, jealousy takes over. Multiple pleas, sincere apologies, or offers of restitution will not satisfy the passion that has been incited in a husband's heart. He will not be settled until the wrong has been made right and the adulterer has paid.

Like a husband's jealously, so too passionate lust is loath to be easily appeased: "Just when we think we're safe from him, he raises up his ugly head and smirks, and there's no river in the world flows cold and strong enough to strike him down."[3] So began a most open and revealing article, "The War Within: An Anatomy of Lust." The author proceeded to give his personal account of a married Christian man's intense struggle with sexual lust.

He begins, "I am writing this article anonymously because I am embarrassed. Embarrassed for my wife and children, yes, but embarrassed most for myself. I will tell of my personal battle with lust, and if I believed I were the only one who fought in that war, I would not waste emotional energy dredging up stained and painful memories."[4]

---

3. Anonymous, "The War Within: An Anatomy of Lust," *Leadership: A Practical Journal for Church Leaders* 3, 4 (Fall 1982): 31.
4. Ibid.

This man proceeds to bare his soul concerning the lustful cravings that overwhelmed his heart and body. It began mildly as an adolescent boy; he remembers how he had "drooled though Playboy, sneaked off to my uncle's room for a heart-thumping first look at hard-core pornography, and done my share of grappling and fumbling with my fiancée's clothes."[5] But it was not until later, as a married man, that a deep, enslaving lust was born in him because of a decisive commitment to follow its driving desire.

His first business trip away from home signaled his decline into slavery. "As I sat in a dingy motel room near the airport and flipped through the city guide of what to do in Rochester, New York, I kept coming back to one haunting photo of an exotic dancer, a former Miss Peach Bowl winner, the ad said. She looked fresh and inviting: the enchanting kind of Southern girl you see on TV commercials for fried chicken—only this one had no clothes on."[6] With each successive trip away from home, he continued to follow his passion into deeper experiences of sexual satisfaction.

He rationalized these with "Christian" justification. If Jesus spent time ministering to prostitutes, he could, too. Besides, he reasoned, "Nudity is art. . . . *Playboy* and its kin have great articles. . . . Some stimulation will help my sex life. . . . Other people do far worse. . . . What is lust anyhow, I kept asking myself. Is fantasizing wrong in itself?"[7] But guilt plagued his every step. He was constantly fearful that someone would see him and that he would be found out, so he became suspicious of everyone, including his wife and children. As his hormones continued to rage, he remembered how "Mark Twain railed against God for parceling out to each human a source of universal joy and pleasure, then forbidding it until marriage and restricting it to one partner."[8] Bitterness grew in his heart toward God. This man was so enslaved to the mastery of sex that he found himself seeking every possible opportunity to secretly fulfill his desires. For a time, he

5. Ibid.
6. Ibid.
7. Ibid., 35–36.
8. Ibid., 33.

was able to keep it from affecting his attitude toward his wife, but as this monkey on his back grew into an ape, its slavish demands made him incredibly self-centered. Even his attitude toward sex dramatically changed. "Most of this time I hated sex," he wrote.[9] Yet by this time it had such a commanding control on him that he could not say no.

Eventually, after several years of enslavement, he told his wife. This proved to be a significant turning point in his battle. He had repented and was helplessly broken for his sin against God and the unknowing pain it had brought to his wife. To him, the genuineness of his repentance included coming clean to his wife.

> Perhaps my impurity had kept our own love from growing in the same way it had blocked the love I could experience with God. We lay side by side on our bed one steamy summer evening. I talked about nothing, in a nervous, halting voice, for an hour or so, trying to break the barrier that held me back, and finally about midnight I began. I told her nearly everything, knowing I was laying on her a burden she might not be able to carry. I have wondered why God let me struggle for a decade before deliverance . . . . I hurt her—only she could tell how much I hurt her. It was not adultery—there was no other woman for her to beam her resentment toward, but perhaps that made it even harder for her. . . . But still, in spite of that pain and the vortex of emotions that must have swirled around inside her, she gave to me forgiveness and love. She took on my enemy as her enemy too. She took on my thirst for purity as her thirst too. She loved me, and as I type this even now, tears streak my face because that love, that awesome love is so incomprehensible to me, and so undeserved.[10]

Was his repentance genuine after ten years of sexual enslavement? After that night with his wife, when he unburdened his soul and experienced her forgiveness and love, the commanding hold of those desires

9. Ibid., 37.
10. Ibid., 45.

began to die. He recognized that he was living in the undeserved grace of God and his wife. He realized that a miracle of grace had taken place in his life. A year after the confession, he found himself alone in an area of San Francisco known for its strip bars and peep shows. He said, "I felt myself pulled—it felt exactly like that—into another of the twenty-five cent peep shows to watch an undulating girl on a revolving table for three minutes. Not ten seconds had passed when I felt a sense of horror. My head was pounding. Evil was taking over. I had to get out of there, immediately. I ran, literally ran, as fast as I could out of the North Beach district. . . . I prayed for strength and walked away. Other than that encounter, I have been free of the compulsion."[11] This was something that had not happened for over eleven years. The gracious love of the Lord, and his wife, had changed him. You can be changed, too, and God can give you the grace "to renounce ungodliness and worldly passions, and to live self-controlled, upright, and godly lives in the present age" (Titus 2:12).

What began as a simple temptation grew into a demanding desire that enslaved him because he already had a preconditioned reason of self-reward in his heart. After all, he was a hard-working husband and father, and he deserved a little self-indulgence occasionally. This was the rationale of his sinful heart. But it was an awful, grotesque sin that saddled him with horrible guilt while funneling all his productive thought and energy into self-gratification. Lust has the potential to destroy everything you hold dear.

MAINTAINING THE PURITY OF MARRIAGE

Remaining pure in marriage involves more than physical faithfulness: marital faithfulness is an issue of the heart. According to Jesus' teaching in the Sermon on the Mount, everyone who has lusted is a sexual deviant in the heart and has broken his marital covenant (Matt. 5:28). Like a loving husband, God is a jealous God when it comes to the single-minded loyalty, worship, and devotion of his elect. He

11. Ibid., 47.

requires nothing less than sole, restricted ownership of his people (Ex. 20:1–5; Deut. 4:23–24; 11:16). This is the reason that New Testament lists of iniquities commonly warn against immorality and greed, deeming it idolatry.[12]

Furthermore, the proper place for holy lust is in a monogamous marriage. That is the reason marriage is analogous to the close relationship God enjoys with his people.[13] There cannot be any promiscuity in either relationship. Each is a picture of the other (Eph. 5:22–27). Paul describes the importance of intimate purity to the Christians at Corinth:

> For I feel a divine jealousy for you, since I betrothed you to one husband, to present you as a pure virgin to Christ. But I am afraid that as the serpent deceived Eve by his cunning, your thoughts will be led astray from a sincere and pure devotion to Christ. (2 Cor. 11:2)

The J. B. Phillips New Testament translates the last phrase of this verse as "single-hearted devotion to him." To be single-hearted means that your heart has no idols that will diminish your devotion to God. It is a heart of simplicity (ἁπλότης, sincerity) and purity (ἁγνότης, unadulterated), without moral defect. God is a jealous lover who expects absolute purity in the heart of his bride. There is not even room for an *imaginary* lover.

> The exclusiveness and uniqueness of the marriage relationship, in which a man and woman give themselves sexually to one another only (as a unifying bond signifying their belonging to one another in every other way as well) obviously rules out casual, hedonistic sex with other people [real or imaginary]—both before and after marriage. To ignore or flaunt this idea of exclusiveness is abhorrent to God—if for no other reason than that the institution of marriage is a

12. Dietrich Bonhoeffer, *The Cost of Discipleship* (New York: Macmillan, 1963), 194.

13. See Song of Solomon and Hosea.

means of helping mankind catch some small glimpse of the singular devotion and undivided loyalty God requires of those who enter into a covenant relationship with him. . . . The single-hearted devotion of a husband and wife who have reserved the sexual expression of love for marriage, who know they have shared their bodies with no one but each other, and who are pledged to be faithful to one another always, provides us with a picture of the singleness of mind and heart that God requires in the Christian's relationship to him.[14]

How can a couple maintain single-heartedness in their faithfulness to God and one another? What must be happening in the Christian marriage to establish and maintain purity? Five biblical guidelines of sexuality are necessary in marriage.

SCRIPTURE ENCOURAGES PASSIONATE LOVEMAKING IN MONOGAMOUS HETEROSEXUAL MARRIAGES.

Being fully captivated by your spouse is the best impediment to sexual idolatry. If unholy lust is to be put off, then holy lust must be put on. The lover and the beloved were surely enthralled with one another in the Song of Solomon. In Proverbs 5, a husband is to exercise self-discipline in focusing his love on his wife. His sexual energies are described as cisterns, wells, springs, and fountains (Prov. 5:15–18). These everyday elements store, channel, and control water. In a similar way, the husband is admonished to store (save), channel (direct toward), and control (restrain) his sex drive for his wife.

According to 1 Corinthians 7:3, the goal of sexuality for the believer is to fulfill, satisfy, and be a refreshment to his spouse. The New American Standard Version translates this verse, "must fulfill his duty to his wife, and likewise also the wife to her husband." You are probably not accustomed to the intimacy of marriage being described as a "right" or "duty" you render for your spouse. This is because you view the sexual experience as a joy you *receive* rather than a joy you

14. Letha Scanzoni, *Sex and the Single Eye* (Grand Rapids: Zondervan, 1968), 110–11.

give. But God makes it clear that it is your duty, or main purpose, to fulfill your spouse. This is the main purpose of a godly marital union—bringing joy to your spouse! And yet it is not wrong to enjoy this ministry. In fact, it is encouraged in Scripture.

Solomon encourages husbands, "Let your fountain be blessed, and rejoice in the wife of your youth, a lovely deer, a graceful doe. Let her breasts fill you at all times with delight; be intoxicated always in her love" (Prov. 5:18–19). Ecclesiastes encourages husbands to "enjoy life with the wife whom you love, all the days of your vain life that he has given you under the sun, because that is your portion in life and in your toil at which you toil under the sun" (Eccl. 9:9). Paul says, "Do not deprive one another, except perhaps by agreement for a limited time, that you may devote yourselves to prayer; but then come together again, so that Satan may not tempt you because of your lack of self-control" (1 Cor. 7:5). This is the type of holy passion God intends in marriage.

A MARITAL COVENANT MEANS THAT SEXUAL ACTIVITY IS NOT FOR SELF-FULLFILLMENT PURPOSES BUT FOR THE FULFILLMENT OF YOUR SPOUSE.

Spouses who practice sexual *self*-gratification are operating from a covetous heart. There should be no room in the Christian marriage for self-seeking sex. Selfish attitudes place personal needs above one's spouse instead of placing the spouse's needs above one's own. Self-seeking husbands and wives are not interested in fulfilling their conjugal rights with their spouse; they are interested in being fulfilled. That is not love; it is greed. Christlike love gives unilaterally, without expecting anything in return.

Paul's instruction also gives insight into gender distinctiveness in marriage: "The husband must fulfill his duty to his wife, and likewise also the wife to her husband" (1 Cor. 7:3 NASB). Selfishly motivated sex is a breeding ground for masturbation, homosexuality, lesbianism, incest, rape, and other sexual deviancies. God-honoring marital partners understand that they were created uniquely as male or female, not for self-gratification purposes but for the specific duty of fulfilling their spouses. A considerable amount of marital infidelity (real or imagined) would be eliminated if spouses took this admonition seriously and began to aggressively pursue fulfilling their partners.

Repenting of a self-gratifying attitude toward intimacy in marriage is the beginning of profound and abundant changes in your life. When your thinking changes concerning your approach to your spouse, you can more clearly see the selfish motivations of your heart that have made it easy to indulge your sexual sin. Your eyes are opened to your own predispositions of anger, self-pity, discontentment, fear, self-reward, flattery, power/control, and comfort. You better understand how your specific rationalizations for sexual sin enabled you to satisfy your demanding heart with ease.

MARITAL SEX IS NOT IMMUNE FROM SINFUL LUST IF SPOUSES ARE USING THEIR IDOLATROUS FANTASIES FOR AROUSAL AND PERFORMANCE PURPOSES.

Purity of the heart in your monogamous marriage compels you to find joy in your spouse, not in an imaginary partner. Conversely, heart idolatry will rob your marriage of joy. It will enslave your conscience and hinder the true mutually satisfying expression of sex that God intended. The author of Ecclesiastes elaborates: "And I find something more bitter than death: the woman whose heart is snares and nets, and whose hands are fetters. He who pleases God escapes her, but the sinner is taken by her" (Eccl. 7:26). Whether this woman is an actual adulteress or the product of a fertile and erotic imagination, intimacy in the marriage is undermined. If you give in to your fantasy of a real or imaginary lover, you reveal that your heart is not pure; it is an idolatrous heart that is not single in its devotion. You must ensure you are single-hearted in your devotion first to God and then to your own spouse.

Bringing lustful desires into a marriage will often result in a form of marital rape. Is it possible for a married couple to be having relations with only each other and still be in sin? The answer to this question is absolutely, yes! This happens when a husband or wife forces themselves on their unwilling spouse to satisfy a deep desire to fulfill their own lust. Selfishness has been brought into the marriage bed. "Let marriage be held in honor among all, and let the marriage bed be undefiled, for God will judge the sexually immoral and adulterous" (Heb. 13:4). The marriage bed is defiled when your selfish heart takes over. Your focus must always be fulfilling your spouse, not self!

RECURRENT AND UNINTERRUPTED SEXUAL RELATIONS IN MARRIAGE ARE INSURANCE AGAINST LUST-DRIVEN SEXUAL TEMPTATION.

Scripture gives married couples clear instruction about the importance of maintaining an ongoing sexual relationship. Paul says, "Do not deprive one another, except perhaps by agreement for a limited time, that you may devote yourselves to prayer; but then come together again, so that Satan may not tempt you because of your lack of self-control" (1 Cor. 7:5). He gives three clear guidelines for not having sex:

(1) By agreement—there must be mutual agreement that it is not a good time for sexual relations.

(2) For a limited time—both husband and wife understand that it is only for a limited time of cessation.

(3) You may devote yourselves to prayer—certain emergency situations ("present distress" or persecution in this context, 1 Cor. 7:26) in which prayer is warranted are good times to abstain from sex.

Therefore, the question for Christian spouses is *not*, "When do we have sex?" It is, "When do we *not* have sex?" Continuous, ongoing sexual relations is assumed in a Christian marriage because the respective spouses are looking out for one another's needs and not their own.

You may question how to determine the frequency of sexual relations in a Christian marriage. The answer to this question is always tied to the "satisfaction" principle. Is your mate satisfied? If your mate is not satisfied, then frequency should increase. If your mate is satisfied, then you are doing your job. In some cases, there may be an equitable agreement between you and your spouse to entirely cease relationships because of a chronic illness, disease, or old age. This should always be by loving, mutual agreement. Certain pharmacological drugs may decrease your spouse's desire for intimacy or physical ability to function, so it is important to have a degree of understanding and kindness rather than viewing it as a rejection of yourself. Obviously, if your main goal is your mate's satisfaction, not self-centered satisfaction, you will find it easier to have a compassionate attitude.

COUPLES MUST BE OPEN AND HONEST ABOUT THEIR SEXUAL DESIRES.

Nothing should inhibit Christian spouses in the discussion of sexual preferences and frequency of desire. Inhibitions pave the way for misunderstanding and failure. Anger, resentment, and bitterness will gain the advantage, while unfulfilled bodily desires may drive a mate back to his lust-filled idolatrous ways. Your ability to maintain a right relationship is directly dependent on your honest communication with your spouse. Serious disagreements, arguments, and interpersonal conflicts during your marriage will challenge your communication with one another. However, a humble, loving, and forgiving attitude will quickly restore your communication. "Husbands, love your wives, and do not be harsh [embittered] with them" (Col. 3:19). Of course, the same is true for a wife in relation to her husband. Bitterness provides the environment for Satan to gain a foothold in your marriage.

For instance, one Christian wife allowed her deep-seated anger against her husband to bring an end to their intimacy. She withheld herself from him for several months because of a dispute they had had over money. Later, when she caught her husband practicing masturbation, she was horrified and acted as if he had committed the unpardonable sin. As far as she was concerned, his sin was grievous, but she saw herself as justified and innocent of any wrong. Her sinful attitude and approach to their sexual relationship had paved the way for her husband's sin. Unless there is a continuous physical relationship, Satan gains ground in marriage and the heart.

MAINTAINING PURITY WHILE SINGLE

Remaining pure while single is a matter of daily seeking God's grace while immersing oneself in passionate service for Christ's kingdom. Having said that, it is apparent that those who remain single and actively serve Christ still may have struggles of a sexual nature. Those who have no marital prospects must guard their hearts against idolatrous desires and the predispositions of anger and self-pity. These desires can become the rationalization for yielding to the seemingly relentless pressures of lust.

Singles who are given the gift of celibacy will not be hampered by the tension of sexual fulfillment (1 Cor. 7:7). This is not to say that they are sinless and idol-free. It means that they, like Paul and Jesus, will not be prone to lustful sexuality. But a single person who is pressured with sexual desires does not have the gift of singleness. In speaking to the disciples concerning marriage and sexual temptation, Jesus gave a clarification: "For there are eunuchs who have been so from birth, and there are eunuchs who have been made eunuchs by men, and there are eunuchs who have made themselves eunuchs for the sake of the kingdom of heaven. Let the one who is able to receive this receive it" (Matt. 19:12). Notice how Jesus describes some as "eunuchs who have made themselves eunuchs for the sake of the kingdom of heaven." They are not eunuchs because of a birth defect or because someone else mutilated their body. These are the eunuchs (celibate singles) who have a single-hearted devotion to the kingdom of heaven. They have no personal time for, or interest in, marriage or sex. These singles have thoroughly immersed themselves into passionate service for Christ's kingdom.

Often the passage in 1 Corinthians 7:9 is given as counsel to singles to marry if they burn with lust. Yet, in the context, that is not the teaching of the passage. Paul is dealing with the question of whether two people should get married given the present state of persecution that Christians were enduring (1 Cor. 7:26). He is saying to the unmarried that they should not feel pressured to get married because of this time of unusual distress. Many people do that today before soldiers go off to war—they marry out of desperation. But in verse 8, Paul says they should remain single, as he was. Verse 9 is the exception: if they are in a relationship and are strongly attracted to each other, then do get married. Verse 9 is not teaching that getting married cures lust, as some think. You have already seen that married people can still sinfully lust while having sex with their spouse.

What is the biblical help for the one who desires to marry but has no opportunity? This single person must actively pursue and cultivate a grateful spirit. A greedy heart will be his greatest downfall, causing him to be overcome with discontentment and ingratitude. As a result, misery and guilt will plague his life. His focus must be on all he possesses in Christ, not on what he lacks (Eph. 5:3–5). Devoting himself to giving, rather than fixating on receiving, is also critical to his change.

Masturbation is far too common among Christian singles of both sexes. This is a self-gratifying sexual activity that relies on lustful erotic pictures (for men) and romantic stories (for women) that become deeply ingrained in the flesh. While many Christians view masturbation has harmless, this sexual practice is impossible without committing "mental" adultery (Matt. 5:27–28). Additionally, masturbation is similar to homosexuality because it is sex with the same sex! It is an aberration of gender-distinctive copulation purposed by God in original creation.

Once a single is accustomed to self-touch, with the instant awareness of the most pleasurable spots and caresses, enjoyment in marital sex—should the Lord bring this to pass—will not even come close to the intensity of self-stimulation. As a result, your spouse will never be able to reproduce the most satisfying responses that you became accustomed to through your own immediate, tactile movements because of the immediate bio-feedback that accompanies it. Once built, the idol of pleasurable comfort and excitement is hard to tear down.

MATE SELECTION AND SEXUAL LUST

The choice of a marriage partner should be a spiritual choice, revealing purity of the heart. But the same desires and cravings of the heart that set up a person for sexual failure can also influence unwise mate selection. Some Christians marry out of anger just to prove their parents wrong, saying in effect, "We can make it, we will show them!" Others marry out of self-pity—"No one else I want will marry me, so I might as well marry her!" It is not uncommon for a person to marry out of fear or to escape miserable conditions at home. Still others may be restless, somehow thinking that marriage will solve their general discontentedness with life. Men might marry an "arm trophy" to be praised and flattered by other admiring and jealous men. Women do the same. Some marry because they know they can control their spouse for their own purposes and desires. Then there are those who marry for self-reward—the ones who have selfish, pleasurable purposes ruling in their hearts. Of course, many marry for comfort reasons. They see their future mates as bringing security to their lives and the comfortable lifestyle they have always desired. In each case, idols of the heart are controlling the selection of a lifetime mate.

When these idols are expressed sexually in lustful mate selection, the problem is compounded. Early Christians had the same problem with choosing future wives based on sex appeal. In doing so, they were not pleasing to the Lord. This is the argument of the apostle Paul to the Thessalonian Christians. On the negative side, they were to "abstain from sexual immorality" (1 Thess. 4:3). But on the positive side, he said that each man should "know how to take a wife for himself in holiness and honor."[15] John Eadie comments, "The Thessalonian believers were to abstain from all forms of illicit sexual intercourse, and were in one way to preserve themselves from it, by each not simply getting a wife, but getting to himself his own wife according to God's ordinance in purity and honour (Heb. 13:4; Gen. 1:28; 2:24)."[16] Christians are not to make mate-selection choices on the basis of "the passion of lust" (1 Thess. 4:5), the way that pagans choose a mate.[17] Jay Adams explains the meaning this text would have

15. The Revised Standard Version New Testament (New York: Thomas Nelson, 1946), 436.

16. John Eadie, *Commentary on the Greek Text of the Epistle of Paul to the Thessalonians* (Grand Rapids: Baker, 1979), 130.

17. The English translation of 1 Thessalonians 4:4 in the English Standard Version, "that each one of you know how to control his own body in holiness and honor," is not my preferred translation. The Greek term that is translated "body" is possible but not probable. It is the term *vessel* (σκεῦος) that speaks of a clay jar. It is the same word used in 1 Peter 3:7 to speak of a wife. Also, the term *control* (κτάομαι) is a business term better understood as "to acquire, get or procure." You do not acquire your own body, but you do acquire a wife. It is believed that this understanding better fits the contextual argument of the apostle Paul.

had in the historical context of the original recipients. He starts in the hypothetical voice of the apostle Paul.

> All the ways in which pagans acquire a wife, that are contrary to the *instructions* I gave, are now to be eschewed. . . . Getting a girl pregnant in order to obligate her for marriage would obviously be proscribed. Having sexual relations with her before marriage would also be included. The *honorable* way to acquire a wife is through a proposal that is honored before and after marriage. The *passion of desire*, mentioned in verse 5, is the principle way in which one wrongly acquires a wife. It is not romantic or sexual factors that should be uppermost in the matter. *Pagans, who don't know God,* make sexual attraction the basis for marriage—a very shaky one! Christians must not. One wonders if it isn't because Christians have failed to observe this instruction by Paul that so many marriages are falling apart today. . . . Lust, in whatever form it takes, is the last reason for contracting a marriage.[18]

Sexual idolatry that controls the mate-selection process does not bring about a marriage that glorifies the Lord. Choosing a spouse who has great sex appeal comes from a motivation of covetousness and is driven by a craving for comfort, self-reward, power/control, and flattery. Christians are to be substantially different, and this is especially true when finding a mate for life.

This does not mean that a Christian couple should not be sexually attracted to one another. Rather, Paul is saying that the process should not be driven by sexual lust. The things that should drive the mate-selection process are everything falling under the categories of being holy (pure) and honorable (respectable—of high moral quality and virtue). The choice of a life partner should be driven by issues like commitment to Jesus Christ, godly character, faithfulness, mutual goals,

18. Jay E. Adams, *The Christian Counselor's Commentary: Romans, Philippians, 1 Thessalonians, 2 Thessalonians* (Hackettstown, NJ: Timeless Texts, 1995), 204 (emphasis original).

theological understanding, and heritage. No perfect mate exists, of course, because men and women are sinners, and this is what makes the process difficult (Eccl. 7:26–29). However, it is a worthwhile endeavor if done God's way. "He who finds a wife finds a good thing and obtains favor from the LORD" (Prov. 18:22). If you are single and do not possess the gift of singleness, then your search for a spouse must focus on the godly criteria of holiness and honor. Does your relationship to her result in mutual sanctification (holiness)? Is your relationship to her honorable in God's eyes and the eyes of those who know you?

SEX EDUCATION FOR CHILDREN

This is a distressing contemporary issue for Christians throughout the world. Pressure is on the public school system because of the prevalence of preteen and teenage pregnancies as well as a multitude of sexually transmitted diseases. The post-Christian paganism of modern education in many countries has ruled in favor of giving children whatever sexual liberties they desire, such as freedom to explore their own sexuality, abortion on demand, encouragement to question their biological gender, and a seemingly limitless expression of sexual deviancy. Most psychological answers to perceived sexual problems revolve around mechanical and biological problems that result in increased promiscuity, rather than moral issues that restrain wickedness of a sexual nature. When the Christian psychologist James Dobson is asked by parents, "What should I talk about when I discuss sex with my preteenager?" he responds with ten items:

1. The role of intercourse in marriage.
2. Male and female anatomy and physiology.
3. Pregnancy and the birth process.
4. Nocturnal emission ("wet dreams").
5. Masturbation.
6. Guilt and sexual fantasy.
7. Menstruation.
8. Morality and responsibility in sex.

9. Venereal disease.
10. Secondary sex characteristics which will be brought about by glandular changes—pubic hair, general sexual development, increasing interest in sex, etc.[19]

However, Christian parents must view their children as more than a composite of biological urges. More substantial issues supersede the biological expressions of these sexual urges and their consequences. Parents need to address the hearts of their children to adequately deal with sexual curiosity and interest. The heart determines the activity. If the heart of the child can be trained in purity, then no matter how great the urges, the conduct will be pure as well.

Teach children to know their own hearts. Help them to identify the cravings and desires that direct all their actions and sexuality. What is their heart telling them? What does it want? Help your daughter understand what her heart desires when she is willing to "go all the way" with that young man. Help your son understand what is motivating his heart when he has repeated sexual fantasies about the pretty young woman in his class. Explain to them what God desires for them. Explain to them how they can instill serious character flaws if they give in to their bodily desires and do not learn self-control (Eccl. 11:9; 12:1, 13–14). Accordingly, Solomon admonishes his son in Proverbs 5–7. The job of Christian parents—not the school, Christian school, or youth pastor—is to teach children to know their own hearts. It is an important part of discipleship parenting.

KEY CONCEPTS

lust stirs jealousy
"Christian" justification
slavish demands of sex
faithfulness of the heart

19. James Dobson, *Dr. Dobson Answers Your Questions* (Wheaton, IL: Tyndale House, 1982), 93.

holy lust in marriage
single-hearted devotion to Christ
exclusiveness of marriage
goal of sex to satisfy spouse
idolatrous fantasies
continual marital relations
communicating sexual desires
gift of celibacy
cultivating gratitude
lustful mate selection
teaching children

STUDY QUESTIONS

1. Discuss how the doctrine of total depravity, as seen in Romans 3:10–18, is clearly illustrated in the story line of the movie *Indecent Proposal*. How does this teaching in Romans highlight the truth of the statement, "Long before the opportunity presented itself to the rich man and the wannabe-rich couple, idolatrous cravings existed in all their hearts, providing the perfect preconditions for adultery."
2. Many Christians believe they can justify their sexual sin. But once they are enslaved by it, they find themselves overcome by an avalanche of sins against God and others. From the examples in this chapter, make a list of some of the more obvious sins. Then use the book of Proverbs to give examples of how Scripture has warned about these very things.
3. Many Christians believe that their sexual escapades are private indulgences, to the point that when they finally repent they believe they do not need to confess their sin to their spouse. Explain from Scripture why this is an unbiblical view of sin, repentance, and reconciliation.
4. "You are probably not accustomed to the intimacy of marriage being described as a 'right' or 'duty' you render for your spouse." Discuss why this *seems* so wrong. What expectations

reign in the heart that lead one to desire intimate relations based purely on passion and insatiable appetite?

5. "This single person must actively pursue and cultivate a grateful spirit." In counseling a single person who desires to be married, a good homework assignment would be to make a long list of things to be grateful for. Suppose that you are this single person and make such a list. Beware of allowing bitterness of heart to enter into this list-making!

FOR FURTHER READING

Jones, Peter. *The God of Sex: How Spirituality Defines Your Sexuality.* Colorado Springs, CO: Cook Communications Ministries, 2014.

Peace, Martha. *The Excellent Wife: A Biblical Perspective.* Bemidji, MN: Focus Publishing, 2005.

Powlison, David. *Seeing with New Eyes: Counseling and the Human Condition through the Lens of Scripture.* Phillipsburg, NJ: P&R Publishing, 2003.

Scott, Stuart. *The Exemplary Husband: A Biblical Perspective.* Bemidji, MN: Focus Publishing, 2002.

Street, John. ed. *Men Counseling Men: A Biblical Guide to the Major Issues Men Face.* Eugene, OR: Harvest House, 2013 (see chap. 13, by Melvin Dirkse; chap. 14, by Jim Newheiser; chap. 17, by Nicolas Ellen; chap. 18, by Daniel Kirk; chap. 19, by Ben Marshall; chap. 21, by Wayne Mack).

Street, John, and Janie Street. *The Biblical Counseling Guide for Women.* Eugene, OR: Harvest House, 2016 (see chap. 16 on transgenderism).

CONCLUSION

Becoming pure of sexual idolatry is difficult because the heart is multilayered, constantly changing, and self-deceived. Such diversity flourishes so profusely in the heart that at times it seems beyond comprehension. By-products of sin's effect on the heart—like anger, self-pity, discontentment, fear, self-reward, flattery, power/control, and comfort—can exist as a sinful predisposition in the heart prior to any indulgence in sexual sin. These entanglements often create the perfect condition in the heart to make way for fertile ground for lust and immorality. But the Word of God brings light, understanding, and hope when applied skillfully (Ps. 119:104–105; cf. Jer. 17:9).

Sexual lust is a sinister temptation because its cravings cannot be permanently satisfied. When lust is indulged, it only hungers for more. Like a wild animal devouring all it sees and craving for more, lust soon consumes and controls everything in life (Eph. 4:19). Similar to Cain's struggle with anger, lust's "desire is for you, but you must rule over it" (Gen. 4:7).

God has nothing but utter contempt and judgment for those who would trivialize the sin of sexual lust and thereby justify continual indulgence. This is because lust robs you of a passion for godliness and righteousness; it replaces holy lust with unholy lust. It promotes a love for self above love for God and others. It assaults your conscience, weakening your sense of guilt and culpability, and sears it with the hot iron of indifference. It defiles your character and opens the floodgates of doubt, jealousy, and distrust. To lust-driven men, God says, "They were well-fed, lusty stallions, each neighing for his neighbor's wife. Shall I not punish them for these things? declares the LORD; and shall I not avenge myself on a nation such as this?" (Jer. 5:8–9). To lust-driven women, God says, "I myself will lift up your skirts over your face, and your shame will be seen. I have seen your abominations, your adulteries and neighings, your lewd whorings, on the hills in the field. Woe to you, O Jerusalem! How long will it be before you are made clean?" (Jer. 13:26–27).

The apostle John concludes Revelation with a curse on those who have given themselves over to sensuality, with no possibility of eternal blessing. "Outside are the dogs and sorcerers and the sexually immoral and murderers and idolaters, and everyone who loves and practices falsehood" (Rev. 22:15). Christians must take sexual lust seriously. This begins by examining every predisposition and compromise of the heart that has allowed godless idols to take the place of true worship of God and has predisposed one to sexual sin.

In conclusion, you can use a sevenfold summary while working through sexual enslavement:

1. What idolatrous cravings of the heart have your sexual lusts and habits revealed? Behavioral changes will never break the habituation of sexual sin until the functional gods that feed these sins are addressed (Matt. 5:27–28).
2. What is your theology of sex? What is your understanding of the purpose of sex? Self-gratification is an idolatrous god of covetousness, and you must repent (1 Cor. 7:3–5).
3. Are you willing to die to that which has become precious to you? Demanding desires of comfort, self-reward, and flattery are especially difficult to extinguish. Yet this death-type experience is necessary for breaking the hold of sexual lust (Rom. 7:14–25). The gospel of Jesus Christ is critical to the identification and attainment of new holy desires.
4. Are you willing to re-engage the battle and train yourself to focus all your sexual energies and desire on your partner? If

you are single, are you willing to pour yourself into service for Christ until God sends along a partner (Prov. 5:15–20; 1 Cor. 7:8–35; Heb. 12:7–13)?

5. You must remember that even though sexual lust can easily be hidden for years, God sees the X-rated theater of the mind (Prov. 5:21–23; Luke 12:1–3).

6. The inner life—the inner thoughts and desires—defines the true person. This inner life is what God sees and is truly reflective of a person's character (Prov. 23:7).

7. You must be ready to replace immoral lustful thoughts and desires with God-honoring thoughts and desires that absorb the inner man.

8. What absorbs the thinking and desires of the inner man?
   • Provocative thoughts that excite the imagination.
   • Productive thoughts that require development and creativity.
   • Pure thoughts that are sanctifying and honorable.

Substantial and lasting change in your life requires wisdom, diligence, and care. Change should never be a simple process of mere behavior adjustments. You must be ready to go to battle in the heart, with all its sinful predispositions and compromises, by using all the biblical insight that can be gained to defeat this foe. You must accept the rules of engagement, as God has defined them, and be willing to fight until the last lustful enemy is dead. Success is not measured by instantaneous perfection; it is determined by your faithfulness in carefully applying the Word to your own heart. It is a matter of the Holy Spirit bringing about conviction and change—which includes a wholehearted willingness to go to battle as a spiritual soldier for righteousness. The passions of your heart must change by his transforming grace and truth.

Make the following your humble prayer before the Lord this very day:

Conclusion

LORD JESUS,

I sin—Grant that I may
   never cease grieving because of it,
   never be content within myself,
   never think I can reach a point of perfection.
Kill my envy, command my tongue,
   trample down self.
Give me grace to be holy, kind, gentle, pure, peaceable,
   to live for thee and not for self,
   to copy thy words, acts, spirit,
   to be transformed into thy likeness,
   to be consecrated wholly to thee,
   to live entirely to thy glory.
Deliver me from attachment to things unclean,
   from wrong associations,
   from the predominance of evil passions,
   from the sugar of sin as well as its gall,
   that with self-loathing, deep contrition,
     earnest heart searching
   I may come to thee, cast myself on thee,
     trust in thee, cry to thee,
     be delivered by thee.
O God, the Eternal All, help me to know that
   all things are shadows, but thou art substance,
   all things are quicksands, but thou art mountain,
   all things are shifting, but thou art anchor,
   all things are ignorance, but thou art wisdom.
If my life is to be a crucible amid burning heat,
   so be it,
   but do thou sit at the furnace mouth
   to watch the ore that nothing be lost.
If I sin wilfully, grievously, tormentedly,
   in grace take away my mourning
     and give me music;

remove my sackcloth
   and clothe me with beauty;
still my sighs
   and fill my mouth with song,
then give me summer weather as a Christian.[1]

1. Arthur Bennett, ed., *The Valley of Vision: A Collection of Puritan Prayers and Devotions* (Edinburgh: Banner of Truth, 2002), 146–47. Used by permission.

GLOSSARY

The literary meaning of a word or phrase is always colored by the surrounding literary context. This glossary is provided as an aid to the reader's understanding on how I am using key terms and concepts within the context of this book. These definitions will often go beyond the typical etymological definitions found in standard dictionaries and lexicons because of the focused subject matter of this book. Often Scripture references are supplied to further support and illustrate the definition.

antinomianism. An approach to sanctification that rejects willful obedience to the law of God as a means of walking a more holy path, often emphasizing only the believer's knowledge of his identity in Christ as the sole means of sanctifying grace (Rom. 7:25; 1 Cor. 9:21; Gal. 6:2).

behaviorism. A focus on external Christian obedience and practices that conform to biblical standards without consideration of any true internal change of heart (Isa. 29:13; Matt. 5:21–22, 27–28).

biological determinism (genetic determinism). It is a belief that the bio-chemical processes and/or genes of the human body determine behavior, especially in thinking and decision-making. Belief in the immaterial human soul existing independently of the body is denied (Prov. 16:24; Matt. 10:28).

blind to weakness. A person's inadvertent or willful ignorance of a propensity to personal sin and guilt resulting in continued ungodly attitudes or actions (Prov. 16:2; 21:2; 1 Cor. 4:4).

coercive nature of desire. Deep cravings of longing to acquire something or someone for personal satisfaction that place one under domination to fulfill the obsession, no matter the destructive consequences. In Scripture, it is referred to as being controlled by corrupting fleshly desires (Prov. 21:10; Rom. 13:14; Eph. 4:22).

cognitive-behavioral therapy. An approach to psychotherapy that seeks to challenge thoughts, beliefs, and attitudes (thought disorders and maladaptive behaviors) that are irrational and to develop strategies to address destructive goals and decrease the severity of symptoms for a disorder.

competing lusts and ambitions. Equally strong sinful desires in a person that demand satisfaction and form rival aspirations promising a similar outcome of reward (Ps. 119:113; James 1:8; 4:8).

covetousness or greed. It is an insatiable longing or inordinate desire of the heart for unnecessary and selfish gain through sinful attitudes, words, and actions. This avarice involves the inability to control "wants" that are often misidentified as "needs" (1 Cor. 5:11; Eph. 5:3; 2 Peter 2:14).

cravings that rule. These are the sinful desires of the heart that dominate all other desires and reign as supreme. They are the idolatrous desires that take control of a person's life, channeling their thoughts, words, and actions away from God and toward self-gratification (Rom. 6:12–14; 1 Cor. 10:6–8).

death to self. Killing the desire to live for one's self and its selfish desires, then turning to live for Christ (Matt. 16:24–26; Luke 9:23–25; Rom. 6:6–7, 11).

deep longing of lust. This is an intense inward desire of the heart that is deeper than the physiological desire of the body for sex, even though it will often accompany it. It is a strong, controlling passion to find fulfillment in immoral gratification (Prov. 11:6; Ezek. 16:36; 1 Thess. 4:4–5).

depraved desire. The motivational longing that stems from the fallen sinfulness of humanity. A sense of craving that is excited by the thought of obtaining gratification from something or someone that is biblically inappropriate (Rom. 3:10–18; 2 Peter 1:4; 3:3).

discipline of grace. This is the understanding of the Christian, who knows he has been saved solely on the merits of the grace of Jesus Christ and his substitutionary atonement, which grants the believer underserved salvation and eternal life that is the central motivation of everlasting gratefulness to live a life of righteousness (Eph. 2:8–10; Titus 2:11–12; 3:3–8).

Docetism ("Illusionists"). A theological system of belief among a small group of self-professing Christians during the first four centuries A.D. advocating that all matter was innately evil and the immaterial spirit was innately good. Their goal was to escape this material world and their sinful material bodies. Therefore, since Jesus Christ was perfect, he could not have come in real flesh. His physical body was only an illusion. If he did not come in the flesh, then he did not die a real death or shed real blood. It was a system of philosophic thought that undermined the apostolic gospel (1 Tim. 4:4; 1 John 4:2–3; 2 John 7).

dynamic and reflexive. In reference to the Old Testament Hebrew, the dynamic and reflexive senses are mentioned in relationship to the term *desire* (חֶמְדָּה). The *dynamic* sense of this word is used in the Old Testament, carrying the idea of a very strong longing or lust demanding satisfaction, like any obsessive desire for sexual fulfillment (Ex. 20:17; Deut. 5:21). The *reflexive* sense of this word is used in the Old Testament to refer to a detached appreciation of beauty or innate attractiveness, like the appreciation of a work of art (1 Kings 20:6; Lam. 2:4). The dynamic sense is used mostly in sinful desires, while the reflexive is used as a holy appreciation of symmetry and beauty.

enabling grace. It is the grace of God that provides the ability to accomplish his will for the Christian's life and ministry. Without his enablement, the Christian alone would not able to achieve anything worthwhile for God's glory (Rom. 12:6; 2 Cor. 12:9; Eph. 2:10; Col. 1:29). This is not the historical concept of prevenient grace that is rooted in Arminian theology.

endorphins. Morphine-like chemicals produced in the central nervous system and pituitary gland (endogenous opioid neuropeptides and peptide hormones) that function to both inhibit painful sensations and produce an exhilarated experience of euphoria. These intense feelings of pleasure are often released during a sexual climax (orgasm) or in anticipation of one by bathing the neurons of the brain.

escape (mental). The mental diversion of creating an alternative reality, usually involving a fictitious and sensualizing sexual story, to avoid an unpleasant life or situation.

euphoria. It is the experience of intense pleasure or happiness. Within this context it is the experience often associated with a real or imagined sexual experience that activates the pleasure centers of the brain (Eccl. 2:1–2; Ezek. 16:37; 2 Tim. 3:4).

false memory. This happens when a person recalls an event or experience from the past that never occurred. Often forms of regression therapies, using repeated suggestion, produce false memories in a client of past sexual abuse that never actually occurred.

forced laborer. This is a biblical concept that comes from ancient warfare terminology, in which enemies are captured and enslaved for hard labor against their will. It is used as an analogy of a Christian who has been captured by the enemy of lust and feels helpless to resist (Prov. 5:22; John 8:34; Rom. 7:14–25).

Godly sorrow. Such sorrow is a deep inward remorse or grief over offending a righteous and holy God. It always results in genuine repentance from sin and includes a willful desire never to repeat the sin again (2 Cor. 7:10–11).

habituation. This is a form of adaptive behavior or thought that God gives to enable a person to perform repeated, often mundane behaviors without conscious thought. Because of the sinful propensities of the human condition, this capacity has been distorted to the practice of repeated ungodly behaviors or thought patterns. For anything to be a habit, it must be practiced automatically, comfortably, and unconsciously. Such is often the case with sinful sexual practices (2 Cor. 12:21; 2 Peter 2:14).

heart context. This is a description of the central core of a person's immaterial soul. It is viewed in Scripture as the control center of a person's thoughts, purposes, and intentions. All sexual sins come out of a person's heart context. The outer, material body of a person, including attitudes and intentional behaviors, functions only with the permission of the heart (Matt. 15:19; Mark 7:21–23; Luke 6:45).

heart hermeneutics. This refers to the biblical principles and guidelines used to interpret critical motivations of the immaterial human heart. Properly understanding these motivations that fuel sinful sexual behavior is critical to repentance and purifying the heart. Because of ignorance, the unbeliever is uninterested in his own heart (Prov. 20:5; Mark 12:33; Eph. 4:18).

heart idolatry. Any strong desire or worshipful longing that reigns over all others in a person's thinking that is not worship of the Creator. God created the hearts of all human beings to worship, but the defilement of the sinful heart replaces worship of God with worship of something, someone, or some experience. To worship anything or anyone that is not the God of heaven is the false worship of an idol. These idols will always feed sinful attitudes and actions in a person's life (Ezek. 14:1–8; 1 Cor. 10:6–14; Eph. 5:3–5).

heart of an adulterer. This is the description of the deep inner sensual desire of a person to be intimate with someone who is not his or her spouse. The heart of the lustful person and the heart of the adulterer is the same heart, only the latter has acted on sinful desire and the former has not (Jer. 5:7–8; Matt. 5:27–28).

heart of man. In Scripture, it is the immaterial core of the human soul involved in thinking, purposing, intending, desiring, craving, and planning. This contrasts with the contemporary Western view of the heart that is more related to emotions and romance. These longings or intentions may be righteous or unrighteous (Gen. 6:5; Prov. 20:5; Mark 7:21).

hedonistic greed. This is the description of a life in pursuit of selfish goals to maximize pleasurable experiences. The ethic of goodness to honor God or the good of others is subordinate to the ultimate purpose of personal satisfaction and pleasure (1 Cor. 5:11; 2 Thess. 2:11–12).

high self-esteem. The elevated belief about the importance of oneself that stems from human depravity. People do not practice sexual sin because of an essential low opinion of self. It is what they believe they deserve. A person may dislike certain aspects of themselves (too tall, too short, too fat, too skinny, etc.), but the fact they are miserable about it shows an intrinsic love of self (Matt. 22:37–40; 2 Tim. 3:1–2).

holy desires and passions. These are sincere, godly aspirations to live a sanctified and pure life for God's glory. Only the Christian with a redeemed heart can have such aspirations (Ps. 19:12–14; 1 Peter 1:12).

homeborn slave. This is a biblical concept that comes from ancient warfare terminology, in which a person is born into slavery. Such a person knows nothing but slavery and is comfortable being a slave. It is used as an analogy of an unbeliever who has lived his entire life as a captive of lust and believes there is no need to change (Eccl. 2:7; John 8:34).

hope. Biblical hope is a certain hope, especially as it applies to change in the believer's heart when it comes to stubborn sexual sins. This certainty is based on the promises of God in progressive sanctification (Ps. 33:18; Prov. 10:28; Rom. 15:4, 13).

hungering heart. This is the heart that is constantly dissatisfied with life. It is always seeking to find satisfaction and happiness in the sensual indulgences of this world (Prov. 11:6; 2 Peter 2:9–10).

hurting heart. This heart is overwhelmed with a deep sense of emotional pain that seeks relief through sinful sexual activities that are motivated by anger, self-pity, discontentment, and fear (Gen. 12:10–20).

idolatrous fantasies. These are mental images, thoughts, or story lines that dominate the thought life of a person sexually. They are an idol of desire worshiped in the heart. A person's corrupt imagination, memory, or external stimulation from pornographic literature, pictures, or provocative objects can feed these impure mental fixations (2 Sam. 11:2; Prov. 11:23).

image of God. Every person was created in the image and likeness of God (Gen. 1:26–27; 5:1; 9:6; 1 Cor. 11:7; Eph. 4:24; James 3:9). Since God is Spirit, this is not a physical likeness. Man was not created as a god but does have essential communicable attributes of God, such as ruling over creation through rational thought, understanding right and wrong, loving, and grieving. Nevertheless, man will never be omnipresent, omniscient, or omnipotent as the infinite God. Man will always remain finite.

insatiable appetite. Although it is common to speak of a glutton as having an insatiable appetite, here it is used in a metaphorical sense, speaking of the continual lust of the heart for more and more satisfaction yet never being satisfied (Prov. 13:25; 30:15–16; Rom. 13:14; Gal. 5:16–17, 24).

judicial forgiveness. God the righteous Judge grants full and complete forgiveness of a sinful life to believers when they are regenerated by the Holy Spirit and confess and repent of their sinfulness, clinging to Jesus Christ as their only hope of salvation and eternal life. No longer is any sin—past, present, or future—judicially held to their account (Acts 2:38; 10:43; Heb. 10:18). An entire lifetime of sin is covered by the atoning sacrifice of Jesus Christ (Heb. 9:26; 10:10, 12, 14).

justification. When a sinner's entire guilt and culpability is removed by God by the once-for-all atoning sacrifice of Jesus Christ on the cross, making him forever righteous. This is accredited to the sinner only through faith and is not based on any merited works of his own, otherwise Christ's atoning death would have been insufficient (Rom. 5:9–10; Eph. 2:8–9; Heb. 10:14; 1 Peter 1:5).

layers of motivations. The human heart is dynamic and multilayered in its purposes and intentions. Because it is depraved it is also clever and calculating in hiding them. Frequently the motivation behind sexual sinfulness can possess multiple rationales. For example, an unmarried young woman may consent to premarital relations with a young man to simultaneously please the young man so he will remain her boyfriend and give away her virginity to hurt her parents with whom she is angry (Rom. 1:24–32).

materialistic view of humanity or cosmology. This is a reductionistic assumption of atheism. Reality simply consists of the material universe, and there is no God or spiritual reality. Therefore, a person simply consists of a body and nothing more. There is no immaterial soul. The Old Testament Hebrew idiom for such a view is used by the author of Ecclesiastes, life from an "under the sun" perspective (Eccl. 2:11, 17–20).

motivations that predispose (negative and affirmative). Often the sinful desires of lust are unseen until a person acts on his or her desires. These impure motivations of the heart are part of the cognitive bias that prejudices a person for moral failure. When it comes to ungodly predispositions to sexual sin, four *negative* motivations are described in this book: anger, self-pity, discontentment, and fear. There are also four *affirmative* motivations: self-reward, flattery, power/control, and comfort.

muscle memory. God created the body so that muscles that repeat the same behavior are conditioned by procedural memory through repetition to provide maximum efficiency of time and effort (e.g., riding a bicycle, playing a musical instrument). Often repeated sexual sins condition the body to impure actions by becoming automatic, comfortable, and unconscious (2 Peter 2:2–3, 14).

myopic. It is a form of spiritual near-sightedness and is used in this book as a metaphorical way of describing a person who has a selfish view of life. Many Christians who struggle with stubborn sexual sins often possess an indulgent self-centeredness (James 3:16).

mysticism. This describes a person who lives based on subjective experiences and intuition rather than living by the standard of biblical truth. Personal experiences are not unimportant, but they are a very unreliable guide for life. Experience must be measured by God's truth (John 14:6; 17:17, 19; 2 Peter 1:16–21).

out-of-awareness mind (subconscious). This is a theorical aspect of a human being held by many psychologists and psychiatrists who argue that a very powerful awareness exists underneath layers of conscious thought. For many psychoanalysts, it is a place in which certain hidden associations and impulses are key to a person's well-being. Supposedly they are the reason behind improper sexual behavior, fits of anger, phobic reactions, and so on. Therefore, only a trained psychotherapist is equipped to peel back the layers of consciousness and bring them to the conscious level. No hard science exists to demonstrate its existence, neither is there any biblical reference to such a hidden state of human consciousness. Biblically, there is only consciousness and unconsciousness, no subconsciousness (Prov. 3:24; 1 Thess. 5:6; Heb. 10:2).

out-of-body human consciousness. God created the human being to be both material and immaterial. The material part of a person is the body. The immaterial part of the person is the soul. When the body dies and the soul departs, this immaterial aspect of a person becomes spirit. The spirit without the use of a physical brain still maintains consciousness and has the capacity to think, intend, and purpose (2 Cor. 5:8–9).

parental forgiveness. Once a person has been judicially forgiven, they become eternal members of God's family as his children. Sin does not remove them from God's family, but it is against their loving heavenly Father. Confession and repentance of sin to the Father restores the child's relationship and relieves him or her from temporal chastisement (Matt. 6:9–13; 1 John 2:1).

past psychological trauma. It is a type of impressionistic damage to the mental recall of a person who has experienced a very disturbing event. Anything or anyone who triggers a recall of such an event may cause this person to be overwhelmed with severe stress resulting in their inability to cope with life. Depending on the severity of the event and the recall of the person, he or she may develop what has been labeled post-traumatic stress disorder (PTSD).

penance. External acts that the Christian imposes on himself to repay a sin to show God and others his seriousness in dealing with a sin and its guilt. Penance is often seen in external acts of denial, various forms of self-flagellation, long periods of sullen depression, and so on. This is an unbiblical practice that denies Jesus' full payment of sin on the cross, and it circumvents the chief process of dealing with God and others: confession, repentance, and seeking forgiveness (Matt. 18:15; Luke 17:3–5; 1 John 1:9–10).

personal rights. These are assumed to be fundamental things owed to a person. The right to be happy, to have a comfortable life, to have an attractive spouse, to have obedient children, and many more are among them. These expectations often become the seedbed for idolatrous cravings when they are denied. Sometimes even legitimate rights can be elevated to sinful, demanding rights (Prov. 29:7; Jer. 5:28; 1 Cor. 7:3).

pleasing people. It is a personal desire for approval. When this becomes greater in a person's life than seeking God's approval, it becomes idolatrous. Then a person will fear men more than they fear God (Prov. 29:25; Eccl. 12:13; Heb. 13:6).

pornography as an innocent indulgence. Many believe that pornography is a morally neutral activity as long as it is not hurting anyone else. For men it is more often sensual pictures; for women it is often sensual stories. Scripture says it is feeding the sinful covetousness of the heart, pulling the heart away from God and enslaving the person to the endorphin rush it provides (Eph. 5:3–5).

precondition of the heart. This phrase is used to describe weaknesses or strengths in the heart prior to an occasion of sexual temptation. A pure heart, free from negative and affirmative motivations, cannot be tempted, because it worships God alone. An impure heart already worships one or more of these motivations and therefore will yield to temptation (Prov. 5:22; 7:25; Matt. 5:27–28).

presumption of innocence. It is an assumption that a person is free from the guilt of sin(s) or a specific sin that has been called into question (Luke 23:47; Acts 18:6; 2 Cor. 7:11).

recompense. This is a form of paying back what is duly owed to another. One can never pay God back, in any measure, for the salvation he provides in Jesus Christ. This debt is too great, and our payment is too defiled. But Scripture is clear that when a believer owes another man, it is his duty to provide restitution (Ex. 22:1; Lev. 5:15; Luke 19:1–10).

relief from stress. Sexual activity releases chemical endorphins in the body that relieve pain and provide pleasure. Often a person will enter into a sinful sexual activity to handle difficulty in life rather than turning to Christ (Ps. 18:6, 41; Heb. 4:16).

repentance. Biblical repentance is such a complete change of mind concerning one's sin that it always leads to a complete change of thinking, acting, and speaking away from sin and toward greater holiness (Matt. 3:8; Acts 20:21; James 4:8–10).

sanctification. The Lord works through the conflicts, difficulties, and losses of life to make the Christian more holy. It is not instantaneous or a passive experience but rather a progressive experience of grace, as obedience grows, to bring the believer into greater Christlikeness (Prov. 4:18; Heb. 12:7–11).

self-assessment. The capacity to analyze or appraise one's own attitudes, desires, intentions, longings, words, and actions in a biblically accurate way. It often involves a metacognitive approach, using particular strategies for learning how to live a more sanctified life or resolve a sinful problem with Scripture as the guide (Ps. 139:3, 23; Eccl. 7:25).

self-deceived. The tendency of the sinful human heart to be self-righteous in evaluating its own holiness or lack thereof (Ps. 36:1–4; Prov. 16:2; 21:2; Titus 1:15).

self-destructive obsessions. A person can become so fixated on a sexual experience that he is willing to risk loss of wealth, marriage, home, children, and health to acquire it. But the greater loss for the Christian is always his fellowship with the heavenly Father, who will bring chastisement (Prov. 13:15, 21).

self-determination. A commitment to a way of life that assumes all circumstances are under a person's control. Although the Bible says that man should plan his way, it is the Lord who determines his steps (Prov. 16:1, 9; 19:21).

self-knowledge. The cognitive ability to have an honest evaluation of one's own life, especially as one stands before an absolutely holy God. It fairly answers the question, "Who am I?" To know anything about oneself, one must first know God's view of self (Jer. 12:3; 1 Cor. 4:4).

self-pity. It is an emotional state or feeling that assumes the source of all problems to be something outside of oneself, and it usually causes a downward spiral in one's mood. Such a person is always a victim of others or circumstances and is frequently seeking attention.

self-righteousness. A false assumption of sanctimoniousness that comes from one's errant belief about the goodness of oneself, a common false belief of depravity, that results in a sense of moral superiority (Matt. 7:1–5; Luke 6:42).

sexual captivity or enslavement. This is the point in which a person's resistance to sexual temptation falls below his craving for the experience. Even though he still has the capacity to willfully change through repentance, he is self-convinced that he is unable to change (Prov. 5:20; Rom. 6:6; 2 Peter 2:19).

sexual conquest. A desire to experience a sexual relationship with another person as an achievement of prowess or honor. In an extreme sense it may also involve violence and is more of a statement of power than pride (2 Sam. 13:1–19).

solace. An experience of consolation or emotional comfort provided by a sexual experience. A person who wants to be loved may consent to having sinful sex to receive the consolation he or she seeks.

total depravity. The inherent corrupting sinfulness of every person, extending to every aspect of one's nature, both body and soul. Although every aspect of man's nature is blighted by sin's deadening effect, it does not mean that such a person is as bad as they could be. One can become more corrupt when indulging his depraved nature. It means that no fallen sinner is spiritually good in relation to God (John 5:42; Rom. 7:18, 23; Eph. 4:18).

transgender. Relating to the rejection of an individual's gender identity by which they were conceived and the adoption of the identity of the opposite sex. Some may go as far as having sexual reassignment surgery, which simply changes the soft tissue of the body.

Then the person must take hormones of the opposite sex for the rest of his or her life, even though their skeletal structure remains the same as their birth gender. It is a system that says "God has made a mistake in creating me with my gender, and I know better what my gender should be" (1 Tim. 4:4).

unrealized expectation. When a person earnestly desires to achieve a craving but is disappointed. This can occur with ungodly sexual expectations. When this happens the person may become angry, hostile, or hateful. The person may withdraw, become sullen or moody, or be overcome with severe depression (Jer. 23:16; 1 Tim. 6:17).

vanity. A person's obsessive belief in one's own capabilities or attractiveness. He is consumed with his own strength or sex appeal because his heart is full of pride (Ps. 10:4; Prov. 8:13; Mark 7:22).

voyeurism. The practice of secretly observing others who are privately involved in intimate behavior, undressing, or sexual activity. Occasionally this term refers to habitually fantasizing of having a sinful sexual relationship with another unsuspecting person or imagining them undressed (Lev. 18:6–23; Rom. 1:21).

worldly sorrow. An attitude that shows remorse or sorrow over the consequences of sin, on the one hand, but regrets having abandoned the behavior, on the other. The heart will still long to be practicing the sin that it did not wish to cease practicing in the first place. It may be accompanied by many tears and external signs of grief, but there is no genuine repentance (Gen. 19:26; 2 Cor. 7:10).

BIBLIOGRAPHY

Disclaimer: The listing of these books or articles does not necessarily mean an endorsement of every position each author presents.

Aalders, G. Charles, *Bible Student's Commentary: Genesis*. Vol. 2. Translated by William Heynen. Grand Rapids: Zondervan, 1981.

Adams, Jay E. *The Biblical View of Self-Esteem, Self-Love and Self-Image*. Eugene, OR: Harvest House, 1986.

———. *The Christian Counselor's Commentary: Romans, Philippians, 1 Thessalonians, 2 Thessalonians*. Hackettstown, NJ: Timeless Texts, 1995.

———. *The Christian Counselor's Manual*. Grand Rapids: Zondervan, 1986.

———. *How to Help People Change: The Four-Step Biblical Process*. Grand Rapids: Zondervan, 1986.

———. *Winning the War Within*. Woodruff, SC: Timeless Texts, 1996.

Aharon, Itzhak, Nancy Etcoff, Dan Ariely, Christopher F. Chabris, Ethan O'Connar, and Hans C. Breiter. "Beautiful Faces Have Variable Reward Value: fMRI and Behavioral Evidence." *Neuron* 32 (November 8, 2001): 537–51.

Alleine, Richard. *Instructions about Heart Work*. Morgan, PA: Soli Deo Gloria, 2003.

Allestree, Richard. *The Whole Duty of Man*. London: W. Pickering, 1842.

Ames, William. *Conscience with the Power and Cases Thereof*. 1639. Facsimile reprint. Norwood, NJ: Walter J. Johnson, 1975.

Anonymous. "The War Within: An Anatomy of Lust." *Leadership: A Practical Journal for Church Leaders* 3, 4 (Fall 1982): 30–48.

B., D. *An Antidote against Discord betwixt Man and Wife*. 1685. Reprint, Warrenton, VA: Edification Press, 2013.

Bates, William. *Spiritual Perfection, Unfolded and Enforced. 2 Cor. 7:1.* In *The Whole Works of the Rev. W. Bates*, 2:287–526. Harrisonburg, VA: Sprinkle Publications, 1990.

Baumeister, Roy. "Violent Pride: Do People Turn Violent Because of Self-Hate, or Self-Love?" *Scientific American* (April 2001): 96–101.

Bayly, Lewis. *The Practice of Piety: Directing a Christian How to Walk, That He May Please God*. Morgan, PA: Soli Deo Gloria, 1994.

Beale, G. K. *We Become What We Worship: A Biblical Theology of Idolatry*. Downers Grove, IL: InterVarsity Press, 2008.

Beeke, Joel R. *Living for God's Glory: An Introduction to Calvinism*. Lake Mary, FL: Reformation Trust, 2009.

Bennett, Arthur, ed. *The Valley of Vision: A Collection of Puritan Prayers and Devotions*. Edinburgh: Banner of Truth, 2002.

Berger, P. L., and T. Luckmann. *The Social Construction of Reality*. Garden City, NY: Anchor Books, 1966.

Bonhoeffer, Dietrich. *The Cost of Discipleship*. New York: Macmillan, 1963.

Bourne, Immanuel. *A Golden Chain of Directions, with Twenty Gold-links of Love, to Preserve Love Firm between Husband and Wife, during Their Lives*. London: J. Streater for George Sanbridge, 1669.

Breidenbaugh, Joel R. "Docetism." In *The Popular Encyclopedia of Apologetics: Surveying the Evidence for the Truth of Christianity*. Edited by Ed Hindson, Ergun Caner, and Edward J. Verstraete. Eugene, OR: Harvest House, 2008.

Bridges, Jerry. *The Discipline of Grace*. Colorado Springs, CO: NavPress, 1994.

Brooks, Thomas. *Precious Remedies against Satan's Devices*. Carlisle, PA: Banner of Truth, 1990. First published 1652.

Brown, Colin, ed. *The New International Dictionary of New Testament Theology*. Vol. 1. Grand Rapids: Zondervan, 1975.

Brown, Francis, S. R. Driver, and Charles A. Briggs, eds. *A Hebrew and English Lexicon of the Old Testament*. Oxford: Clarendon Press, 1978.

Bruce, F. F. *The Epistle to the Hebrews*. New International Commentary on the New Testament. Grand Rapids: Eerdmans, 1964.

Burgess, Anthony. *Spiritual Refining*. Part 1, *The Heart Established by Grace*, 316–33. Ames, IA: International Outreach, 1991.

———. *Spiritual Refining*. Part 2, *Of Uprightness of Heart, or the Heart without Guile*, 65–98. Ames, IA: International Outreach, 1991.

Burk, Denny. *Transforming Homosexuality: What the Bible Says about Sexual Orientation and Change*. Phillipsburg, NJ: P&R Publishing, 2015.

Burroughs, Jeremiah. *The Beatitudes*. Edinburgh: James Nichol, 1867.

"Buttafuoco Blames His Crime on Lust," *Dayton Daily News*, November 17, 1993.

Calvin, John. *The Epistles of Paul the Apostle to the Romans and to the Thessalonians*. Calvin's New Testament Commentaries. Edited by David W. Torrance and Thomas F. Torrance. Translated by Ross Mackenzie. Grand Rapids: Eerdmans, 1973.

———. *A Harmony of the Gospels Matthew, Mark and Luke and the Epistles of James and Jude*. Calvin's New Testament Commentaries. 3 vols. Edited by David W. Torrance and Thomas F. Torrance. Translated by A. W. Morrison. Grand Rapids: Eerdmans, 1972.

———. *Institutes of the Christian Religion*. Edited by John T. McNeill. Translated by Ford Lewis Battles. Vol. 1. Philadelphia, PA: Westminster Press, 1960.

Challies, Tim. *Sexual Detox: A Guide for Guys Who Are Sick of Porn*. Adelphi, MD: Cruciform Press, 2010.

Chavez, Linda. "Self-Esteem's Dark Side Emerges." *USA Today*, February 21, 1996.

Coyle, Rachel. *Help! She's Struggling with Pornography*. Wapwallopen, PA: Shepherd Press, 2017.

de Vaux, Roland. *Ancient Israel*. Vol. 1. New York: McGraw-Hill, 1965.

DeYoung, Kevin. *The Hole in Our Holiness: Filling the Gap between Gospel Passion and the Pursuit of Godliness*. Wheaton, IL: Crossway, 2014.

Diagnostic and Statistical Manual of Mental Disorders. 4th ed. Washington, DC: American Psychiatric Association, 1994.

Dobson, James. *Dr. Dobson Answers Your Questions*. Wheaton, IL: Tyndale House, 1982.

Dod, John. *A Plain and Familiar Exposition of the Ten Commandments.* London: Thomas Man, Paul Man, and Jonah Man, 1632.

Duvall, Scott J., and J. Daniel Hays. *Grasping God's Word.* Grand Rapids: Zondervan, 2012.

Dyke, Daniel. *The Mystery of Selfe-Deceiving: A Discourse and Discovery of the Deceitfulnesse of Mans Heart.* London: Richard Bishop, 1642.

Eadie, John. *Commentary on the Greek Text of the Epistle of Paul to the Thessalonians.* Grand Rapids: Baker, 1979.

Elliot, Elisabeth. *Passion and Purity: Learning to Bring Your Love Life under Christ's Control.* Ada, MI: Revell, 2013.

Ferguson, Sinclair B. *The Christian Life: A Doctrinal Introduction.* Carlisle, PA: Banner of Truth, 2013.

———. *The Grace of Repentance.* Wheaton, IL: Crossway, 2011.

Frame, John M. *The Doctrine of the Word of God.* Phillipsburg, NJ: P&R Publishing, 2018.

Gallagher, Steve. *At the Altar of Sexual Idolatry.* Dry Ridge, KY: Pure Life Ministries, 2000.

Ganschow, Julie, and Bruce Roeder. *The Process of Biblical Heart Change.* Kansas City, MO: Pure Water Press, 2013.

Gataker, Thomas. "A Good Wife God's Gift." In *Certain Sermons.* London: John Haviland, 1637.

———. "Marriage Duties." In *Certain Sermons.*

———. "A Marriage Prayer." In *Certain Sermons.*

———. "A Wife in Deed." In *Certain Sermons.*

Hemfelt, Robert, Frank Minirth, and Paul Meier. *Love Is a Choice.* Nashville, TN: Thomas Nelson, 1989.

Heyer, Walt. "If California's LGBT Therapy Ban Had Been Law 30 Years Ago, I Might Have Killed Myself." *The Federalist,* April 25, 2018. http://thefederalist.com/2018/04/25/californias-lgbt-therapy-ban-law-30-years-ago-might-killed/.

Hillerstrom, P. Roger. *Intimate Deception: Escaping the Trap of Sexual Impurity.* Portland, OR: Multnomah Press, 1989.

Hopkins, Ezekiel. *An Exposition upon the Commandments.* In *The Works of Ezekiel Hopkins,* edited by Charles W. Quick, 1:413–26. 1874. Reprint, Morgan, PA: Soli Deo Gloria, 1995.

Hughes, Kent R. *Disciplines of a Godly Man*. Wheaton, IL: Crossway, 1991.

Jenni, Ernest, and Claus Westermann, eds. *Theological Lexicon of the Old Testament*. Vol. 1. Translated by Mark E. Biddle. Peabody, MA: Hendrickson, 1997.

Jones, Peter. *The God of Sex: How Spirituality Defines Your Sexuality*. Colorado Springs, CO: Cook Communications Ministries, 2014.

———. *The Other Worldview*. Bellingham, WA: Kirkdale Press, 2015.

———. *The Pagan Heart of Today's Culture*. Phillipsburg, NJ: P&R Publishing, 2014.

Kittel, Gerhard, ed. *Theological Dictionary of the New Testament*. Vol. 3. Translated by Geoffrey W. Bromiley. Grand Rapids: Eerdmans, 1965.

Kruger, Melissa. *The Envy of Eve: Finding Contentment in a Covetous World*. Focus for Women. Scotland, UK: Christian Focus Publications, 2012.

Lambert, Heath. *Finally Free: Fighting for Purity with the Power of Grace*. Grand Rapids: Zondervan, 2013.

———. *A Theology of Biblical Counseling: The Doctrinal Foundations of Counseling Ministry*. Grand Rapids: Zondervan, 2016.

Lane, Timothy S., and Paul David Tripp. *How People Change*. Greensboro, NC: New Growth Press, 2008.

Ley, David J. "Sex Addiction: Rejected Yet Again by the APA." *Psychology Today*. December 5, 2012. https://www.psychologytoday.com/intl/blog/women-who-stray/201212/sex-addiction-rejected-yet-again-apa.

Longman, Tremper, III. *The Book of Ecclesiastes*. Grand Rapids, MI / Cambridge, UK: Eerdmans, 1998.

Lundgaard, Kris. *The Enemy Within: Straight Talk about the Power and Defeat of Sin*. Phillipsburg, NJ: P&R Publishing, 1998.

———. *Through the Looking Glass*. Phillipsburg, NJ: P&R Publishing, 2000.

Lye, Thomas. "What May Gracious Parents Best Do for the Conversion of Those Children Whose Wickedness Is Occasioned by Their Sinful Severity or Indulgence?" In *Puritan Sermons, 1659–1689*, 3:153–84. Wheaton, IL: Richard Owen Roberts, 1981.

MacArthur, John. *How to Live for God's Glory*. Wheaton, IL: Good News Publishers, 2003.

———. *The Gospel according to Jesus*. Grand Rapids: Zondervan, 2008.

Mack, Wayne, and Joshua Mack. *Courage: Fighting Fear with Fear.* Phillipsburg, NJ: P&R Publishing, 2014.

———. *A Fight to the Death.* Phillipsburg, NJ: P&R Publishing, 2006.

Minirth, Frank, Paul Meier, and Stephen Arterburn. *The Complete Life Encyclopedia.* Nashville, TN: Thomas Nelson, 1995.

Moulton, James Hope, and George Milligan. *The Vocabulary of the Greek New Testament: Illustrated from the Papyri and Other Non-Literary Sources.* Grand Rapids: Eerdmans, 1982.

Murray, Andrew. *Humility: The Beauty of Holiness.* Pensacola, FL: Chapel Library, n.d..

Ohlschlager, George, and Peter Mosgogian. "Sex Therapy in the Body." *Christian Counseling Today* 2 (Summer 1994): 9–13.

Pass It On: The Story of Bill Wilson and How the A.A. Message Reached the World. New York: Alcoholics Anonymous World Services, 1984.

Peace, Martha. *The Excellent Wife: A Biblical Perspective.* Bemidji, MN: Focus Publishing, 2005.

Piper, John, and Justin Taylor. *Sex and the Supremacy of Christ.* Wheaton, IL: Crossway, 2005.

Powlison, David. *Dynamics of Biblical Change Class Notebook.* Glenside, PA: Westminster Campus Bookstore special printing, 1997.

———. *Making All Things New: Restoring Joy to the Sexually Broken.* Wheaton, IL: Crossway, 2017.

———. *Seeing with New Eyes: Counseling and the Human Condition through the Lens of Scripture.* Phillipsburg, NJ: P&R Publishing, 2003.

Pratt, Richard L., Jr. *He Gave Us Stories: The Bible Student's Guide to Interpreting Old Testament Narratives.* Phillipsburg, NJ: P&R Publishing, 1993.

Priolo, Lou. *Discontentment: Why Am I So Unhappy?* Phillipsburg, NJ: P&R Publishing, 2012.

———. *Pleasing People: How Not to Be an Approval Junkie.* Phillipsburg, NJ: P&R Publishing, 2007.

The Revised Standard Version New Testament. New York: Thomas Nelson, 1946.

Rienecker, Fritz, and Cleon L. Rogers, Jr. *A Linguistic Key to the New Testament.* Grand Rapids: Zondervan, 1980.

Ryken, Philip Graham. *Ecclesiastes: Why Everything Matters.* Wheaton, IL: Crossway, 2010.

Ryle, J. C. *Holiness: Its Nature, Hindrances, Difficulties, and Roots.* 7th ed. Durham, England: Evangelical Press, 1993.

Scanzoni, Letha. *Sex and the Single Eye.* Grand Rapids: Zondervan, 1968.

Scott, Stuart. *The Exemplary Husband: A Biblical Perspective.* Bemidji, MN: Focus Publishing, 2002.

———. *From Pride to Humility.* Bemidji, MN: Focus Publishing, 2002.

Scudder, Henry. *The Godly Man's Choice.* London: Matthew Simmons for Henry Overton, 1644.

Sibbes, Richard. *The Pattern of Purity.* In *Complete Works of Richard Sibbes,* 7:505–16. Edinburgh: James Nichol, 1864.

———. *The Tender Heart.* Carlisle, PA: Banner of Truth, 2011.

Sproul, R. C., Jr. *One Holy Passion: The Consuming Thirst to Know God.* Nashville, TN: Thomas Nelson, 1987.

Steele, Richard. "What Are the Duties of Husbands and Wives towards Each Other?" In *Puritan Sermons, 1659–1689,* 2:272–303. Wheaton, IL: Richard Owen Roberts, 1981.

Street, John, ed. *Men Counseling Men: A Biblical Guide to the Major Issues Men Face.* Eugene, OR: Harvest House, 2013.

Street, John, and Janie Street. *The Biblical Counseling Guide for Women.* Eugene, OR: Harvest House, 2016.

Struthers, William M. *Wired for Intimacy: How Pornography Hijacks the Male Brain.* Downers Grove, IL: InterVarsity Press, 2009.

Swinnock, George. *The Christian Man's Calling.* In *The Works of George Swinnock,* 1:464–528. 1868. Reprint, Edinburgh: Banner of Truth, 1992.

Tenney, Merrill C., ed., and Steven Barabas, assoc. ed. *The Zondervan Pictorial Encyclopedia of the Bible.* Vol. 1. Grand Rapids: Zondervan, 1975.

Thorne, Helen. *Purity Is Possible: How to Live Free of the Fantasy Trap.* Live Different. Purcellville, VA: The Good Book Company, 2014.

Viars, Steve. *Putting Your Past in Its Place.* Eugene, OR: Harvest House, 2011.

Welch, Edward T. *Addictions: A Banquet in the Grave; Finding Hope in the Power of the Gospel.* Phillipsburg, NJ: P&R Publishing, 2001.

———. "A Discussion among Clergy: Pastoral Counseling Talks with Secular Psychology." *The Journal of Biblical Counseling* 13, 2 (Winter 1995): 23–34.

———. *When People Are Big and God Is Small: Overcoming Peer Pressure, Codependency, and the Fear of Man.* Phillipsburg, NJ: P&R Publishing, 1997.

Whately, William. *A Care-Cloth or the Cumbers and Troubles of Marriage.* 1624. Reprint, Norwood, NJ: Walter J. Johnson, 1975.

Wilson, Gary. *Your Brain on Porn: Internet Pornography and the Emerging Science of Addiction.* Kent, UK: Commonwealth Publishing, 2014.

Wragg, Jerry, and Paul Shirley. *Free to Be Holy: Conference Edition with Selected Chapters.* CreateSpace, 2017.

INDEX OF SCRIPTURE

Song of Solomon
(whole book) 42, 243, 244

Isaiah
3:16—143
3:16–17—145
3:16–24—164
4:1—143
29:13—263
31:8—45
51:12—108, 132
55:11—18
58:2—43

Jeremiah
2:14—45
5:7–8—169, 267
5:8–9—258
5:28—275
7:9—169
12:3—274
13:26–27—258
17:9—5, 257
20:12—5, 8
23:16—275
49:16—5, 7

Lamentations
1:1—45
2:4—43, 265
3:32–33—118
3:37–40—118

Ezekiel
12:24—162
14:1–8—267
14:6–7—217

14:7–8—75
16:36—264
16:37—266
24:16—43
24:21—43
24:25—43

Hosea
(whole book) 243n13
1–3—170n6
1:2—170
2:5—170
2:6—170
2:7—170

Obadiah
1:3–5, 7

Habakkuk
2:5—166
2:15—166

Matthew
1:3—132
3:8—273
5:3–12—89
5:8—xix, 19, 41
5:19—82
5:20—82
5:21–22—263
5:22—122
5:27–28—5, 81, 86, 206, 250, 258, 263, 267, 272
5:27–32—42
5:28—32, 83, 214, 242
5:29–30—90, 232
5:32—83

5:43–48—133n11
5:48—154
6:9–13—271
6:12—17
7:1–5—274
7:13–27—89
7:20–23—33
10:28—263
12:34—33
12:34–36—228
15:19—42, 140, 267
16:24–25—209
16:24–26—264
16:24–28—90
18:15—272
19:9–12—42
19:12—249
22:37—41
22:37–40—24, 33, 268
23:25–28—110
24:13—209
27:4—21

Mark
(whole book) 19
7:20–21—32
7:21—267
7:21–23—110, 228, 267
7:22—275
12:33—267

Luke
3:8—ix
4:8—30
6:42—274
6:45—228, 267
9:23—227

INDEX OF SUBJECTS AND NAMES

hungering heart, 148, 157, 172

hurting heart, 147–48

layers of reasoning, 178

layers of self-righteous rationalizations, 9, 222

negative, 116, 144, 148

negative ruling desires, 116

pleasure, 13, 18, 34, 58, 62, 116,
123, 152, 165, 167–71, 196,
199, 205, 226, 228

self-pity, 25, 104, 109, 116, 123,
125, 127–28, 130, 132–34,
144–45, 148, 150, 171, 178,
180, 200, 204–5, 225, 246,
249–50, 257

solace, 104, 116, 128, 130, 144,
167, 178, 200

helplessness, xvi, 52, 159, 230

heterosexual relationships, 45, 71,
179, 198, 214

holiness, xi, 6, 15, 17, 22–23, 29,
32, 34, 41, 43, 73, 85, 90,
119, 167–68, 173, 192, 208,
220, 223–25, 228–29, 243–
45, 252, 255, 257–58, 260

Holy Spirit, 19, 26, 45, 48, 50, 69,
93, 101, 103, 106, 142, 154,
191, 207, 210, 223, 259

homosexuality, 20, 45, 71, 76, 104,
122, 135, 139, 151, 157,
196–97, 211, 216, 245, 250

hope, 19, 44, 47, 58, 61, 75, 85,
135, 143, 145, 192, 210–11,
216, 220–21, 231, 233, 257

hopelessness, 48, 52, 54, 61, 76,
191–92, 194, 229

humbling, 8, 218, 221

humility, 8, 75, 207, 212, 219, 233

hypothalamus, 84

idolatry, 21, 26, 29, 33–37, 40, 44,
48, 57–58, 61–62, 66–67, 75,
77, 80–81, 85–86, 90–96, 99,
105, 109–10, 113, 131, 157,
169–70, 191, 193–95, 197,
199, 202, 205–7, 209, 217,
223–27, 238–39, 243–44,
246, 248–49, 252, 255,
257–58

illicit thoughts and behavior, 43,
49, 72, 75, 78, 125, 131, 141,
170, 218, 251

image of God, 3, 30, 57

impurity, 20, 29, 72, 103, 105,
199, 218, 224–25, 241

innocence, 9, 13–14, 26, 35, 57,
65, 79–80, 104, 163, 202,
213, 233, 248

irresistible sexual desire, 45–46, 51,
230–31

jealousy, 30, 55, 75, 161, 237–38,
242–43, 251

Jesus Christ, x–xiii, xix, 5–6, 12,
17, 19–21, 23, 25, 28, 32, 41,
61, 81–84, 104, 108, 132–33,
153–54, 177, 190, 193, 200,
207–11, 221–22, 226–27,
230–32, 240, 242, 249, 252,
258, 260

justification

in Christ, 176

self-justification, 123

self-interest
  self-concern, 200
  self-opinion, 119
selfishness, 24, 49, 55–56, 71–72,
    83, 103, 141, 163, 166–67,
    202, 228–29, 246–47, 251
  self-pleasure, 18
self-love, xvii, 122
  self-absorbed, 71
  self-dignity, 122
  self-esteem, 119–20, 144–45,
    155, 172, 216
  self-favoring, 12, 22, 26
  self-image, 119, 215
  self-seeking, 116, 245
self-made, 6, 25, 153, 226
  self-appointed, 25
  self-determined, 4
  self-diagnostic, 14
  self-generated, 38
self-pity, 25, 109, 123, 125, 127–
    28, 130, 132–34, 144–45,
    148, 150, 171, 178, 180, 200,
    204–5, 225, 246, 249–50, 257
self-righteousness, 5, 10, 12, 14, 22,
    26, 29, 47, 57, 70, 84, 86,
    122, 131, 150, 154, 207, 217
self-worship, 31
sensual
  activities, 72
  demands, 72
  desires, 5, 12, 26, 43–44, 50, 54,
    94, 230
  enjoyment, 120
  excitement, 165
  feeding the sensual slide show, 134
  fulfillment, 95

furnishings, 160
gratification, 48
heart, 5
illicit, 48
impulses, 73
impurity, 23
indiscretions, 123
indulgence, 144, 169
passions, 40, 80
pleasure, 65, 152
self-seeking greed, 116
sins, 13
temptation, 41
thought life, 48, 148–49
ungodliness, 42
unrighteousness, 46
ways, 218
sensuality, 46–47, 52, 77, 103, 105,
    152, 194, 210, 218–19, 258
sex, 34, 36, 39–43, 49–53, 55–56,
    58, 62, 70, 72, 79–81, 84, 86,
    90, 93, 95, 104, 108, 117–18,
    120, 127–29, 131, 133–35,
    139, 142–43, 157, 163, 165–
    66, 169–71, 179–82, 194–95,
    197–98, 202, 204–6, 214–16,
    219, 222, 230, 234, 237–38,
    240, 243–47, 249–55, 258
sexual activity, 52, 91, 128, 250
sexual addiction, 50, 155, 213
sexual conquest, 100, 181, 183, 274
sexual immorality, 32, 34, 55, 83,
    95, 103, 105, 111, 135, 157,
    199, 218, 223, 225, 251
sexual indulgences, 46, 143, 214
sexual obsession, 45, 47, 57, 69, 71,
    213, 215, 217

sexual perversion, 52, 55, 135
shame, 20, 22, 55, 57, 68–69,
  71–73, 75, 80, 107, 143, 190,
  224, 258
sinful
  activity, 91
  anger, 104, 117, 122
  attitudes, x–xi, xiii, xviii, 5, 12,
    16–17, 20, 22, 24–25, 31,
    34–37, 39–44, 46, 52–53, 62,
    64–69, 72, 77, 79, 81, 86–88,
    90–92, 95, 103–5, 107–8,
    116–17, 119–22, 125, 141,
    148, 154, 166–67, 175–77,
    179, 181–82, 191, 195, 197,
    199, 201, 205, 207, 209–11,
    214–15, 221–22, 228, 242,
    248, 257, 259
  behavior, 41, 66, 68, 175
  believers, 77
  compromises, 12
  condition, 12
  corruption, 154
  cravings, 12, 34, 36, 201, 210
  demanding heart, 37
  demands, 167
  desires, x–xi, 22, 24, 35, 87, 167
  dominating desires, 20
  and enslaving, 62
  fantasy, 18, 48, 54, 55, 79, 117,
    133, 156, 165, 172–73, 204,
    237, 246
  flesh, 154, 207
  habits, 64, 69, 90, 92, 95, 107,
    176, 214, 221
  habituations, 69, 87–88, 92, 95,
    214

heart, xiii, 17, 25, 31, 66, 72, 81,
  104, 120, 125, 199, 242
idolatry, 197, 211
imaginations, 122
incentives, 166
innately, 37, 41, 166
intentionality, 177
lust, 65, 86, 177, 179
mind, 16, 39
motivations, 182, 221–22
passion, 44, 177
practices, 108
predisposition, 257, 259
presumption, 42
pride, 181
propensities of the heart, 16
self-gratification, 166
self-satisfying sex, 103, 119
sensual desires, 24, 50
sex, xviii, 35, 39–41, 46, 77, 88,
  105, 116–17, 125, 148, 166,
  179, 182, 228
sexual activity, 46
sexual behavior, 77, 228
sexual desires, 35, 166
sexual indulgence, xviii
sexuality, 182
sexual pleasure, 168
sexual satisfaction, 148
tendencies, 191, 215
the thought of sin is not sinful, 50
ways, 209
when does a thought become sinful?, 41–42
sinfulness, 6, 19, 22, 33, 103–4, 108
slave, 45–47, 49, 51–52, 63, 70–73,
  75–76, 80, 151–53, 208–9,
  227, 230